THE JOURNEY TO WORK

The Journey to Work

IAN MANNING
Research Fellow
Urban Research Unit
Australian National University

SYDNEY
GEORGE ALLEN & UNWIN
LONDON BOSTON

First published in 1978 by
George Allen & Unwin Australia Pty Ltd
Cnr Bridge Road and Jersey Street
Hornsby NSW 2077

National Library of Australia
Cataloguing-in-Publication entry:

Manning, Ian.
The journey to work.

Index.
Bibliography.
ISBN 0 86861 200 6 Paperback: $7.95 Aust.
ISBN 0 86861 192 1

1. Commuting — Australia. 2. Urban transportation — Australia. I. Title.

380.5′0994

Library of Congress Catalog Card Number 78-57601

Set in 10 on 12 point Times by G.T. Setters, Sydney
Printed by Hogbin Poole, Sydney

Preface

This book owes its origin to two things: the debate about urban transport — freeways, transport deficits, excessive journey times and costs — and the existence of an hitherto unanalysed body of data which could be used to focus the issues of the debate. The data is that collected at the 1971 census and in the course of the Sydney Area Transportation Study, and the questions addressed to it include such as these:

> Do people *have* to work so far from home? Is it forced on them, or is it their free choice?
>
> Should there be a policy of job dispersion in Australian metropolitan areas, or should the dominance of city centres be maintained?. . .and
>
> Are there any policies which would attract people out of their motor cars towards a means of transport less expensive in public and environmental costs?

The discussion is in terms of Australia's largest metropolis, Sydney, but the arguments are equally applicable to other Australian cities, and in many cases to cities in other western countries.

Since its arguments are based on statistics, this book is one end result of the labours of the anonymous officers of the Australian Bureau of Statistics and the Sydney Area Transportation Study, and was further made possible by the long-suffering public who answered the statisticians' questions. I also wish to thank Richard Davis, Jenny Norman and Vân Phan for helping me to extract numbers and maps from the computer, and all members of the Urban Research Unit for comments in writing about them — particularly Max Neutze and Peter Harrison, who read the manuscript and made many valuable suggestions. Thanks are due as well to June Harries, Jenny Nocella and Lyn Smith for typing. The remaining errors and shortcomings are my own.

Ian Manning

Contents

LIST OF TABLES

Tables refer to Sydney, 1971, unless otherwise indicated

MAPS

All maps cover the Sydney Metropolitan Area, and relate to 1971.

GRAPHS

CHAPTER 1

An Introduction to the Journey to Work

Not many Australian workers live on the job; most have a daily journey to work, out in the morning and back at night. For some this journey is a pleasant interlude, separating the two worlds in which they live, but others resent the time it consumes, the money it costs, and the discomfort it imposes. Again, from a public point of view, provision for the journey to work is an important item of government expenditure and at times, as with the argument about freeways, an important element in political debate.

On the face of it, this concern is well justified. Three out of every five Australians aged over fifteen are in the workforce (Year Book 1975/76, p.692) and, apart from a proportion unemployed and a proportion who work at home, all of these people travel to work.[1] The work journeys of those who live outside the capital cities are no great burden — the typical duration is ten minutes (Chapter 12) — but in the big cities the situation is quite different. There and back, work travel typically absorbs an hour of each Sydney worker's time each weekday (Chapter 9). People in the Sydney metropolitan area typically live nine kilometres from where they work — some more, some less, this is the average distance (Chapter 3). Each weekday in 1971 the people of Sydney travelled a total of more than 20 million kilometres on their journeys to and from work (Chapter 3), burning more than a million litres of petrol in the process. At this rate, the journey to work was responsible for around half the total person-kilometres of travel carried out in Sydney, Monday to Friday. Most of this travel occurred during the two daily peak periods, straining the capacity of the public transport system and clogging the roads.

A mass movement of this magnitude and timing entails considerable private and public expenditure (Neutze, 1977, ch. 5). As an expense to individuals, the

1. The proportion unemployed in 1974 was about 1.6 per cent of the workforce (Year Book 1975/6 p 692). Excluding farmers, 8 per cent of those at work worked at home or in jobs where work starts at the front door (e.g. taxi drivers, repairmen) (ABS Journey to Work 1974). After allowance for these two effects, a little less than 60 per cent of all urban residents aged over fifteen would have had journeys to work.

journey to work in 1974/5 cost an average of $6 a week for each worker in Sydney, and absorbed around 5 per cent of total household expenditure (Chapter 11). At a rough guess, a similar proportion of the total expenditure of the NSW state government was devoted to the maintenance and building of roads primarily to carry people to work in Sydney, and to meet public transport deficits partly attributable to work travel (Chapter 11).

The costs of the journey to work in a large metropolitan area, both in time and in money, are thus considerable. What do people gain by it? The obvious benefit is that home and workplace can be separated; factories can be kept out of residential areas and offices can be staffed by clerks who live, not in penthouses but in single family dwellings. Jobs can be grouped together in the city centre, suburban centres and industrial zones. Journeys to work are thus partly a consequence of the different locational patterns of housing and employment. But this is not all. Many people travel further than they need, in the sense that they bypass the nearest suitable job and travel to one further afield. It may be that the further job was available when they happened to be looking for work, or that it was in some way better — better pay, promotion prospects and so on. Again, sometimes people shift to a better house without changing their workplace to match. In all these cases the benefit of the longer-than-necessary journey to work is that of choice, for the greater a person's willingness to put up with a long journey to work, the greater his choice both of workplaces and of places to live.

Both the geographic separation of workplaces and residences, and the tendency to bypass the nearest job in pursuit of choice, are at their most acute in the largest metropolitan areas. This study accordingly concentrates on Sydney, though many of its findings, particularly those concerning human behaviour rather than city layout, are true of other Australian cities, and probably of cities in other countries with a similar level of economic development (Chapter 12). It begins with an account of the geographic separation of workplaces and residences in Sydney, and then proceeds to an examination of the pattern of work travel between the two. In effect it starts out with the hypothesis that work travel is due to the failure to match jobs and housing locationally, but continues to argue that much work travel is due to the deliberate choice of long journeys. There is, therefore, scope for reducing the burden of the journey to work by better planning of job locations in relation to residential areas, but this scope is limited. Much of the burden of the journey to work is shouldered voluntarily.

The Separation of Workplaces and Dwellings

In the long history of urban settlements it has been usual for people to live close to their work. The craftsman lived by his workshop and the burgher over his warehouse. Even when the workshop was replaced by the dark Satanic mill it was usual for the mill owner to provide housing nearby for his workers

(Mumford, 1961, ch. 15). As 19th century industrial plants grew, it became impossible for all their employees to live next door without considerable residential congestion. At the same time, social reformers saw that the smoke and grime from nearby factories was not good for people's health. Improvements in transport — the train, bus and motor car — provided the means by which people's dwellings could be separated from their workplaces, and so from the late 19th century onwards it became usual to plan residential extensions to the city physically away from centres of employment, and without any specific relation to any of them. Housing no longer went with the job; the age of the suburb had begun (Mumford, 1961, ch. 16). In Australia, as in other parts of the Western world, this resulted in the concentration of employment in the inner suburbs, while housing was dispersed around it. In each of the five State capitals of the Australian mainland half the jobs lie within the inner 12 to 16 per cent of the urban area (Harrison, 1977, p.19). Much more than half the population lives outside this inner area, resulting in a daily tide of journeys to work, in in the morning and out in the evening.

Why is it that employment is relatively centralised and housing relatively spread out? It is often put forward that the centralisation of employment in Australian urban areas is largely due to inertia (Neutze, 1977, ch. 2). In each capital city the commercial core lies at the point of first settlement and the surrounding warehousing and industrial areas continue where they were established a century or more ago. Some of this locational conservatism can be put down to the long life of buildings, and the expense of converting them from one use to another. It is extremely expensive to shift a fully equipped factory to a new site, or to change the location of a transport terminal. Again, many locational decisions are incremental — a government department adds a new bureau, a factory a new process — such additions being more easily accommodated by extension rather than by starting out again somewhere else. The complementarity of different activities also adds to the inertia. Lawyers need to be near the courts, senior public servants need to be near one another to join in committees, executives like to be near their club, and speciality shopkeepers benefit from being among a number of shops of different specialities. Once such complementarities have been established in an area it is very difficult for any single enterprise to break clear of them. The hive can become exceedingly overcrowded, but a new queen is never found to lead a swarm away to start afresh (Stretton, 1975, ch. 9, part 1).

The role of the transport system in maintaining the centralisation of employment is more ambiguous. As the builders of the Warringah Expressway and Eastern Suburbs Railway have found, inserting new transport routes into the existing urban area is extremely expensive. It is therefore necessary to make do with the routes that exist, and by and large these are radial, built to carry heavy loads in and out. In this sense, the transport system favours centralisation; the city centre is the point of maximum accessibility. However, the recent switch from public transport to the motor car for passengers, and from horse-drawn waggons to the truck for goods, has reduced the centralising power of the radial transport system. In the inner areas the roads do not have the capacity to carry all the motorists who would like to use them, thus causing people to ponder the benefits of employment and shopping away from the city centre. In response department stores have been set up in the suburbs, adding their employment to the small-scale retailing that was already there. At the same time the motor truck has liberated factories from the need to be near the wharves and railway terminals of the inner areas. Factories are now built single-storeyed on expansive sites in the middle and outer suburbs. With retailing and manufacturing employment now breaking away from the central area, some would predict that the separation of workplaces and dwellings is righting itself, and that in due course they will come into a balance which will reduce the burden of the journey to work.

There are several arguments against this optimistic prediction. First, the element of voluntary choice in the journey to work is strong, and increasing the accessibility of employment in the outer areas will not necessarily prompt people to shorten their journeys; they may instead choose their jobs from among a larger pool (Liepmann, 1944, p.11). Second, the decentralisation of employment has not extended as strongly to office work, which remains obstinately tied to the city centre. Third, even among those kinds of employment which have decentralised, the balance between jobs and residents is very patchy, with some suburbs having a relative self-sufficiency of jobs and others having very few. This is not surprising, since there has been very little effort to coordinate the location of workplaces and of dwelling construction. At the moment those who decide the location of new employment are under no compulsion to consider the effect of their decisions on the journeys to work of their employees, while those who develop new residential areas are under no obligation to try to arrange nearby employment. In Sydney only the Macarthur Development Corporation, in its plans for Campbelltown, is really making an effort to develop employment and residential areas concurrently and in relation to each other.

Despite the ambitions of the town planners, decisions as to where employment will be located are made by employers, public and private. Travel to and from work is conducted in the employees' own time and mostly at their own expense, much of the rest of the cost being borne by the taxpayer through the provision of roads and the financing of public transport deficits. None of these costs impinge directly on the accounts of the businesses and government agencies which employ people. There is an acute contrast between the care with which a retailer considers his customers' convenience and many employers disregard for their employees' work journeys; between the efforts of the education department to ensure that schools are convenient for their pupils and the inertia that has resulted in the concentration of government offices in central Sydney.

The costs of work travel may be divided into those borne publicly and those borne privately in time, discomfort and cash. Occasionally private travel costs may have some influence over the siting of economic activity. The owner of a business may, for example, locate it to suit his own convenience — hence the proliferation of consulting firms in North Sydney close to the consultants' homes in the high status area of Ku-ring-gai. Again, an employer may find that by careful location he can obtain a more reliable or perhaps more efficient workforce. Such a benefit is claimed for the shift of the Australian Taxation Office to Parramatta (Lanigan 1976). However, the inconveniences of the journey to work are not severe enough to make such indirect effects compelling. At most locations in the urban area an entrepreneur can obtain the labour he needs, even in times of full employment.

Location decisions are even less frequently influenced by the public costs of the journey to work — the roads, the transport deficits. Only occasionally, and usually when there is a major public contribution to the direct cost, does a proposed development precipitate a round of negotiations between the authorities involved, such as the bargaining over Port Botany. Otherwise the only way that public costs are brought to bear on the decision-maker is by land use controls, often weakly enforced and tenuously connected to the costs involved.

In one respect, however, land use controls are quite effective. This is in maintaining the purity of areas of residential land use. Led by the town planners of two generations ago, the public has accepted that residential areas should contain no employment, except for schools and neighborhood shopping centres. This means that very few jobs are found within walking distance of the houses in any residential development (as distinct from redevelopment) designed in the past four or five decades. The best that can be done is to reduce distances to the order of a few kilometres. However, with the honourable and recent exception of Macarthur, not even this has been tried. Long journeys were taken as an inevitable part of the price of the single-family dwelling, set in its own spacious garden and among its own kind. Residential developers were under no obligation to see to it that their houses were close to jobs; and indeed such was the public desire for a house and garden, and such the willingness to put up with a long journey to work, that fringe development was profitable in areas a long way removed from workplaces.

The result of this lack of coordination is that there is a considerable geographic imbalance between the location of residential and employment areas in Sydney. Table 1.1 shows the number of resident workers in each local government area, and the number of jobs. A few areas have surplus jobs, though only in the City of Sydney and Municipality of South Sydney do jobs outnumber residents at all strongly. In most places, and particularly the outer suburbs, there are more resident workers than workplaces. Even so, if people put first priority on taking a job within the same local government area, 65 per cent could do so. Such is the willingness to travel in pursuit of choice that only 29 per cent actually work in the local government area they live in.

TABLE 1.1 *Jobs and Residents in Sydney. Census 1971.*

Local Government Area	Resident Workers '000	Jobs '000	Excess Jobs '000	Excess Residents '000
INNER SUBURBS				
City of Sydney	23	279	+256	
South Sydney	14	70	+ 56	
Botany	16	30	+ 14	
Marrickville	36	34	+ 2	
Leichhardt	27	29		- 2
	116	442	+326	
EASTERN SUBURBS				
Woolahra	25	12		- 13
Waverley	29	9		- 20
Randwick	51	26		- 25
	105	47		- 58
MIDDLE SOUTHERN AND WESTERN SUBURBS				
Drummoyne	13	8		- 5
Ashfield	18	9		- 9
Burwood	13	9		- 4
Concord	10	14	+ 4	
Strathfield	11	15	+ 4	
Auburn	19	38	+ 19	
Parramatta	42	51	+ 9	
Canterbury	52	26		- 26
Rockdale	34	19		- 15
Kogarah	19	9		- 10
Hurstville	27	16		- 11
Bankstown	66	55		- 11
	324	269		- 55
NORTHERN SUBURBS				
North Sydney	26	32	+ 6	
Willoughby	21	27	+ 6	
Ku-ring-gai	33	13		- 20
Warringah	57	30		- 27
Manly	15	7		- 8
Mosman	13	5		- 8
Lane Cove	12	8		- 4
Hunters Hill	5	3		- 2
Ryde	36	25		- 11
Hornsby	33	15		- 18
	251	165		- 86
OUTER SOUTHERN AND WESTERN SUBURBS				
Sutherland	56	28		- 28
Liverpool	27	21		- 6
Campbelltown	11	7		- 4
Fairfield	40	19		- 21
Holroyd	29	16		- 13
Blacktown	51	22		- 29
Penrith	20	17		- 3
Windsor	6	7	+ 1	
	240	137		-103

All persons who failed to nominate a workplace are excluded

Source: Census 1971, per P.E.C. '*Work Places and Work Trips 1971*'.

Factors Influencing the Journey to Work

The fact that far fewer people work in their home local government area than could shows that work travel in Sydney is caused by more than the mere geographic separation of workplaces and dwellings. Confronted with a geographic distribution of jobs and houses over which they individually have very little control, the workers of Sydney choose to travel further than they might. This decision will be discussed by taking firstly the choice of a job starting from a fixed dwelling, and secondly the choice of a house by people who have a fixed job.

Those who are looking for a job without wanting to change their dwelling include most young people seeking their first job, wives returning to the workforce, and indeed anybody changing jobs who is committed to a particular dwelling through home ownership, the convenience of others in the household, or simply an attachment to the home locality. They confront the geographic array of jobs from a fixed point, from which they will have to travel daily to whichever job they choose. The factors which may influence this choice begin with the willingness to travel, which depends mainly upon the urgency of other calls on the traveller's time. We may guess that people with domestic responsibilities (housewives, single parents) will be more anxious than others to minimise time spent travelling (Liepmann, 1944, p.40). Willingness to travel is also a matter of the ability to pay for it, depending in turn on wage rates (economists can enjoy themselves intersecting travel cost gradients with wage gradients, both increasing with distance) and the urgency of other financial commitments. If a person's income is already heavily committed he may seek to economise on travel spending, either by switching to slower but cheaper means of transport (thus trading time for money) or seeking a closer job. Average travel distances will be shorter in kilometres if not in minutes among those who, for lack of a licence or financial stringency, do not own a car: the young just embarking on their first job, the ill-paid perhaps and those whose incomes are fully committed to maintaining a family or buying a house.

While work journeys will tend to be long if people are willing to put up with the time and cash costs of travel, a wide local choice of jobs can make such travel unnecessary. This choice is not just a matter of number, but of suitability, depending in turn on the characteristics of the job and the worker; his degree of attachment to a particular kind of job, and his willingness to accept inferior local jobs in preference to better work at a greater distance. Again, a worker's chance of acquiring a nearby job depends on the competition for these jobs. If the turnover of suitable local jobs is high, and there is not much competition, a worker who so desires has a good chance of a short journey to work. On the other hand, if the turnover is low, as in a recession, (Schaeffer & Sclar, 1975, p.3) and if the number of locals far exceeds the number of local jobs, he is likely to have to go further afield. The limitations to this are reached when suitable jobs are available only at such a distance that the worker finds it worthwhile to shift his dwelling (this in turn depends on the cost of shifting house, which varies greatly from family to family); or when there is no suitable work, in which case he either revises his idea of what is suitable, withdraws from the labour market (a course forced on many working wives during recessions) or joins the reserve army of the unemployed.

As soon as a change of dwelling is at issue, the factors influencing the journey to work become more varied. Shifting house is usually both costly and troublesome, so it is most frequent among renters (provided they are not locked in by below-market rents or neighborhood associations) and among people buying their first home. People may change their house when they change their workplace, but this would not be common for changes of workplace within the metropolitan area. In addition, there may be owners who sell and buy to upgrade their accommodation. Such changes are probably not frequent in the life of any family, though in the aggregate they may contribute a significant proportion of total moves (Urban Research Unit, 1973, p.64).

According to the accepted theory of residential location, an individual considering where to live balances his distaste for the journey to work against his demand for a pleasant house and his ability to pay for it (Evans, 1973, chs. 3 to 7). Thus all the factors influencing the choice of work from a fixed dwelling come into play, with some extra as well.

If a worker's job lies in an area of cheap low-density housing — which according to the theory means that it is probably in a place where jobs are few — conflict between housing costs and travel costs does not arise. If, however, he works in an area where housing is cramped and expensive (which in all probability is an area where many other people work as well) he can but trade travel costs (in money and time) against housing costs and the quality of the housing on offer. Apart from individual preferences, the demand of space is likely to increase with family size (Evans, 1973, ch. 9). Again, of all people, the man who can leave a housebound wife to perform the domestic chores is most likely to be willing to lengthen the working day with long travel. The theory therefore predicts that those with the longest journeys to work will tend to be the heads of families where only one adult works, while single parent workers and single people will try harder to save travel time. The position is, however, complicated by the money costs of housing and travel. A low income may not be enough both to pay for a long journey to work and to cover the mortgage on even the cheapest house on the spacious fringe. Workers on low incomes may therefore squeeze their perhaps large families into cramped quarters within walking distance of work (Evans, 1973, ch. 8). By contrast, the wealthy family man can afford a large purchase of space (in which he gets best value at a distance) and the speediest form of travel. This may result in a long journey to work. However, at present levels of traffic congestion there is a limit to the extent to which money can buy speed, so some of the wealthy, particularly those with a taste for urbane living, may opt to buy a house near their workplace.

These fine calculations of optimal journey distance become less certain when other factors are taken into account (Wheaton, 1977, p.360). In many families, for example, the wife works in a different place from her husband, and they may seek a house that is convenient to both. Again, accessibility to work is not the only consideration in choosing a place to live. There is also accessibility to other destinations, and the attractions they offer — the schools and universities, the more specialised entertainments of live theatres and orchestras. Further, for some people the immediate surroundings of the house are more important than its location in relation to the services and activities of the rest of the city — topography, neighbours and the snob rating of the suburb (Evans, 1973, ch. 8). Of course, pleasant topography and prestigious neighbours are not necessarily incompatible with short journeys to work. Wealthy people who want to live close to the employment opportunities and diversions of the central city have established high class residential suburbs in parts of the inner areas. Again, the surroundings of a centre of employment may or may not be attractive topographically. These forces serve mainly to concentrate demand in particular areas (Davis and Spearritt, 1974, Maps 1 and 48). On the other hand, insofar as a lack of local employment is a necessary attribute of a prestige suburb, the well-paid are likely to have long journeys to work.

In Sydney it is normal for families to strive for home ownership. Given the disruption involved in shifting house, having once achieved home ownership people tend to stay put (Neutze, 1971, p.14). Housing in the older suburbs thus comes available for resale or redevelopment rather slowly. In a growing city, many first-time buyers will have to go to the fringe — a trend which will be encouraged if finance is more easily arranged on new houses than old. Not for them any fine balancing of the utility of space against the disutility of work travel. At the most, the location of the workplace will influence their choice of the sector of the fringe in which to buy. Further, if this has been going on for some time (as it has in Sydney) the length of a man's journey to work will depend as much on his age as on his family size or income.

Though when considering the factors which influence the journey to work it is thus helpful to distinguish the choice of a workplace from a fixed dwelling and the choice of a dwelling from a fixed workplace, the patterns actually observed in Sydney combine the journeys that result from these two different kinds of decision. Further, the available statistical data gives only dwelling, workplace, occupation, industry, sex and means of transport. Drawing on the list of factors, some tentative predictions are possible as to the length of work journeys for different groups. Other things being equal (and this includes the distribution of job opportunities):

1. Where the distinction is by sex, women should have the shorter work journeys, because their time out of working hours is more valuable, and because they tend to be less well-paid.
2. Where the distinction is by workplace, people who work in the city centre should have longer journeys to work than the rest. From a housing market

point of view this is because there is not enough room for all those who work in the city centre to live close by. From a labour market point of view, this is because there are not enough local jobs to go round in most residential suburbs and those who cannot work locally will have to travel longer distances to places where more jobs are available.

3. Where the distinction is by occupation, people in the more skilled jobs should have the longer work journeys, due to the narrower, more specific labour markets in these occupations and to their higher incomes. This generalisation, however, has to be modified in that some kinds of work are spread throughout the metropolitan area, and others are concentrated. People in the widespread occupations (schoolteachers, local government employees) should have shorter journeys to work.
4. Where the distinction is by place of residence, people in areas with plentiful local employment should have the shortest journeys to work, specially where the local labour market is not subject to competition from job-deficit areas outside.

Before moving on to see whether these predictions are accurate it is best to look at the data on which the subsequent discussion will be based.

The Data

Most of the discussion in this book depends on the 1971 census. It is true that another census has been taken since, and it is also true that in some respects the pattern of the journey to work has been changing rapidly. However, the data from the 1976 census will not be available for several years yet, and even when it is published it is likely to be technically inferior (the intended zonal classification is coarser). Again, the most rapid changes in journey patterns concern the mode of travel (car, bus, etc.), not so much the pattern of origins and destinations, and even less people's habits of choice — the ways in which some groups tend to prefer long journeys, and others short. 1971 data is still relevant for what it reveals about choice, and for the generalisations it makes possible. Finally, the maps in this study complement those previously published in the Urban Research Unit's atlas of *Sydney at the Census, 1971* (Davis and Spearritt, 1974). The maps in the atlas are all by residential area, and provide a description of the population of Sydney when it is at home; those in the present study show the characteristics of the population at work.

The data derives from the following census questions, asked of every working Australian:

> What is the full trading name of this person's own or employer's business? What is the name of the Division, or Branch, or Section (if any) in which he works?
>
> What is the full address of the Division, or Branch, or Section (if any) or

business at which he works? (Persons with no fixed place of work last week, e.g. taxi drivers, airline pilots, etc., write 'N.A.')

What kind of industry, business or service is carried out at that address?

What was this person's occupation (kind of work) last week?

The answers to these questions enable us to cross-classify workers by industry, occupation and workplace. In addition, from other census questions, sex and place of residence can be added to the cross-classification.

Though this census data on workplaces and their relation to residential areas is by far the most comprehensive available, it suffers from several limitations.

1 *Unknown workplaces*

In Sydney, 11 per cent of the male workers, and 8 per cent of the female, responded to the invitation to write 'N.A.' and thus gave no workplace. Such workers without named destination were concentrated in the construction and transport industries (up to a quarter without destination) and lived mainly in the inner suburbs (up to 20 per cent of the male labour force resident in parts of the City of Sydney gave no work address). The statistics and maps in this book omit such persons and jobs entirely.

The fact that significant numbers of people failed to nominate a workplace explains the lack of any historical comparisons in this study. Though the 1966 and 1961 censuses carried a question on the location of workplace, the specific invitation to write 'N.A.' was added only in 1971. This resulted in an increase in the numbers giving no fixed place of work, particularly in transport and construction. The changes brought about by the alteration of the question are large enough to outweigh any trend in the location of workplaces, and disentangling the two is very difficult.

2 *Zones*

Workplaces and residences could not be allocated more finely than to a zone. There were 552 of these, with considerable differences in size. Those in the City of Sydney ranged between ten and fifty hectares, those in the inner suburbs between thirty and a hundred hectares, and so on until the outer suburban range was between a hundred and five hundred hectares, with occasional zones larger than a thousand hectares. The zones were irregularly shaped, so the largest of them were up to five kilometres across at their greatest dimension. However, the general run of outer suburban zones were less than two kilometres across, and those in the inner areas less than one kilometre across.

The maps in this book were prepared from data at a zonal level by a process described in *Sydney at the Census, 1971* using the Symap computer program. In a few mainly outer suburban cases the zonal boundaries (which respected local government boundaries but were otherwise matters of administrative convenience) were so drawn that the maps give a misleading picture. This is particularly so with the maps showing jobs per hectare. Here, where zonal boundaries were drawn tightly round a group of workplaces (say a shopping centre) a high density peak results, but where the zone boundaries included areas of parkland or housing, the concentration of employment may simply fail to show. The worst example of this is the zone which included Liverpool shopping centre. Stretching from Warwick Farm racecourse into the residential areas on the other side of the shops, it included perhaps 50 hectares of quite high employment density and 1200 hectares of housing and open space. The resulting average jobs per hectare scarcely ever show as a peak on the maps.

The boundary of the area mapped approximates that of the Sydney urban area, with the omission of suburbs to the west of the Nepean River (i.e. beyond Penrith). With this exception, all residential areas with a population density of more than 200 persons per square kilometre are shown, and their residents appear in the tables. However the maps and in some cases the statistics exclude several peripheral concentrations of employment which lie just outside the urban area so defined. The two most important of these are the Moorebank/Holsworthy industrial and defence area near Liverpool, and the RAAF base near Richmond.

Among people included as having stated an address were a few whose workplaces could not be properly located on a map. These included several thousand who named a GPO box as their workplace and maybe a thousand who gave 'City of Sydney'. These were all assumed to work near the city centre.

3 *Distances*

This study includes maps of the proportion of the population working within three kilometres of home; it includes graphs of workers by distance travelled, and tables of average and median journey lengths. In each case these distances are based on the straight-line distance from zone centroid to zone centroid, with no allowance for any deviations from a straight line caused by the street pattern or by obstructions like the harbour. The only exception to these rules is that where both workplace and residence lay within the same zone an arbitrary estimate of one kilometre is used, reasonable in the outer suburbs but perhaps too long in the inner areas. The estimate by this method for the median journey to work for all Sydney was 6.4 kilometres, whereas according to the Sydney Area Transportation Study the actual median in 1971 was of the order of 9 kilometres. A difference of this order would vitiate the analysis for some purposes (e.g. calculating energy consumption) but in this book distances are merely used to compare suburb with suburb and occupation with occupation. Provided the straight-line and actual distances do not diverge too much, such comparisons are meaningful. The most obvious divergence arises when travellers have to cross a water obstacle: thus estimates for journey distances from Sutherland Shire may be particularly low since they take no account of deviations to cross the George's River.

A second, less serious drawback of the estimates of median and average distance is that they do not take into account journeys which either begin or end outside the urban area. As a result figures given for some of the fringe areas are probably too low.

The maps and tables of the proportions of people working within three kilometres of home, or living within three kilometres of work, are likewise dependent on centroid to centroid straight-line distances. By and large three kilometres is too short a distance for obstacles to matter, but the method means that the maps and tables are dependent on the chance that a centroid to centroid distance may be just over or just under three kilometres. This does not matter very much in the inner areas, where the zones were small, but may change the estimated proportions appreciably in a few outer suburban areas.

4 *The occupational and industrial classifications*

Not all the workers who stated the location of their work could be allocated to a specific industry or occupation. However, the proportion of such cases was under one per cent.

Occupations and industries were classified according to the Bureau of Statistics codings. As will be explained in Chapter 2, these were not always entirely appropriate for the work in hand, but they must be taken as given.

5 *Means of transport*

The census does not give any information on how people travel to and from work. However, this can be made good from the Sydney Area Transportation Study home interview survey, which was conducted at about the same time as the census. The tables and maps in Chapters 9 and 10 therefore derive mostly from a survey rather than a complete enumeration. However, the data was checked by road counts of traffic, and by surveys of public transport passengers, and is certainly reliable enough to give a broad picture. It will be further described where it is used.

Despite these limitations, the census provides a rich source of information for those evolving a strategy for the good planning of Sydney, both the planning of land use (especially the relation of workplaces to housing) and the planning of transport. So far census information on the location of workplaces and on the journey to work has been underexploited, though it has been published in booklets issued by the N.S.W. Planning and Environment Commission (P.E.C. 1976). The following chapters attempt to make better use of the available information, but by no means exhaust it.

CHAPTER 2

The Location of Jobs

The theme of this book is that people in Sydney travel further to work than they need, partly because they choose to do so, and partly because dwellings and workplaces are unnecessarily far apart. This excess distance between residential and employment areas arises basically because employment is more centralised than housing. Sydney comprises an inner core (the city centre and inner suburbs) with jobs well in excess of resident workers, and a periphery where resident workers generally outnumber the jobs available, with the result that most workers travel in to work in the morning and out again in the evening.

It is not true, however, that all kinds of employment are centralised. Some kinds are widespread; others strongly concentrated. Whether or not a worker has a wide choice of jobs near his house, or of houses near his job, depends on whether he works in a centralised occupation. Most clerks have little choice but to work in the city centre and live in the suburbs, whereas carpenters' jobs are mainly in the suburbs, like their homes. The argument that employment is over-centralised therefore applies only to some occupations, and any efforts to decentralise jobs should be directed towards these occupations. However, planners do not have any direct control over the location of jobs in particular occupations. Locational decisions are made by employers, and must suit the requirements of the industry or administrative activity they are engaged in. Occupations will be centralised most often when they are highly represented in centralised industries. The most that planners can do is to attempt to decentralise occupations indirectly by promoting the dispersal of presently centralised industries, or at least of those parts of presently centralised industries which could move to the suburbs without undue loss of efficiency.

On this argument, the centralisation of employment can usefully be described in two ways. The first concentrates on the identification of centralised industries — those kinds of activity which might be candidates for decentralisation. The second identifies centralised occupations — that is, those occupations which are likely to put a worker to the disadvantage of long work journeys. This second discussion provides background to the subsequent consideration (in Chapter 6) of the extent to which long journeys are due to the separation of workplaces and dwellings, and the extent to which they are due to other factors including voluntary choice.

The Centralisation of Employment by Industry

Conventionally, economic activities are grouped as industries, each industry consisting of a group of establishments playing a more or less similar role in the flow of goods from producer to consumer. In this sense, industries are not confined to primary production and manufacturing, but extend to include transport and services — even government services, and in fact all activities providing paid employment.

For statistical purposes, industries are classified to 'reflect as realistically as possible the way in which activities are actually organised in establishments... The classes represent realistic and recognisable segments of Australian industry' (ABS 1968, p.6). In classifying establishments, the statistician's aim has been to group similar activities and segregate dissimilar, similarity being defined in terms of function within the flow from producer to consumer; in terms of an activity identifiable by its inputs and outputs. Thus retailing is recognisable as a stage in the flow from producer to consumer (the stocking and display of finished goods, and their final sale to the consumer) and from its inputs and outputs (shop buildings, shop assistants' labour, working capital, and value added through services to the customer).

The 1971 Census gives the location of workplaces in Sydney according to a classification of 59 industries. Of these 12 are different kinds of 'unidentified' and 'other', and one (petroleum exploration) is not worth considering for it has but 28 employees. This leaves 47 industries of widely varying employment, from forestry with 163 employees to retailing with 136362. In all cases, the numbers are understated to the extent that workers in that industry failed to nominate the address of their workplace (see Chapter 1).

Excellent though the Australian Standard Industrial Classification may be as a listing of economic activities, it is not quite so apposite in the description of the geographic patterns of employment. For example, one industry, 'retailing', comprises a number of segments each with different locational characteristics. Department stores are far between; corner shops are ubiquitous at least in the older suburbs. Similarly, the 'health' industry includes both general practitioners' surgeries, which are widespread, and general hospitals, which are not. If industries were classified according to similarity of locational pattern, corner stores and doctors' surgeries would quite likely come under the same heading, and similarly department stores and general hospitals. The definitions of several of the 47 industries are unsatisfactory in this way, but such cases do not altogether vitiate the statistics as means of describing the location patterns of economic activity. Employment in some of the industries is recognisably centralised, while in others it is dispersed. In yet others it is neither centralised nor dispersed, but is concentrated in particular suburbs outside the city centre.

In order to classify industries into these three types (dispersed, concentrated in the suburbs, and concentrated in the city centre) two measures are required. The first is a simple measure of centralisation: the proportion of the total workforce in the industry working within the City of Sydney (post-1968 boundaries). It is more difficult to identify industries concentrated elsewhere, but a start can be made by calculating the coefficient of variation of the zonal distribution of jobs in each industry. Other things being equal, this coefficient (the standard deviation divided by the mean) will be high for concentrated industries, and low for dispersed industries. However, before industries can be compared, it is necessary to adjust further for the effect of industry size. If an industry is small, it is likely that its coefficient of variation will be higher than for a large industry. In manufacturing, for example, all the jobs in a small industry may be gathered into one or two factories, resulting in a high coefficient of variation. With factory size remaining the same, a larger, more broadly defined industry would record a lower coefficient. Since these differences are due to definitions which, from a locational point of view, are quite arbitrary, it is best to adjust for them by regressing the coefficient of variation on the total number of employees in each industry. Empirically, the fit is better if the logarithm of the number of employees is used, for the effect diminishes rapidly as industry size increases. Deviations from the trend line then give a rough estimate of whether an industry is more or less concentrated than average, given its size class.

Taking these two criteria, the degree of centralisation in the City of Sydney and the degree of concentration generally, the 47 industries can be cross-classified as shown in Table 2.1. For the sake of completeness the table includes a number of non-urban industries whose total employment in Sydney is low, and in many cases unrepresentative of the industry as a whole, consisting of forwarding depots or head offices and the like. Examples include forestry and coal mining. There are also some low-employment industries which represent incursions of the rural hinterland within the urban boundary — agriculture, fishing and the like. Though included in the table these industries will not be further discussed.

Several observations may be made about this rough classification. Firstly, the expected relationship between the degree of centralisation in the City of Sydney and the general degree of concentration is far from complete. Air transport and insurance are both highly concentrated, but the first has only a third, and the second more than three-quarters of its total employment in the city centre. Similarly, some of the more dispersed industries maintain a substantial presence in the City of Sydney, and others do not. Welfare and religion, for example, has a quarter of its workforce in the City, while household domestic service is hardly found there at all. Although it covers but one per cent of the urban area, the City of Sydney contains 52 census zones, roughly a tenth of the total, and if an industry were spread through these 52 and not elsewhere it would score highly for centralisation in the City without being rated as strongly concentrated.

TABLE 2.1 *The Concentration of Industries in Sydney. Census 1971.*

	Total workforce	Degree of concentration (see note)	% workforce working in the City of Sydney
1. INDUSTRIES OF LOW CONCENTRATION			
1a. Industries with less than 15% of total jobs in the City of Sydney.			
Domestic service (private households)	1,620	-3.7	3
Personal services	13,388	-3.0	13
Special trade contracting (construction industry)	21,714	-2.7	7
Wood, wood products, furniture	14,361	-2.0	5
1b. Industries with 15 to 45% of total jobs in the City of Sydney.			
Welfare and religion	5,847	-3.1	24
Restaurants, hotels and clubs	29,252	-1.9	29
General construction	39,345	-1.6	19
1c. Industries with over 44% of total jobs in the City of Sydney.			
Forestry	163	-1.8	49
2. INDUSTRIES OF MODERATE CONCENTRATION			
2a. Industries with less than 15% of total jobs in the City of Sydney.			
Quarries	1,008	-1.3	4
Agriculture	5,421	-1.2	1
Fishing	193	-1.2	4
Fabricated metal products	33,733	-0.9	3
Leather, rubber and plastic products	21,316	-0.9	10
Textiles	10,651	-0.6	10
Chemical, petroleum and coal products	26,019	-0.5	5
Basic metal products	11,597	-0.3	6
Industrial equipment and household appliances	70,628	+0.4	5
Transport equipment	32,657	+0.5	7
Non-metallic mineral products	14,714	+0.8	2
Non-metallic non-construction minerals	150	+1.5	7
2b. Industries with 15 to 45% of total jobs in the City of Sydney.			
Road transport	22,447	-1.5	16
Community Services not elsewhere included	18,290	-1.2	43
Health services	51,731	-0.8	21
Clothing and footwear	26,464	-0.8	30
Entertainment and recreation	12,421	-0.8	40
Food, drink and tobacco	34,679	-0.6	17

TABLE 2.1 *(Continued)*

	Total workforce	Degree of concentration (see note)	% workforce working in the City of Sydney
2b. (Continued)			
Education, art galleries and museums	39,978	-0.5	19
Wholesale trade	86,844	-0.4	30
Retail trade	136,362	-0.1	18
Services to agriculture	294	0	28
Paper, paper products, printing and publishing	32,334	0	38
Communications	23,949	+1.2	39
Coal mining	305	+1.2	43
2c. Industries with over 44% of total jobs in the City of Sydney.			
Transport and storage not elsewhere included	6,199	-0.9	55
Services to mining	1,345	-0.5	66
Real Estate and business services	54,000	+0.7	46
Electricity and gas	13,812	+1.0	45
3. INDUSTRIES OF HIGH CONCENTRATION			
3a. Industries with 15 to 45% of total jobs in the City of Sydney.			
Defence	19,669	+2.9	33
Air transport	8,891	+8.4	34
3b. Industries with over 44 % of total jobs in the City of Sydney.			
Public administration	39,237	+1.7	66
Water transport	6,537	+2.6	84
Metallic minerals	262	+3.0	89
Rail transport	9,925	+3.3	61
Insurance	19,362	+3.8	79
Finance and investment	34,984	+4.6	61
Water supply, sewerage and drainage	6,537	+5.3	49

Note: The degree of concentration is $Y - Y_c$

where $Y = \frac{\sigma}{\bar{x}}$

$Y_c = 13.53 - 2.23 (\log T)$
$(r^2 = .34)$

$\bar{x}$ = average number of jobs per zone in that industry

T = total number of jobs in the industry

σ = standard deviation of the number of jobs per zone

Source: Census 1971, journey to work tapes.

Industries rated as highly concentrated comprise defence, with its limited number of large installations; transport by water, rail or air, and industries with a high proportion of office employment (the Water Board and public administration in general, and finance, investment and insurance). In several of these cases the industry as a whole rates as highly concentrated even though parts of it are fairly well dispersed: finance has its branch banks, public administration its municipal offices, the railways their individual stations. The industries which lack such a penumbra of dispersion are the most highly concentrated of all — air transport and insurance.

Industries like non-road transport and defence are concentrated (though not centralised) for technical reasons, and would be hard to disperse. Their concentration in particular suburbs undoubtedly creates long journeys to work for some employees, but on the other hand a man who works in a suburban concentration has a better chance of obtaining a single family house near his workplace than one who works in the city centre. It is for this reason that industries which are both concentrated and centralised should be the prime targets for any decentralisation policies. These are almost entirely the office industries.

The dispersed industries, in no need of decentralisation, are of two kinds, building and construction (including wood products), and services like pubs, religion, welfare and laundries. The list of dispersed industries would undoubtedly be swollen considerably if the dispersed parts of retailing, health and education were separated from the concentrated, but given the statistician's definitions this cannot be done.

None of the manufacturing industries are highly concentrated, and few are centralised in the City of Sydney. Indeed, apart from several low-employment industries like fishing, all industries of moderate concentration and low centralisation come under the functional heading of manufacturing. The two manufacturing industries with significant employment in the City are traditional occupants of inner city space — the rag trade and printing and publishing. Even these have less than 40 per cent of their total jobs in the City of Sydney. However, some parts of manufacturing industry may be centralised, for example, head offices.

This leaves the moderately concentrated non-manufacturing industries, nearly all of which are also moderately well represented in the City of Sydney, and so present some but limited scope for decentralisation. As already noted, some of these are not satisfactorily defined from a geographic point of view, but others perhaps deserve their place in the table — entertainment and recreation, for example, with its city theatres and suburban sports grounds.

The Centralisation of Employment by Occupation

Though for planning purposes the concentration of employment is best described by industry, from the individual worker's point of view it is the centralisation of occupations that matters. A similar analysis to that already applied for industries can be used to classify occupations into those centralised in the City of Sydney, those concentrated elsewhere, and those dispersed throughout the metropolitan area. The basic census classification in this instance comprises 67 occupations, defined to group together similar and related skills. Once again the census definitions may have brought together occupations with different geographic distributions, though this is not important if the occupations are close substitutes. Thus the same shop assistant may be able to find dispersed employment in a local milk bar, or concentrated in a department store. On the other hand, some occupational definitions still hide important differences of pattern, such as the difference in the degree of dispersion of the jobs available to primary and tertiary teachers.

Like the industries the census occupations include widely varying numbers of people, with clerks the most common at 151 564 workers, tailing off through mineral treaters (157) to such insignificant occupations as hunter and trapper, engaging two people. Occupations with less than 150 representatives in Sydney are omitted from the analysis. A few other mainly rural occupations, though included for reasons of completeness, are scarcely worth comment because only a few hundred jobs are involved for each.

The analysis of occupations proceeds exactly as in the industry case, and results in a cross-classification according to the degree of concentration, and the degree of centralisation in the City of Sydney. Once again the index of the degree of concentration depends on the relative standard deviation of the distribution by census zones, adjusted by regression on the total number of workers in each occupation. This regression equation is almost the same as that between industry size and relative standard deviation, and similarly reflects the increasing probability of dispersion as the number employed in an industry or occupation increases. Accordingly Table 2.2 presents rough estimates of the degree of concentration of each occupation after allowance for the numbers of people involved, and also shows the proportion of jobs in each occupation in the City of Sydney.

Given that Table 2.2 is constructed in the same way as Table 2.1 it is not surprising to find a fairly close relationship between the degree of concentration of different industries and of the occupations common in those industries. The strongly concentrated industries are non-road transport, defence and the office industries, so it is to be expected that air pilots, railway drivers, ship's officers, servicemen, typists and clerks have highly concentrated occupations. The typists and clerks are especially significant, for together with stenographers they comprise nearly 20 per cent of total employment. Their jobs are not only concentrated, but are also centralised in the City of Sydney. Though many of these typists and clerks work in the office industries, many more work in offices which are part of firms engaged in other industries.

At the other extreme, the dispersed industries are personal services and

TABLE 2.2 *The Concentration of Occupations in Sydney. Census 1971.*

		Total workforce	Degree of concentration (see note)	% workforce in City of Sydney
1.	OCCUPATIONS OF LOW CONCENTRATION			
1a.	Occupations with less than 15% of total jobs in the City of Sydney			
	Athletes, sportsmen, related workers	753	-3.6	9
	Mineral treaters	157	-3.5	3
	Undertakers and crematorium workers	174	-2.8	9
	Miners, mineral prospectors, quarrymen	326	-3.1	7
	Painters and decorators	8,680	-2.1	12
	Farm worker	5,937	-2.0	5
	Carpenters, wood machinists etc.	21,112	-2.0	11
1b.	Occupations with 15 to 45% of total jobs in the City of Sydney.			
	Clergy and members of religious orders	2,042	-3.2	16
	Paramedical workers	3,529	-2.8	17
	Photographers and camera operators	1,111	-2.8	42
	Launderers, dry cleaners and pressers	3,826	-2.3	17
	Biologists, vets., agronomists etc.	1,202	-2.1	37
	Barbers, hairdressers, beauticians	6,082	-1.7	15
	Waiters, bartenders	8,992	-1.7	29
2.	OCCUPATIONS OF MODERATE CONCENTRATION			
2a.	Occupations with less than 15% of total jobs in the City of Sydney.			
	Bricklayers, plasterers, construction workers	8,680	-1.5	11
	Furnacemen, rollers, moulders, metal workers	3,450	-1.5	2
	Stationary engine, excavator, lift operators	10,670	-1.3	13
	Packers, wrappers, labellers	10,438	-1.2	11
	Millers, bakers, food and drink workers	15,776	-1.2	9
	Road transport drivers	31,397	-0.6	13
	Labourers not elsewhere classified	35,237	-0.3	13
	Fishermen	162	-0.3	4
	Teachers	28,841	-0.2	14
	Farmers and farm managers	3,444	-0.1	0
	Chemical, sugar, paper products process workers	8,294	+0.3	4
	Metal and electrical products process workers	31,277	+0.5	5
	Spinners, weavers, knitters, dyers etc.	6,206	+0.5	9
	Rubber, plastic, concrete products process workers	14,102	+0.6	6
	Metal tradesmen, mechanics etc.	85,339	+0.9	9

TABLE 2.2 *(Continued)*

	Total workforce	Degree of concentration (see note)	% workforce in City of Sydney
2b. Occupations with 15 to 45% of total jobs in the City of Sydney.			
Medical practitioners, dentists	4,981	-1.4	28
Service, sport and recreation workers not elsewhere classified	8,243	-1.3	23
Chemists, physicists, other physical scientists	2,104	-1.3	36
Instrument makers, jewellers etc.	4,735	-1.3	40
Caretakers, cleaners of buildings	16,668	-1.2	26
Storemen and freight handlers	25,475	-1.0	24
Commercial travellers, manufacturers agents	12,467	-1.0	27
Housekeepers, cooks, maids etc.	22,679	-0.9	22
Leather cutters, lasters, sewers etc.	3,946	-0.7	15
Fire brigade, police and protective workers	10,040	-0.7	36
Transport and communication workers not elsewhere included	1,700	-0.6	24
Electricians and related workers	29,545	-0.4	22
Nurses including trainees	19,121	-0.2	19
Architects, engineers, surveyors	12,589	+0.2	19
Tailors, cutters, furriers etc.	21,109	+0.2	29
Draughtsmen and technicians	30,276	+0.2	34
Printing trades workers	14,258	+0.4	38
Bookkeepers and cashiers	28,887	+0.5	38
Insurance and real estate salesmen, valuers	7,126	+0.5	41
Employers, managers, workers on own account	83,974	+0.6	26
Proprietors, shopkeepers, retail and wholesale salesmen, shop assistants etc.	69,504	+0.9	20
Transport inspectors, supervisors and controllers	3,588	+1.2	38
2c. Occupations with more than 44% of total employment in the City of Sydney.			
Government administrative and executive officials	1,576	-1.3	55
Artists, entertainers, writers etc.	8,804	-0.4	49
Telephone, telegraph, telecommunications operators	7,051	+0.4	53
Wool classers	229	+0.5	50
Professional and technical workers not elsewhere included	16,344	+1.0	55
Deck and engine-room hands, ship and boatmen	547	+1.3	61

TABLE 2.2 *(Continued)*

	Total workforce	Degree of concen-tration (see note)	% work-force in City of Sydney
3. OCCUPATIONS OF HIGH CONCENTRATION			
3a. Occupations with under 15% of total employment in the City of Sydney.			
Members of the armed services	11,031	+3.5	14
Railway drivers and firemen	994	+3.6	13
Air pilots, navigators, flight engineers	395	+8.1	10
Tobacco product makers	836	+11.5	1
3b. Occupations with 15 to 45% of total employment in the City of Sydney.			
Postmasters, postmen and messengers	6,512	+3.1	26
3c. Occupations with over 44% of total employment in the City of Sydney.			
Stenographers and typists	53,183	+1.6	46
Ships deck and engineers officers	328	+2.2	70
Clerks not elsewhere included	151,564	+2.9	49
Law professionals	3,216	+3.1	79
Railway guards and conductors	504	+4.1	47

Note: The degree of concentration is $Y - Y_c$

where $Y = \frac{\sigma}{\bar{x}}$

$Y_c = 12.79 - 2.42 \text{ (log T)}$
$(r^2 = .34)$

$\bar{x}$ = average number of jobs per zone in that occupation

T = total number of jobs in that occupation

σ = standard deviation of the number of jobs per zone

Source: Census 1971, journey to work tapes.

construction. Clergy, launderers, barbers, waiters, painters and carpenters are all, as a result, working in dispersed occupations.

Manufacturing industries tend to be moderately concentrated outside the city centre, and this is also true of most factory occupations.

Despite the general relationship between industry and occupation, there are occasions when occupations typical of an industry have quite different patterns of dispersion from the industry as a whole. For example, health services are moderately concentrated (index –0.8) but they include paramedical workers, dispersed at –2.8, medical practitioners at –1.4, and nurses whose degree of concentration is average at –0.2. Again, communications are moderately concentrated (+1.2) but postmasters are highly and rather unexpectedly so (+3.1). In the opposite direction, public administration is highly concentrated (+1.7) but government administrative and executive officials are fairly well dispersed (–1.3), perhaps due to a higher proportion of officials in the local government part of public administration. However, sometimes such differences are matters of definition alone: tobacco product makers are highly concentrated at +11.5, yet as an industry tobacco is included with food and drink, the overall index for the industry being –0.6. A tobacco industry by itself would record high concentration.

Despite these differences, the general rule holds, that centralised occupations are those common in the centralised industries, and that the decentralisation of these industries and of the centralised offices of other industries would improve the spread of employment opportunities.

Patterns of Employment

The different geographic patterns of concentrated and dispersed employment are shown on Maps 1 to 4. Three of the maps show employment by industry, as follows:

Map 1: Highly concentrated industries (Part 3 of Table 2.1, including defence, non-road transport, and the office industries).

Map 2: Manufacturing industries (Part 2a of Table 2.1, plus wood products, clothing and footwear, food, drink and tobacco, and paper products).

Map 3: Dispersed industries (Part 1 of Table 2.1, excluding wood products. The main industries included are personal services, restaurants, hotels and clubs, welfare and construction).

The fourth group of industries (moderately concentrated non-manufacturing industries) could also have been mapped, but as pointed out when deriving the classification of industries, this group included many industries which, like retailing, were defined unsatisfactorily from a locational point of view. In lieu of a map of the job distribution for these industries as a whole, Map 4 shows the distribution of saleswomen's jobs.

Each of these four maps, and also the other maps of the location of employment (Maps 5 and 6 for all jobs, and Maps 11 and 12 for men and women separately) has four levels of shading, representing different levels of jobs per hectare. The levels are comparable across the different maps, despite differences in the absolute job-densities represented by the same shading, since the cut-off points used on each map are proportional to the number of workers covered by the map. Thus the number of people working in the manufacturing industries is about 32 per cent of all workers, and the cut-off points for the levels of shading in Map 2 are roughly 32 per cent of those in Map 5 (i.e. 1.3 jobs/hectare and 3.9 jobs/hectare respectively for the upper limit of the lowest level of shading). This means that if the manufacturing industries had the same locational pattern as that of jobs as a whole, exactly the same map would result.

Two words of warning apply to all the maps. Firstly, as noted in Chapter 1, the densities shown depend to some extent on the chances of census zone size and boundaries. Secondly, the highest level of shading usually represents a very wide range of densities. Usually the city centre peak density is many times the minimum represented by the most dense shading. None of the maps, therefore, bring home the fact that job densities in the city centre are much greater than anywhere else in the metropolitan area.

By definition the concentrated industries of Map 1 are by and large confined to a small number of special areas. However, even among these industries there is some scattering of workplaces. Indeed, the distribution is broadly one which will become familiar from later maps — the jobs are concentrated in the city centre and the inner and middle-western suburbs out as far as Bankstown and Parramatta, with only a few outliers beyond. The difference between this and more dispersed distributions is that the mid-western scattering of jobs is less marked.

These concentrated industries are of two kinds: defence and non-road transport, providing four per cent of total employment, and the office industries with ten per cent. Defence installations, railway workshops, the airport and wharves account for much of the suburban employment shown on the map, while office employment concentrates in the city centre, North Sydney and Parramatta. While there are technological reasons for the suburban concentration of defence and non-road transport, the reasons for the centralisation of the office industries have more to do with human habit: the need of administrators to be near one another for ready personal contact; the desire for a prestigious office. Centralisation may also be promoted by economic forces: of all points in the metropolitan area the central city is most easily reached by public transport, though perhaps not by motor car. Again, centralisation may be explained by historical inertia — though this does not tell us why the office industries are the most affected. After all there was a time when all Sydney, including all its manufacturing plant and personal service establishments, lay within the present city centre.

Map 2, showing the location of factory jobs, is different from Map 1 — the pattern is much more dispersed — but the two maps still have much in common. The main areas of employment, in manufacturing as in all else, are in

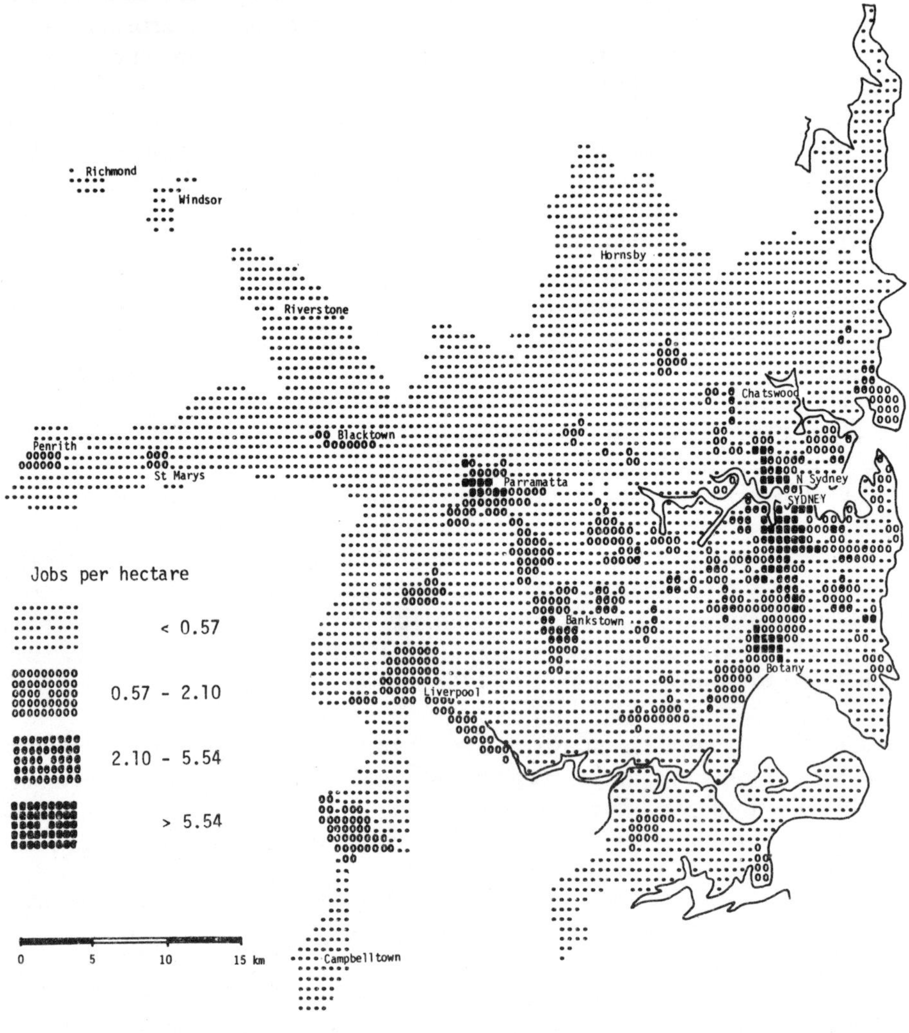

MAP 1. The Location of Jobs in the Concentrated Industries, Sydney, Census 1971 (see text, page 37). As defined in Table 2.1, the concentrated industries include defence, air, water and rail transport, water supply, public administration and insurance, finance and investment. Together they provide 14 per cent of total employment, much of it in the city centre, but with a scattering in the suburbs — including such installations as the airport in Botany and railway workshops in Bankstown.

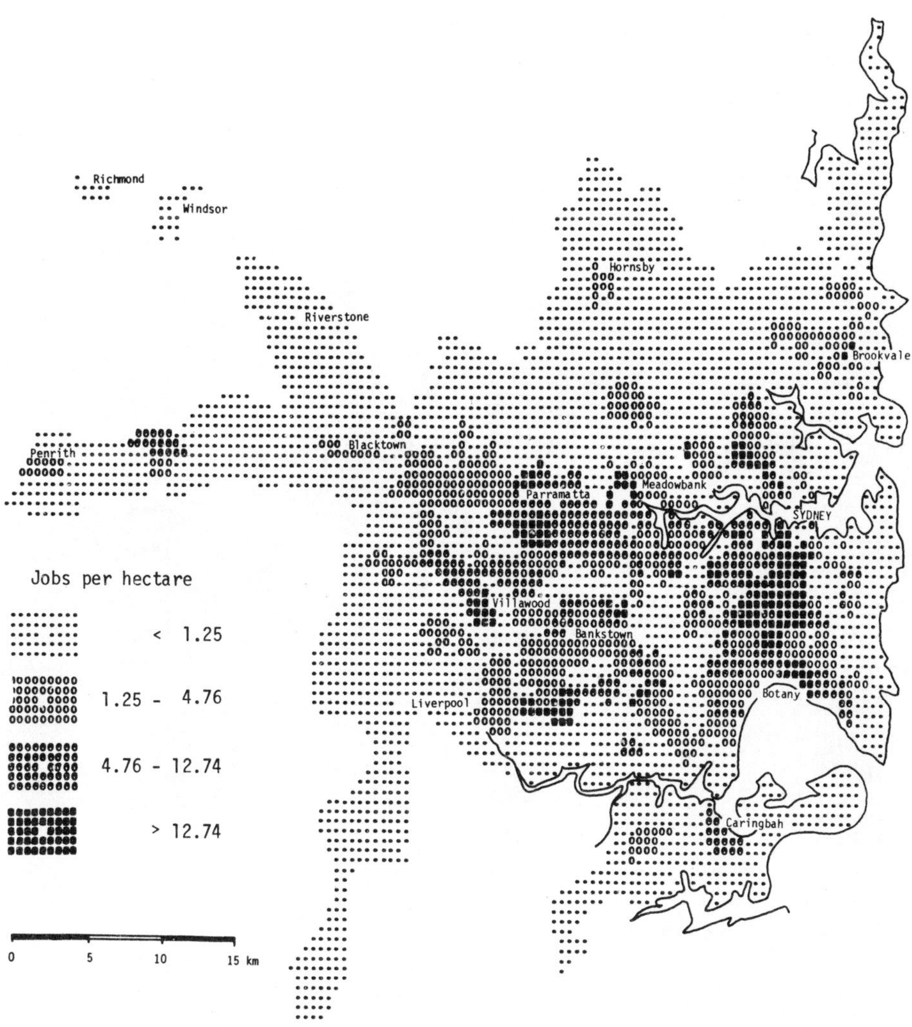

MAP 2. The Location of Jobs in Manufacturing Industry, Sydney, Census 1971 (see text, page 37). Thirty-two per cent of all jobs in Sydney are in manufacturing industry. which by and large is moderately concentrated outside the city centre (Table 2.1). The locational pattern is much more evenly spread than that of the concentrated industries, but even so does not reach into the outer suburbs.

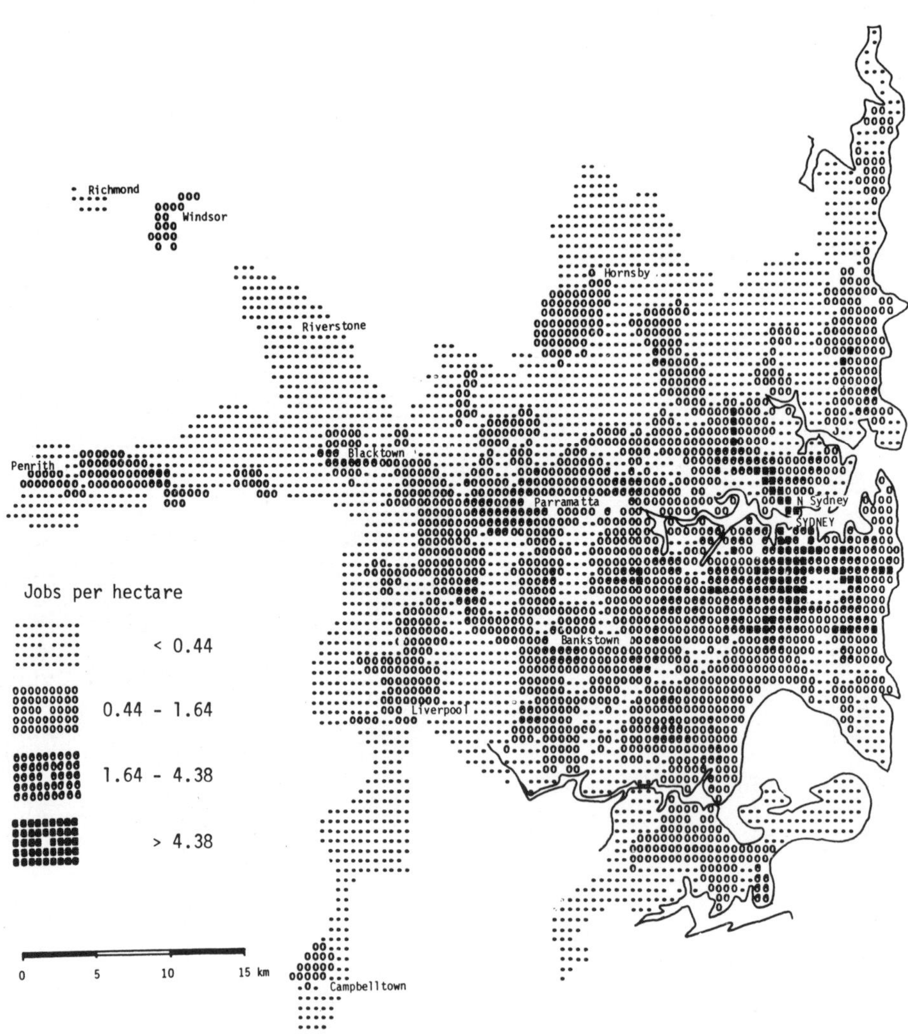

MAP 3. The Location of Jobs in the Dispersed Industries, Sydney, Census 1971 (see text, page 42. Strictly, the dispersed industries shown on this map are domestic and personal services, welfare and religion, restaurants, hotels and clubs and the construction industry, providing in total 10 per cent of all jobs. However their pattern of dispersion is also typical of some segments of retailing, health and education.

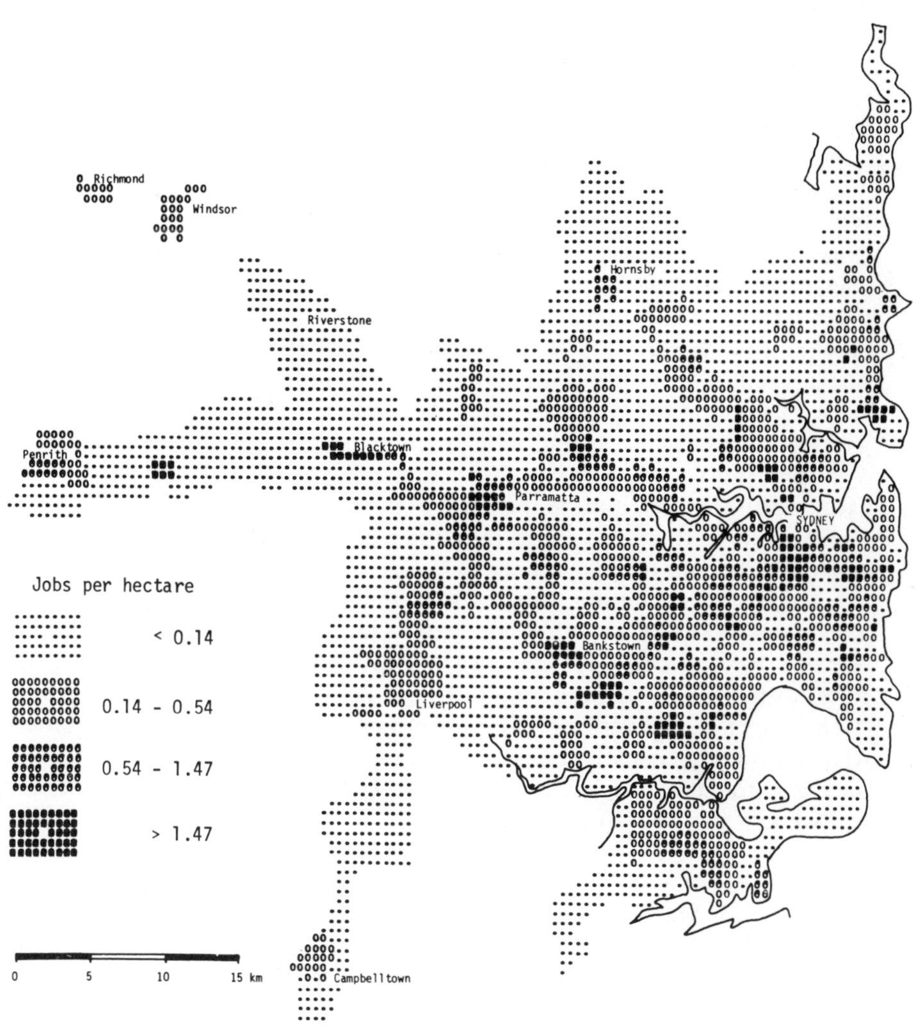

MAP 4. The Location of Saleswomen's Jobs, Sydney, Census 1971 (see text, page 42). Saleswomen's jobs are dispersed throughout the metropolitan area, yet at a regional level are concentrated in the major suburban shopping centres, each of which appears on the map. Though saleswomen comprise only 4 per cent of the total workforce, this pattern of metropolitan dispersion and regional concentration is typical of a number of occupations, including nursing and higher level teaching.

the inner and mid-western suburbs, inside an oval drawn around North Sydney, Botany, Bankstown and Parramatta. Within this area few suburbs are far from a concentration of factory employment, while outside it there are only a few outliers — St Marys, Brookvale (in Warringah Shire) and Caringbah. (Liverpool might also rate a mention, but for technical reasons explained in Chapter 1 it does not show on the map.)

The largest concentrations of factory employment occupy the flatter parts of the inner and mid-western suburbs: the area between the city centre and Botany, and the area at the head of the harbour leading up to Parramatta. Other prominent concentrations lie in Bankstown south of the commercial area, in Villawood (between Bankstown and Parramatta) and in North Sydney, north of the main concentration of offices. Though all these areas are important for factories, the occupations represented in them vary somewhat. The less skilled men's jobs are relatively prominent in the two major industrial areas of South Sydney/Botany and Parramatta/Auburn, while by contrast unskilled women's jobs spread into a number of suburban factory estates with relatively few jobs for men. Notable examples are St Marys, Caringbah, North Sydney and Meadowbank (to the north of the harbour, midway between North Sydney and Parramatta). This may indicate deliberate decentralisation by employers anxious to obtain a cheap and contented labour force. Skilled jobs as a whole form a pattern midway between these two: they are more widespread than men's process work, but do not extend into the outer suburbs as much as women's factory jobs. However, when individual skills are considered, the pattern subdivides and becomes much patchier.

The dispersed industries of Map 3 comprise construction, welfare, hotels, restaurants and personal services. They are indeed more dispersed than either the concentrated industries or the factories, with less emphasis on the inner and mid-western suburbs. However, there is still a degree of concentration among the offices in the city centre, and in North Sydney. On the other hand, the dispersed industries do not account for much employment in manufacturing areas. Though Map 3 applies strictly to but 10 per cent of total employment, and is relevant directly only to workers in services and construction, this dispersed pattern of employment opportunities applies also in certain other occupations, notably business management — for wherever there are economic enterprises managers are to be found.

Map 4, of saleswomen's jobs, illustrates yet another pattern of job opportunities. On this map there are numerous peaks of high density employment, spread over most of the metropolitan area. Each peak represents a shopping centre. Of the important shopping areas, only Liverpool and Campbelltown fail to appear on the map, this being due to the way the census zones are drawn. The office employment areas in Parramatta, North Sydney and the city centre are also shopping centres, though in the last two cases the area of retail activity is more narrowly defined than that for offices. By and large saleswomen are not to be found working in the factory areas, but despite this theirs is a widespread occupation — indeed, in some of the fringe suburbs the only occupation present in significant numbers. The shopping centres shown on Map 4 also have jobs for salesmen but, by contrast with the women, salesmen and storemen often find work in warehouses in the factory areas. This results in their jobs being even more dispersed than saleswomen's.

A pattern of job opportunities similar to that on Map 4 also applies to workers in some of the professions. Once again there are peaks of employment dispersed around the suburbs. Such is true for people who work in hospitals or major educational institutions like universities and technical colleges.

Though they directly cover less than two-thirds of total employment in Sydney, these four maps are sufficient to introduce the main locational patterns exhibited by different occupations and industries. In broad summary, they show that manufacturing is carried on in specialised areas within the inner and mid-western suburbs, while the other kinds of employment tend to concentrate in shopping and commercial centres. In the outer suburbs such shopping centres provide little more than retail employment, but in such places as Parramatta, North Sydney, and overwhelmingly in the city centre, this is supplemented by office jobs. Finally, a scattering of small concentrations of specialised jobs testifies to the peculiar locational requirements of defence and non-road transport, and to the past choices of those who sited the hospitals and universities.

The overall distribution of workplaces is shown on Map 5, with an enlargement of the inner area in Map 6. The addition of the several industrial and occupational patterns gives a central city with a high number of jobs per hectare, a scattering of moderately high figures in the factory and commercial areas of the other inner and mid-western suburbs, and a wide, relatively jobless fringe beyond.

Map 6, the detailed map of the inner suburbs, brings out several features lost on the other maps. One of the most obvious is the way in which jobs in North Sydney are to be found in a narrow belt, along the ridge with the railway and Pacific Highway, from the Harbour Bridge to Chatswood. A lesser arm runs along another ridge towards Mosman. On the city side of the harbour, it is noticeable that the job density falls off abruptly east of the city centre, while to the west and south the decline in job densities is patchier and more gradual, so beginning the mixture of residential, industrial and commercial areas that characterise the western suburbs as far as Parramatta and Bankstown.

If at all possible Maps 5 and 6 should be compared with a map of the residential distribution of the population of Sydney. Such maps are available as Map 39 in Davis & Spearritt, 1974, or included in the sheet 'Major Urban Areas' in the Atlas of Australian Resources. Such a comparison will make obvious the extent to which jobs are centralised more than residential areas. The major factory areas are areas of low residential density, though on either side of South Sydney and of the city centre lie some of the highest density residential areas in Australia. These to some extent provide housing within easy

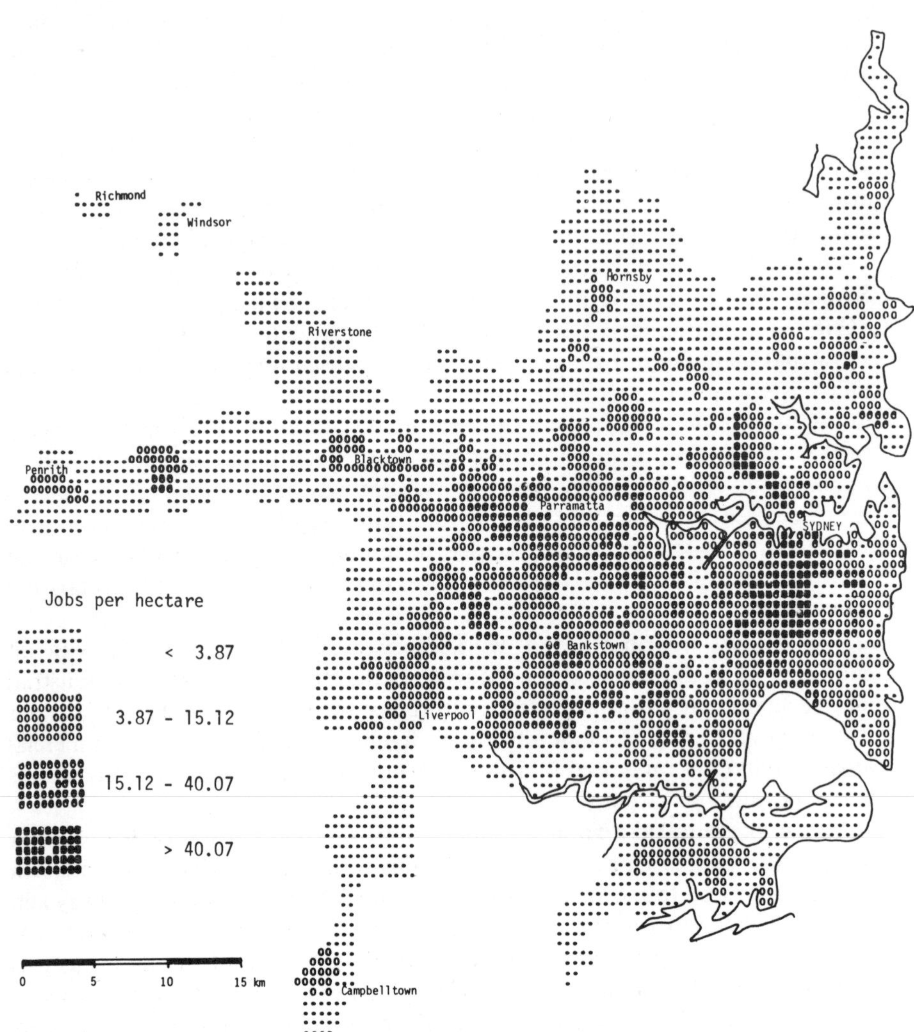

MAP 5. The Location of All Jobs, Sydney, Census 1971 (see text, page 43). This map brings out the basic fact about the distribution of jobs in Sydney: the inner areas have a surplus, while the fringe suburbs have relatively little local employment.

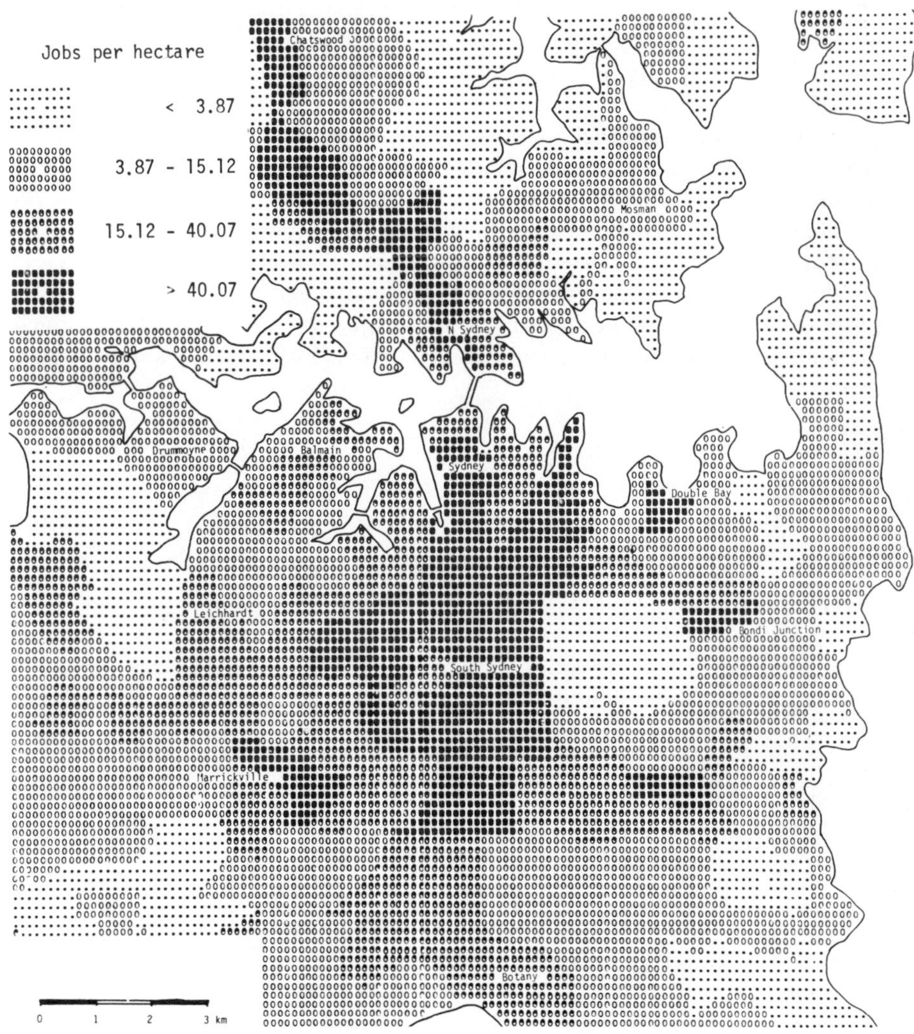

MAP 6. The Location of Jobs in Central Sydney, Census 1971 (see text, page 43). This enlargement of the central part of Map 5 gives the detailed location of workplaces in the inner part of Sydney. The high employment density of the city centre extends into both North and South Sydney — though (and this is not apparent from the map) employment densities in these areas are much less than in the central business district.

reach of the heaviest concentration of jobs. Despite this, only some 40 per cent of the working population of the Sydney urban area lives in the oval bounded by North Sydney, the city centre, Botany, Bankstown and Parramatta — the area mapped as having relatively high employment densities. This area has 70 per cent of the jobs.

Having shown how the distribution of employment in Sydney is more centralised than that of residential areas, we are in a position to enquire how the distribution of jobs affects people's decisions as to where to live and work. To what extent is their travel caused simply by the separation of dwellings and workplaces, and to what extent do they travel further than is strictly necessary? On the answer to this question depends the assessment of job decentralisation proposals, for if it can be shown that the people of Sydney do not put much premium on minimising their work travel, there is little urgency about helping them to do so.

CHAPTER 3

Workplaces and the Journey to Work

Each journey to work starts from a dwelling and proceeds to a workplace. Some journeys to work (and more frequently journeys from work) have diversions on the way, such as visits to shops or hotels, but the census does not provide any data on the frequency of such complications. In it journeys are described by origin, destination, straight-line distance and no more. In this chapter the length of journeys to work is summarised firstly by destination (workplace) and then by origin (dwelling).

Journey Length by Workplace

It was argued in Chapter 1 that the broad pattern of journeys to work in a metropolitan area is predictable; that people take travel into account when deciding where to live and work, and that generalisations can be made about their decisions and verified statistically. The most basic of these generalisations is that a person is less likely to work in any given place the further he lives from that place. As the journey to work lengthens, more and more people are put off by the time and cash costs involved, and either look for work closer to home, or shift to live closer to their work. One way in which this prediction can be checked is to draw rings around each employment area, and find the proportion of the residents of each ring who work in the area. If the prediction is correct, the proportion should decline with distance. That it does is shown in Table 3.1, which proves the point for four major employment areas in Sydney. Overall, slightly over a quarter of the metropolitan workforce works in the City of Sydney, but the proportion declines from nearly 80 per cent of those living in the city centre to only 13 per cent of those living on the fringe of the urban area. Even more marked declines are recorded for the lesser employment areas of South Sydney/Botany, Parramatta/Auburn and North Sydney/Willoughby. On this evidence people are strongly in favour of short journeys to work.

The decline with distance in the probability that people will work in a given employment area means that short journeys to work are the most common. However, this declining probability is to some extent offset by the fact that each

TABLE 3.1 *Percentage of the Metropolitan Workforce Working in Major Employment Areas, by Distance of Residence from Each Area. Sydney, Census 1971.*

Distance of residence from centroid of employment area (km)	Percentage of residents working in employment area			
	City of Sydney	South Sydney/ Botany	Parramatta/ Auburn	North Sydney/ Willoughby
0 < 1	79	62	68	47
1 < 3	55	36	51	32
3 < 6	38	17	36	17
6 < 10	32	11	15	6
10 < 20	25	7	5	4
20 < 30	17	4	2	2
30 & over	13	4	5	1
Overall	27	10	9	6

Source: Census 1971, Journey to work tapes.

ring of constant width around a given employment area is larger in area than its predecessor, and at a given population density will contain more people. It is even possible for the number of workers travelling in from a series of rings drawn round an employment centre to increase outwards, at least until the rings begin to include uninhabited parts of the urban fringe. In practice such increases are rare, being common in only two cases — firstly, where the centre of employment lies in an area where few people live, and secondly in the case of the city centre, where total employment is so great that housing densities would need to be very high to enable a sufficiently large number of workers to live close by. Apart from such cases, the number of workers travelling to a given employment centre declines with distance.

This prediction is confirmed by Graph 3.1, which plots the number of people coming to work in four centres of employment according to the straight-line length of their journey. (Strictly the straight-line distance between the centroid of their zone of residence and that of their zone of employment — see Chapter 1. Where the two zones are the same the distance plotted is one kilometre. This includes persons who worked at home.) The City of Sydney is the most important and most concentrated centre of employment in the metropolitan area, so it is not surprising to find that over the range from two to seven kilometres the number of workers coming to it increases with distance. The seven kilometre band includes such places as Bondi and Mosman; beyond these the number of city centre workers coming from each ring falls away suddenly,

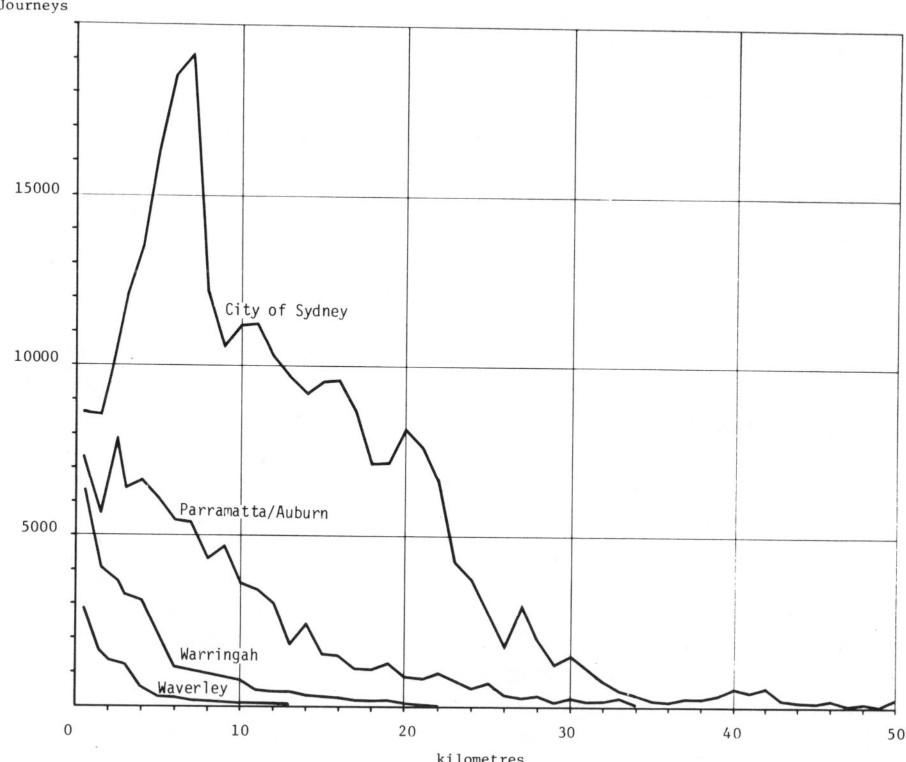

GRAPH 3.1 *Length of Journeys to Work in Selected Employment areas, Sydney, Census 1971.*

and then less rapidly, till by 22 kilometres (the distance of Hornsby, Parramatta and Sutherland) the number is under five thousand for each extra kilometre, and by 32 kilometres (beyond Blacktown and Liverpool) the number is under one thousand. The shape of this distribution reflects the geography of Sydney: the high density inner suburbs finishing at seven kilometres from the city centre; the urban fringe to the north and south occurring at 22 kilometres, and over much of the west at 32 kilometres. In general terms it is as expected; a rise in numbers followed by a fall.

Though much smaller than the City of Sydney in terms of employment, and much less intensely developed, Parramatta/Auburn is still the major free-standing suburban employment area. In its case, however, travel to work declines with distance over virtually the whole range, though there are still significant numbers travelling up to 25 kilometres — this being of the order of the straight-line distance from St Marys to Auburn.

The graph for Warringah Shire combines a number of small employment centres — places like Mona Vale and Narrabeen — and one of moderate size,

Brookvale. None is of more than local importance and few journeys to work in the Shire are of more than ten kilometres. Warringah may be an extreme case, in that it is cut off physically from the rest of Sydney, but a rapid fall in the number of journeys with increasing distance is still typical of employment centres in the other outer suburbs. This fall is even more marked for the smaller places in the inner areas — witness the graph for Waverley Municipality (which includes the important shopping centre at Bondi Junction). Very few people working in this municipality travel more than four kilometres to work.

These four graphs represent all levels of employment concentration, from city centre through major suburban centre to areas of purely local employment, yet the general shape of each graph — the general decline in numbers travelling with distance — remains much the same. Only in a few outer suburban employment zones is the shape much different, and there it is because a few workers coming in from far away lead to a distribution with a very long tail. The general skewed shape of these distributions means that the average distance travelled to work in any employment area is generally greater than the median, and in a few outer suburbs it is very much greater.

Because of the generally similar shape of the distributions in Graph 3.1, the proportion of workers with short trips of less than three kilometres, and of those with long journeys of over ten straight-line kilometres, vary together and closely follow the median (Table 3.2). This simplifies the description and mapping of journey patterns in subsequent chapters.

The fact that average journeys to work in the larger employment concentrations are longer than in the smaller suggests that different sizes of

TABLE 3.2 *Distances Travelled to Major Employment Areas in Sydney. Census 1971.*

Employment Area	Distance travelled				
	0<3 km %	3<6 km %	6<10 km %	10km & over %	Total %
City of Sydney	10	17	21	52	100
Sth.Syd./Botany	19	21	20	40	100
Nth.Syd./Willoughby	30	18	19	33	100
Parramatta/Auburn	24	21	22	32	100
All other areas	39	21	16	24	100
Total	28	20	18	34	100

0<3 km range includes persons who worked at home.

Source: Census 1971. Journey to work tapes.

concentration should be distinguished, in order that the patterns of travel to each might be separately described. The proposed categories are the city centre, inner suburban concentrations of employment (which are in some ways extensions of the city centre), other major concentrations of employment, and the rest — dispersed local employment.

The different centres can be identified in two ways. Firstly, areas of high density employment can be recognised on Maps 5 and 6. Secondly, employment zones of more than local interest will attract journeys of high average and median length.

The city centre is immediately recognisable on Maps 5 and 6, along with its extensions into South Sydney, North Sydney and the inner eastern and western suburbs. The question as to precisely where the city centre ends and its extensions begin will be tackled in Chapter 6. But which extensions should be regarded as major centres of employment in their own right, and which are of but local interest? South Sydney/Botany certainly qualifies: the median journey to work there is 7.7 kilometres, which exceeds the metropolitan median of 6.4 kilometres, though it is below the City of Sydney median of 10.5 kilometres (Table 3.3). The case of North Sydney is a little less certain. Half the workers in North Sydney and Willoughby come from less than 6.5 kilometres away, which is very similar to the position in the metropolitan area as a whole. However, the ridge from the harbour opposite the city centre to Chatswood is prominent on Maps 5 and 6 and is certainly an area of high-density employment. This should be allowed to clinch the issue.

The westward extension of the city centre into Leichhardt and Marrickville

TABLE 3.3 *Median Distances Travelled to Employment Areas in Sydney. Census 1971.*

Employment area	Median journey km	% of total employment
City of Sydney	10.5	26
South Sydney/Botany	7.7	10
North Sydney/Willoughby	6.5	6
Parramatta/Auburn	6.8	8
Strathfield/Concord/Burwood	6.8	3
Bankstown	5.6	6
Marrickville/Leichhardt	5.5	6
All other	4.0	35
All Sydney	6.4	100

Source: Census 1971. Journey to work tapes.

is, according to Map 6, much more patchy, with employment interspersed among residential areas. The median journey to work in these two municipalities is 5.5 kilometres (Table 3.3), well below the all-Sydney median. On this evidence Marrickville and Leichhardt would seem to be employment areas of mainly local interest.

Several suburban concentrations of employment can also be identified on Map 5. The most impressive of these is Parramatta/Auburn, with its relatively high job densities, and its median journey to work of 6.8 kilometres. No other middle or outer suburban concentration is as significant. Strathfield/Concord/Burwood is in some ways an extension of Parramatta/Auburn: it meets the test of long journeys to work (half are more than 6.8 kilometres) but does not account for very many jobs — just 3 per cent of the metropolitan total (Table 3.3). For this reason Strathfield/Concord/Burwood will not be treated as a major employment zone.

The remaining candidates for inclusion as major suburban concentrations comprise three different areas in Bankstown municipality — South Bankstown (light manufacturing industry), Bankstown itself (commerce) and Villawood (manufacturing). Taken together they provide 6 per cent of all metropolitan employment, but separately they are fairly small. The median journey to work in Bankstown is less than that for the metropolitan area as a whole.

According to these criteria there are therefore two major extensions to the city centre, north and south, and one freestanding major concentration, Parramatta/Auburn. Together, these three account for 24 per cent of total employment. Added to the 26 per cent in the City of Sydney, they provide half the jobs in the metropolitan area. The other half are scattered over the rest of the suburbs.

Because journeys to work in the City of Sydney and the other major concentrations of employment are longer than average, they generate more than half the total travel. With 26 per cent of total employment, the City of Sydney is responsible for 36 per cent of total worker-kilometres, while the other three major concentrations, with 24 per cent of the jobs, generate 24 per cent of total travel. The scattered half of total employment occasions but 40 per cent of total journey-to-work kilometres (Table 3.4). Put another way, 40 per cent of all workers who travel more than ten kilometres work in the City of Sydney, 23 per cent in the other concentrations, and 35 per cent elsewhere (Table 3.5). The last figure helps put the difference in perspective: though journeys to work in the city centre and major centres are longer than average, the fact remains that scattered or 'local' employment still attracts a share of long journeys, and indeed this share is not far short of that of the City of Sydney itself.

The Journey to Work from Residential Areas

The fundamental proposition that the probability of a person working in any given place of employment declines the further away he lives from that place

TABLE 3.4 *Proportion of Total Work Travel in Sydney by Workers in Major Employment Areas. Census 1971.*

Employment Area	Employment '000	% of total employment	Implied straight line kms of daily travel.'000 000 km	% of total travel
City of Sydney	271	26.4	6.8	36.3
South Sydney/Botany	99	9.6	2.0	10.8
Nth.Sydney/Willoughby	58	5.6	1.0	5.3
Parramatta/Auburn	86	8.4	1.6	8.1
All other	515	50.0	7.4	39.5
Total	1,029	100.0	18.8	100.0

Note: The use of straight-line kilometres underestimates actual total travel, which would be over 20 million person-kilometres a day.

Source: Census 1971. Journey to work tapes.

TABLE 3.5 *Destinations of Workers Travelling Different Distances in Sydney. Census 1971.*

Employment Area	Distance travelled				
	0<3 km %	3<6 km %	6<10 km %	10km & over %	Total %
City of Sydney	10	22	30	40	26
South Sydney/Botany	7	10	10	11	10
N. Sydney/Willoughby	6	5	6	5	6
Parramatta/Auburn	7	9	10	8	8
All other areas	71	53	43	35	50
Total	100	100	100	100	100

Source: Census 1971. Journey to work tapes.

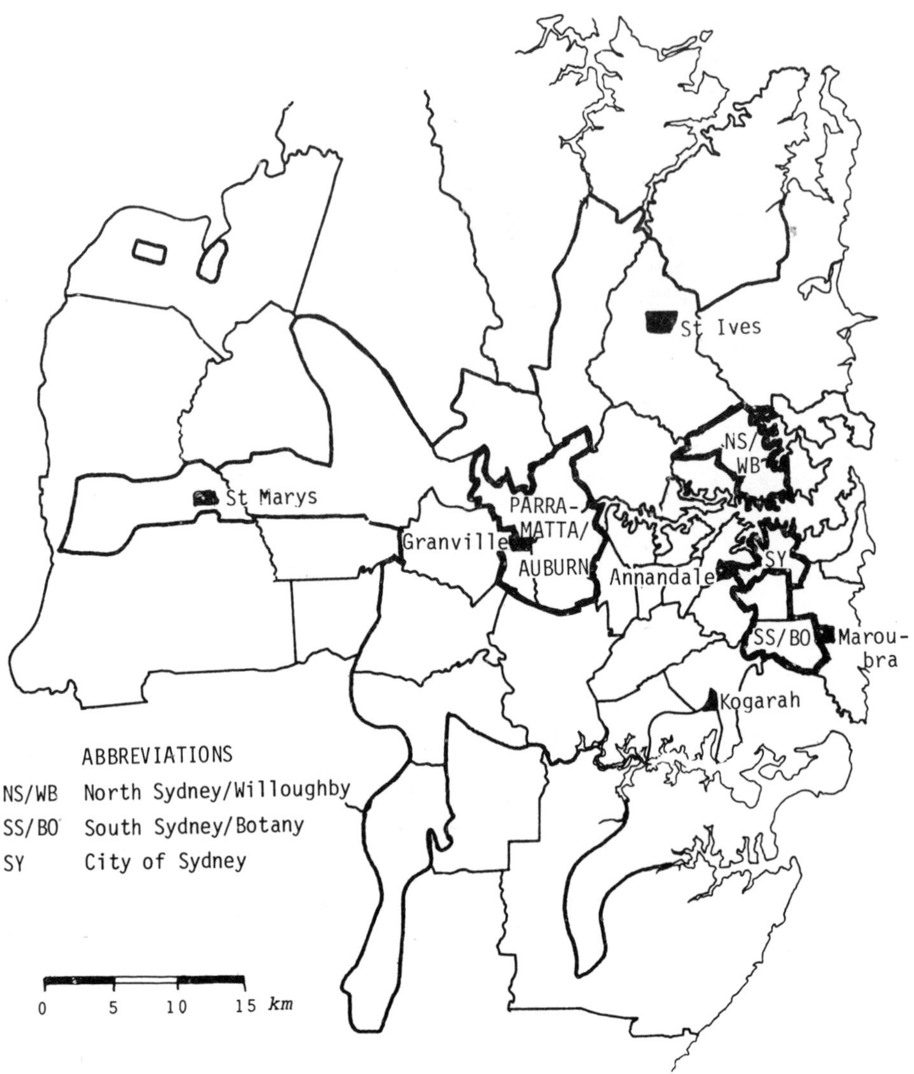

MAP 7. The Major Employment Areas of Sydney (Key map to the tables and discussion, particularly in Chapters 3 and 8). Place names in lower case give locations mentioned in Graphs 3.2 to 3.6 and Table 3.6.

can be checked in a second way. This is by drawing rings round the residential area, and working out the proportion of the jobs available in those rings taken by residents of the designated area. Once again the proportion should decline with distance. Table 3.6 shows that it does, quite regularly and consistently, for four suburbs of quite different character. The residents of St Marys comprise but 0.6 per cent of the total metropolitan workforce, yet they take 33 per cent of the jobs available in their home suburb, declining rapidly to 0.3 per cent of the total jobs available at city centre distance more than 30 kilometres away. Similarly, 1.1 per cent of all workers live in St Ives, yet they fill over 40 per cent of the jobs available in their home suburb, tapering away till virtually none of them work on the far fringe of the metropolitan area.

Reading across the columns of Table 3.6, rather than down them, it can be seen that the probability of filling jobs at various distances differs considerably between suburbs. If Annandale is taken as a representative inner suburb, and if St Ives and St Marys represent the outer suburbs, it would seem that the proportion of jobs at all distances taken by outer suburban residents is higher than for those living nearer the centre of the city. This is not because the two sainted suburbs are more populous than Annandale, but due to the much greater availability of jobs in the inner areas. The desire to work close to home thus interrelates with the availability of jobs to make for a complicated pattern of travel.

TABLE 3.6 *Proportion of Jobs Available at Various Distances Taken by Residents of Selected Suburbs of Sydney. Census 1971.*

Distance of workplace from centroid of residential area. km	Percentages of jobs taken by people coming from:			
	St Marys	St Ives	Maroubra	Annandale
0 < 3	33.0	40.6	13.4	3.3
3 < 6	11.2	10.4	2.9	0.6
7 < 10	6.8	2.5	1.2	0.3
11 < 20	1.2	1.2	0.2	0.1
20 < 30	0.6	0.3	0.1	0.1
> 30	0.3	0.1	0.0	0.0
Overall	0.6	1.1	1.1	0.6

For the location of these suburbs see Map 7.
Source: Census 1971. Journey to work tapes.

GRAPH 3.2 *Jobs by Distance from Annandale, Census, 1971.*

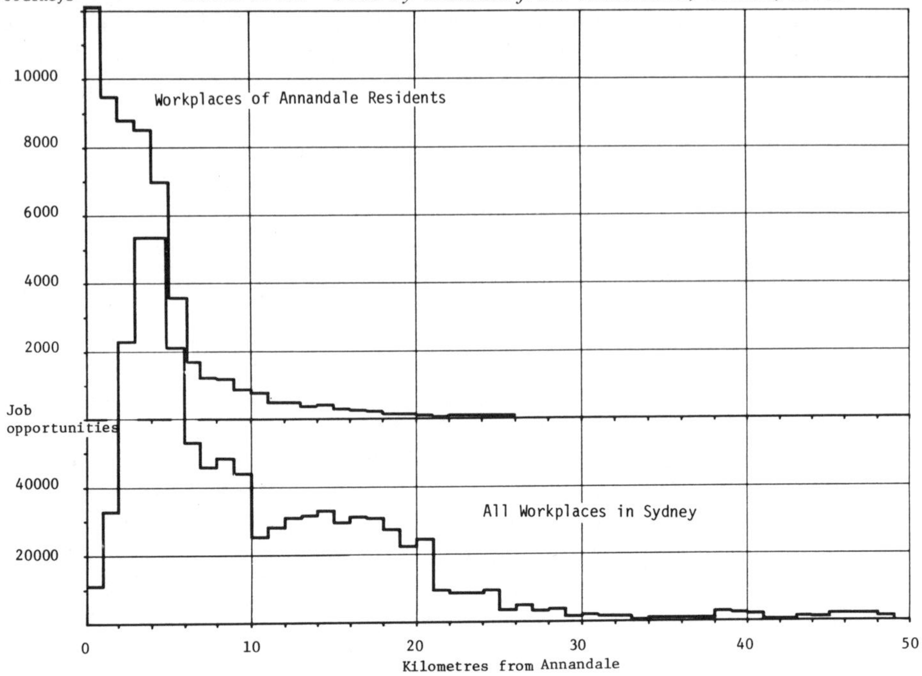

Journeys
10000
8000
6000
4000
2000
Workplaces of Annandale Residents
Job opportunities
40000
20000
All Workplaces in Sydney
0
10
20
30
40
50
Kilometres from Annandale

GRAPH 3.3 *Jobs by Distance from St Marys, Census, 1971.*

Journeys
6000
4000
2000
Workplaces of St Marys Residents
Job opportunities
80000
60000
40000
20000
All Workplaces in Sydney
0
10
20
30
40
50
Kilometres from St.Marys

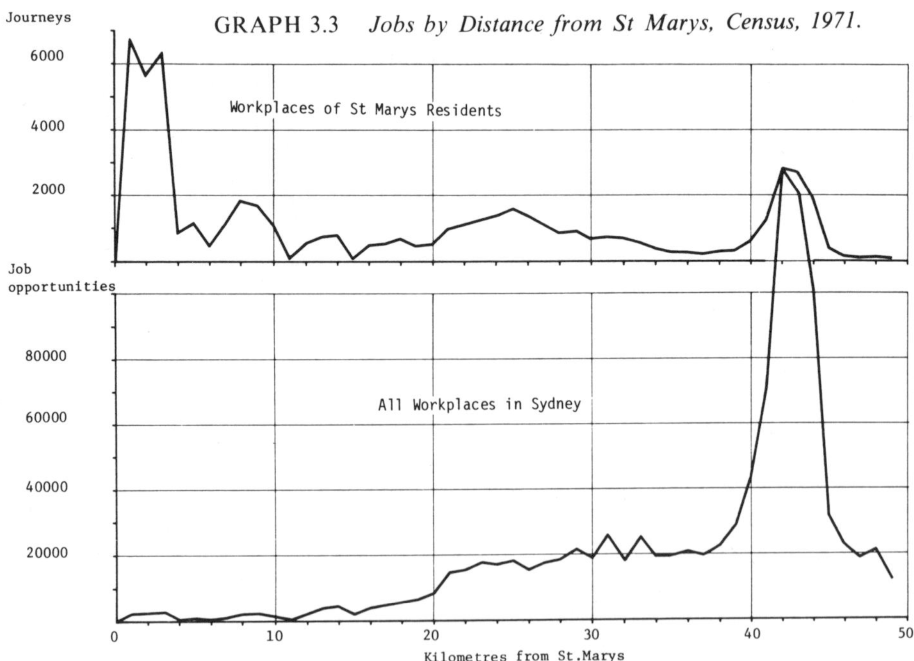

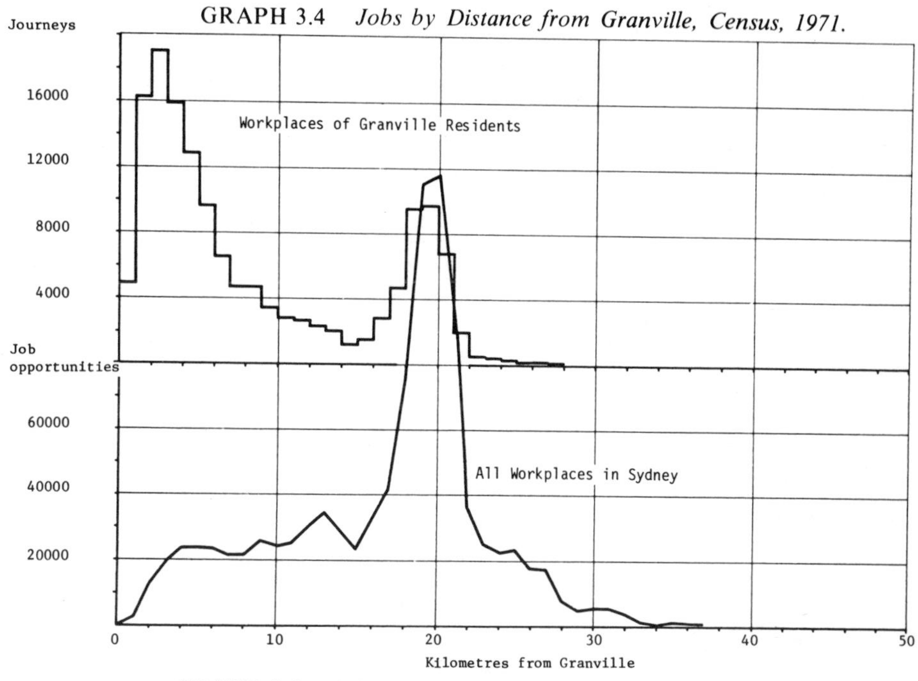

GRAPH 3.4 *Jobs by Distance from Granville, Census, 1971.*

Journeys
16000
12000
8000
4000
Workplaces of Granville Residents
Job opportunities
60000
40000
20000
All Workplaces in Sydney
0
10
20
30
40
50
Kilometres from Granville

GRAPH 3.5 *Jobs by Distance from St Ives, Census, 1971.*

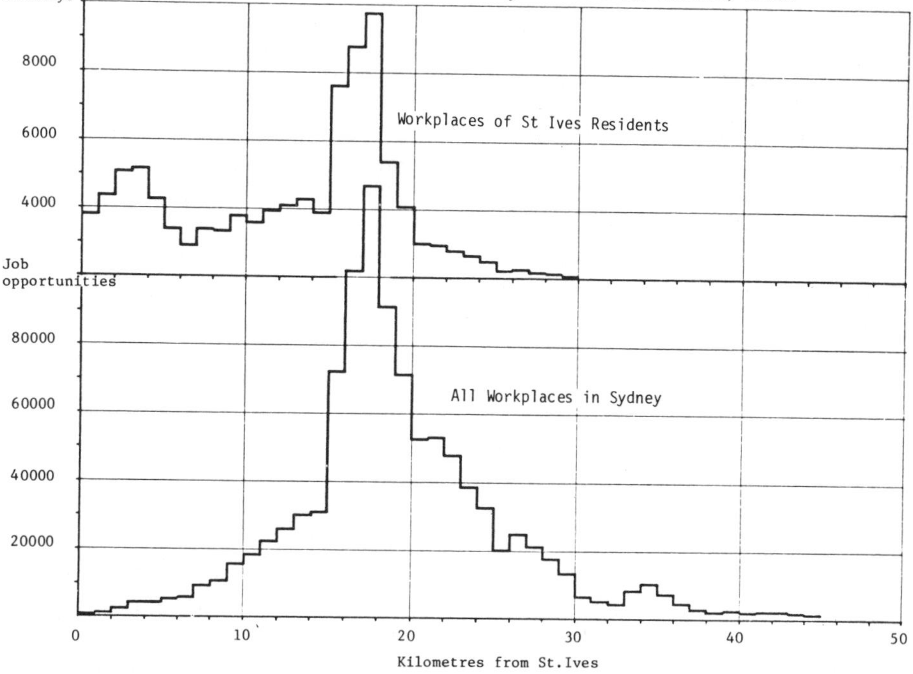

Journeys
8000
6000
4000
Workplaces of St Ives Residents
Job opportunities
80000
60000
40000
20000
All Workplaces in Sydney
0
10
20
30
40
50
Kilometres from St.Ives

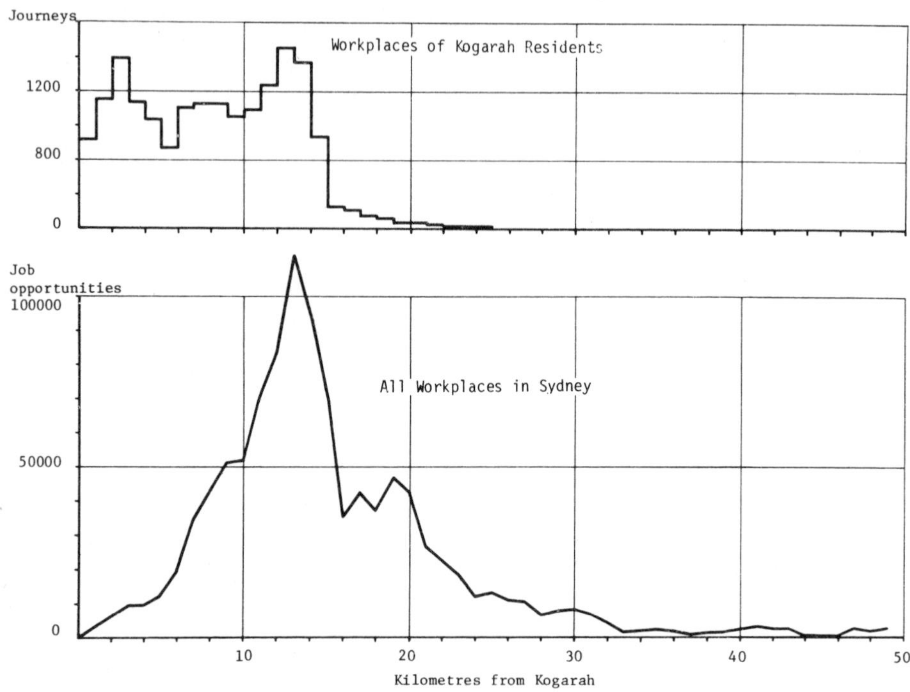

GRAPH 3.6 *Jobs by Distance from Kogarah, Census, 1971.*

The way in which the disinclination to travel interacts with job opportunities can be seen from Graphs 3.2 to 3.6. Each graph represents one suburb which may be located on Map 7. The lower part of the graph records all jobs available in Sydney by distance from that suburb; the upper part shows (on a very much enlarged scale) the jobs actually taken by residents. In all cases the graph of job opportunities has but one peak, and that very high, representing the city centre. North Sydney and South Sydney appear as buttresses to the peak, while (depending somewhat on relative locations) Parramatta/Auburn and other minor suburban concentrations form outliers. These graphs summarise the way the labour market looks from different suburbs. From an inner suburb like Annandale the peak is close at hand (Graph 3.2). At greater distances, but still within 20 kilometres, lie quite large numbers of decentralised jobs, but beyond this distance there is little worth mentioning. The labour market seen from an outer suburb like St Marys is almost the reverse: jobs rather thin on the ground within 20 kilometres, then fair numbers within the middle suburbs rising at last to the city centre peak 40 kilometres away (Graph 3.3). Intermediate suburbs produce intermediate patterns, though it is still instructive to compare Granville (Graph 3.4) with St Ives (Graph 3.5): in the former, job opportunities per kilometre rise quite rapidly to fairly high levels which they maintain till the city centre peak, while in the latter the rise is more gradual, with very few employment opportunities in the first ten kilometres.

The decline with distance in the probability of taking any job combines with the distribution of employment opportunities to produce the actual distribution of residents' job locations by journey length. In any suburb the probability starts relatively high, and falls rapidly for the first few kilometres (see Table 3.6). Thereafter the fall is relatively slow. In some cases (though Table 3.6 is too summarised to see this) the proportion of jobs taken may rise slightly at city centre distance — that is, the probability of taking a job just short of the city centre is less than for a job within the centre itself. This can perhaps be put down to the greater accessibility of the city centre by public transport, and also to its distinctive occupational structure: as explained in Chapter 2, some kinds of work are strongly concentrated in the city centre, and people in these occupations will tend to work there. Beyond city centre distance the probability of taking any job falls right away: few people see the need to travel further than the metropolitan area's biggest concentration of jobs. The result of all this for most suburbs is that at short distances the high probability of taking local work outweighs the small number of available jobs, and there is a peak of short distance travel. At city centre distance the large number of available jobs outweighs the low probability of taking any one of them, and a second peak results. In the inner suburbs, like Annandale, the two peaks coalesce and reinforce one another, while in other places the relative height of the two peaks depends on job opportunities. Where these are relatively abundant nearby, as in Granville, the proportion of the local opportunities taken can be relatively low (Table 3.6) and yet the nearer is still the higher of the two peaks. Again, as in the case of St Marys, the nearer may be the higher because of the great distance of the city centre rather than through any abundance of nearby opportunities. (Such local opportunities as exist are well exploited by local people — Table 3.6). On the other hand, where local opportunities are poor, and even if they are appreciated by the local people, their lack may result in the city centre providing the peak travelling distance. This happens in St Ives. Between the local and city centre peak declining proportions may get the better of job opportunities, and the number of travellers per kilometre decline with distance (Granville), the reverse may happen (St Ives) or some more complicated pattern (St Marys). It is even possible for the number of travellers per kilometre to be fairly constant right through to city centre distance (Kogarah). In all areas, however, the proportion of residents travelling beyond city centre distance is very small — even in Annandale, where this implies a journey of no more than six kilometres.

Bimodal distributions such as these are difficult to summarise by any single measure. Even for a distribution like that for Annandale, which is merely skewed, the median and average are quite different. For others (such as St Ives) the median and average may be close together, but since they lie between two peaks of the distribution they are unsatisfactory as measures of central tendency. Measures of this kind are discussed in the appendix to Chapter 5, but the rest of this book distinguishes between three superimposed labour markets: the city centre, the other major concentrations, and the local markets. City centre employment is covered in Chapter 7, and that in North and South Sydney and Parramatta/Auburn in Chapter 8. In many ways, however, the greatest interest lies in local employment, and to this we now turn.

CHAPTER 4

Local Employment in the Suburbs of Sydney

In Chapters 1 and 2 it was suggested that employment in Sydney is excessively centralised. It was argued that people prefer to work locally; they like to limit the expense of their journey to work, both in time and in cash. One of the main factors preventing them from doing so was seen as the centralisation of employment, and the limited local availability of jobs. If workplaces were more spread around the suburbs, not only would people benefit from shorter journeys, but there would be a saving in public costs — the costs of roads built to carry long-distance commuters, and of railways subsidised to the same end.

There are two arguments against such a policy of job dispersion. The first is that it forfeits the benefits gained when many separate activities, economic, social and cultural, are carried out in the same place, such as the city centre. Many of these benefits are far from measurable, but he who doubts their reality should ask a sample of office girls whether they would rather work in the city centre, where there is much to do of a lunch time, or among the factories of South Sydney (Vandermark, 1970, p.63). However, despite these benefits and despite the highly visible office building boom in the city centre, over the past two decades the trend has been towards the deconcentration of most economic activity. Factory managers, relieved by the motor truck of the necessity to stay close to railway yards and the wharves, have sought suburban acres with plenty of room for expansive single-storey layouts; retailers have shifted their operations to suburban sites with wide open car parks. However, with over a quarter of the jobs in the metropolitan area still (1971) in the City of Sydney, the question remains: has job dispersion gone far enough? Has it sufficiently reached the outer suburbs?

The second argument against the dispersion of jobs is more subtle. It is that the transport benefits of local employment may be more apparent than real. Once the distance covered by workers journeying to dispersed employment rises above an average of a few kilometres, several adverse effects may appear. When people are travelling in various directions, with neither common origin nor common destination, it becomes very difficult to gather them together into a bus, or even in shared private cars. Each traveller is therefore forced to rely on his own vehicle. This is financially expensive for him, and for the government as well, since the provision of roadspace for large, conflicting flows of traffic is costly both in terms of land and concrete. Further, in such travel any person who is unable to drive is at a considerable disadvantage.

Whether these transport costs actually arise depends on people's response to the provision of local employment. If people respond by indeed working locally — meaning within a distance of home so short that both the private and public costs of their travel are low — then it is difficult to gainsay the benefits of the dispersion of jobs. If, on the other hand, they respond by travelling long distances in various directions, then the aim of reducing the burden of the journey to work has not been met.

Defining Local Employment

To assess the response to local employment we need a definition of a local journey to work. The trouble here is that there is no one distance at which travel suddenly starts to become expensive in public and private costs. In the congested inner areas the use of a car for a journey of but one or two kilometres may be expensive both in private costs and in those inflicted on others, whereas in suburbs with quiet streets it may be possible to travel quite long distances by bicycle, incurring very little cost of either kind and indeed experiencing pleasure. The naming of a particular distance as 'local' is therefore rather arbitrary. The particular distance selected for this study is three kilometres.

Though many would object that journeys of up to five or even eight kilometres should be called local, three kilometres is still a useful definition of a short journey. For one thing, the average duration of a journey to work in Sydney is about half an hour, and three kilometres is not much more than the distance that can be covered in this time by the cheapest of all means of transport, walking. Very few Sydney people actually walk when confronted with a distance of three kilometres, but the evidence of the past, and the evidence of the present in countries less wealthy than Australia, is that they could at a pinch — brought on, say, by the next oil crisis. Journeys to work of much more than three kilometres, however, are only walked under duress. Again, a journey of three kilometres can quite likely be aided by a local bus, but as the distance rises so does the probability that there will not be a bus going in the right direction. Once more, journeys by car of up to three kilometres are likely to be largely confined to local streets, and therefore make but small contributions to traffic congestion and conflict, and small demands for public expenditure on roads. Trips of under three kilometres are thus fairly unambiguously cheap, even by car.

This half-arbitrary choice of a three kilometre definition for a local journey to work cannot be imposed directly on the data, for journeys are identified only by origin zone and destination zone. Accordingly, an approximate definition is actually used in the tables and on the maps, namely that a journey is local if it lies wholly within the same census zone (including the zero-length journeys of those who worked at home), or connects zones the centroids of which are less than three straight-line kilometres apart. This means that some truly local journeys are improperly excluded and some of over three kilometres are included (specially since three straight-line kilometres is a little longer in terms of street kilometres — perhaps closer to 3.4 actual kilometres). However, this source of inaccuracy is not important enough to affect the statistics or the pattern on the maps very much.

The Balance between Homes and Workplaces

To prove whether the proportion of the population of any suburb working locally is primarily determined by demand and supply in the local labour market we need a measure of the state of that market. Are there plenty of jobs, or is there a shortage? The measure proposed for assessing the state of local labour markets is the maximum proportion of the population of each zone which could work locally, given the distribution of workers and jobs. This calculation was performed by hand rather than computer, which necessitated the amalgamation of census zones to reduce the total number to manageable proportions. This reduction in the number of zones from 552 to 128 means that tables prepared by this method (Tables 4.1, 5.3, 5.13, 6.2 and 6.3) are less accurate than the other tables in this book; but they have the virtue of internal consistency, and enable comparisons to be made between different regions and (in Chapter 6) different occupations.

The rules for calculating the proportion of resident workers who could work locally were:

1. Workers in each combined zone had first call on the jobs in that zone.
2. After the workers in each zone had been offset against the jobs, some zones would appear with a surplus of jobs, and others with a deficit. Surplus jobs were then allocated to surplus workers living within three straight-line kilometres. If more than one zone with surplus workers was local to a zone with surplus jobs, priority went to the zone radially outwards from the city centre.

   If workers selected their jobs according to these rules, the proportion working locally would be very nearly maximised. The rules are, of course, unrealistic, in that they make no allowance for the suitability of jobs by occupation, or for competition for jobs in mild job-deficit areas coming from workers living in severe deficit areas. However, the rules are not intended to be realistic, but merely to give a consistent indication of the state of the local labour markets of Sydney.
3. After completing this process of allocating jobs in job-surplus zones to workers in deficit zones within local distance, any surplus jobs remaining out of reach of a deficit zone were considered irrelevant to any local labour market. They could not be filled by people travelling three kilometres or less.

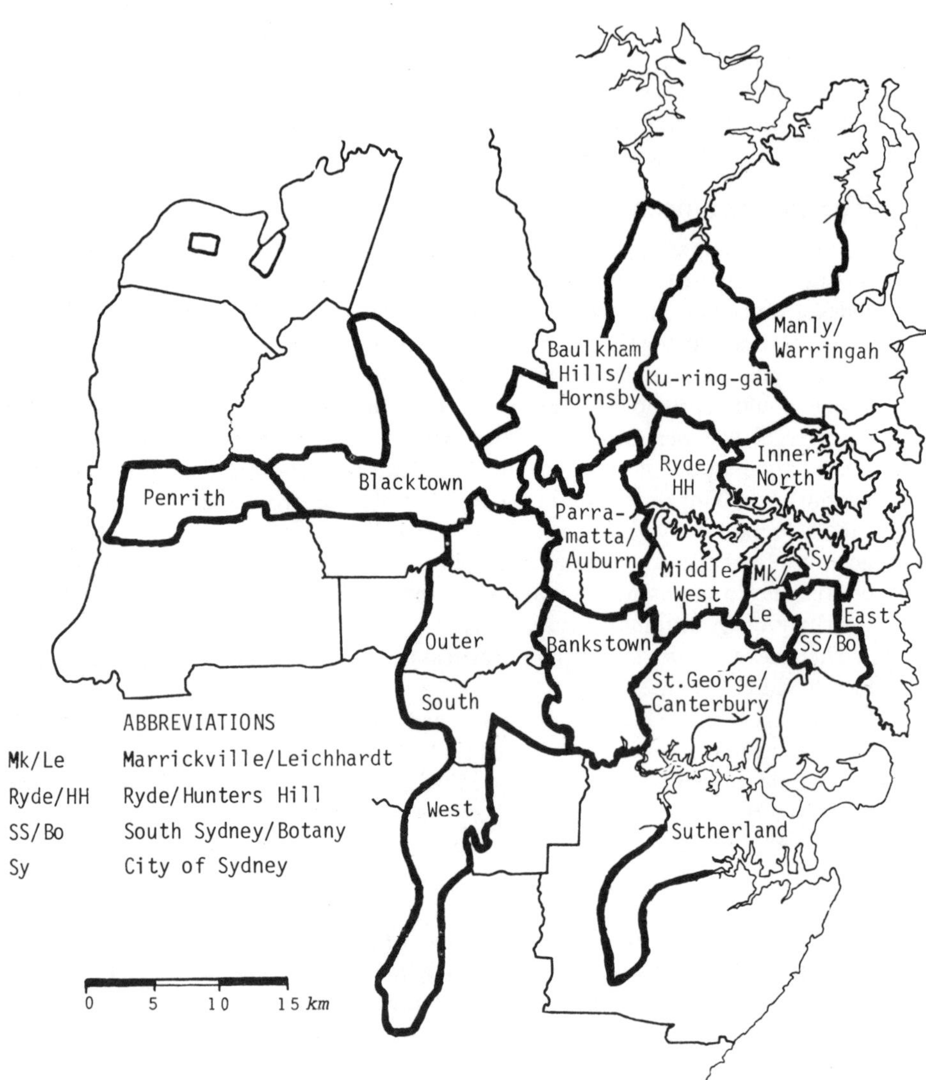

MAP 8. Suburban Regions of Sydney (Key map to the regions used in tables and discussion, particularly in Chapters 4 and 5).

TABLE 4.1 *The Local Balance Between Workers and Jobs in Sydney. Census 1971.*

REGION (See Map 8)	Resident workers '000 1	% able to work locally 2	% actually working locally 3	Response rate (Col.3/Col.2) % 4
Penrith	18	95	32	34
Blacktown	51	44	15	34
Outer South West	103	61	25	41
Parramatta/Auburn	61	95	30	32
Baulkham Hills/ Hornsby	50	48	15	31
Ryde/Hunters Hill	41	69	24	35
Middle West	64	81	28	35
Bankstown	66	82	26	32
Sutherland	56	48	22	46
St.George/ Canterbury	133	60	23	38
Marrickville/ Leichhardt	62	91	48	53
South Sydney/Botany	31	100	58	58
East	105	69	34	49
City of Sydney	23	100	70	70
Ku-ring-gai	34	43	14	33
Inner North	73	89	32	36
Manly/Warringah	70	51	27	53
All Sydney	1038	69	28	41

Source: Census 1971, Journey to work tapes.
Columns 2 and 3 calculated using amalgamated zones.

4. The job deficits in the remaining zones were totalled regionally. The regions used are shown on Map 8; they attempt not to split local labour markets, to use natural boundaries where possible, and local government boundaries at all times. In some regions there were zones with job surpluses and others more than three kilometres away with deficits; in calculating the overall deficit the surpluses were disregarded. The total deficit then gave an estimate of the number of workers in the region who,

with the existing distribution of residences and workplaces, could not work locally due to lack of local jobs.

Table 4.1 presents the results of these calculations. After all the fuss that has been made about the geographical mismatch of jobs and residences in Sydney, it comes as a surprise to find that about two-thirds of the workers in Sydney could work locally if they followed the rules given above. (The true figure may be a little less, for the combined zones used in the hand calculations on average stretched the three-kilometre definition of 'local' more than the small zones used elsewhere in this monograph.) Equally striking, however, are the differences between regions, which range from the City of Sydney and South Sydney/Botany, in which everybody could work locally if they wished, to Ku-ring-gai and Blacktown municipalities, in each of which not many more than 40 per cent of the workers could work locally. In North Sydney/Willoughby (here including Mosman and Lane Cove as well), and in Parramatta/Auburn the proportions able to work locally are high, as would be expected of major employment concentrations: indeed these regions have zones with surplus jobs as well as deficit zones. In view of the centralisation of employment mentioned in Chapter 2, it is not surprising to find that the regions with the worst job deficits are by and large in the outer suburbs, but even here there is an exception to the rule: Penrith municipality has quite a large number of jobs in relation to its population. In 1971 it was only just on the urban fringe, and still had some of the characteristics of a country town.

The Response to Local Employment Opportunities by Region

Despite this regional variation in the balance between homes and jobs, about two thirds of the people of Sydney could work locally if this were their only concern in selecting a job. In fact, less than a third actually do so. Even so, the definition of 'local' at three kilometres or less is strict, and the 28 per cent of all employed people who work within this distance of home is high, specially when it is compared with the 25 per cent who journey from the suburbs to the City of Sydney.

Regional variation in the proportion of workers working locally can to a considerable extent be explained by variation in the local balance between jobs and residents. Over the whole of Sydney a little over 40 per cent of those who could work locally actually do so. However, as can be seen from the last column in Table 4.1, there is a certain amount of regional variation in the response to local employment opportunities. Different explanations seem to fit the situation in different regions.

Very high response rates are recorded in the City of Sydney, in South Sydney/Botany and Marrickville/Leichhardt. This is not surprising. One of the deficiencies of the proportion of workers able to take local jobs as a measure of local labour market conditions is that it cannot go above a hundred per cent, whereas the number of local jobs certainly can. Such excess jobs increase the probability that a worker can find suitable work locally. Alternatively, speaking in terms of housing choices, the excess jobs increase the number of people looking for convenient accommodation, such that only those who place a high premium on residence close to work will live there.

Excess jobs fit well the high response rates in the City of Sydney, South Sydney/Botany and Marrickville/Leichhardt. However, the existence of excess jobs in some of the zones of a region does not guarantee high response. In Parramatta/Auburn they combine with one of the metropolitan area's lowest response rates, and the same is partly true of North Sydney/Willoughby.

A second reason for high response is difficulty of transport to and from the rest of Sydney. This both encourages people to work within their local area, and discourages others from coming in. The most noticeable case is Manly/Warringah, where over half of those who could work locally do so. Sutherland is also cut off from the rest of Sydney, and records high response rates, though a little lower than Manly/Warringah. Two road bridges and a railway line apparently constitute better connections with the rest of Sydney than two roads and a ferry service.

One last area with a high response to local employment opportunities is the eastern suburbs. Here there is no excess of local jobs, though some of the excess jobs in South Sydney/Botany are within local distance of parts of the region. Again the reason for high response cannot be that there are hindrances to the residents' travel — no Middle Harbour obstructs their journey to the west. Rather, the high proportion working locally must be due to lack of competition. Nobody can come in from further out radially, while the numerous job opportunities and hectic traffic of the city centre and inner southern industrial suburbs shield the eastern suburbs from job seekers living in the west.

Over the rest of the metropolitan area the proportion of those actually working locally to those who could is less than average. It is particularly low in Parramatta/Auburn, Baulkham Hills/Hornsby and in Ku-ring-gai. Again, considering the surplus of jobs in some parts of North Sydney/Willoughby, response is rather low in this region.

The low response in Parramatta/Auburn can be traced to the state of competition in the local labour market. The region is surrounded by other areas badly deficient in local employment: Blacktown particularly. The low response in North Sydney/Willoughby, on the other hand, may perhaps be put down to ease and pleasantness of travel to the city centre, which attracts many harbourside residents, leaving the local jobs to be filled by others from further out.

In the case of Ku-ring-gai and of Baulkham Hills/Hornsby, low response is perhaps due to an occupational mismatch. The residents of these suburbs are mostly of high socio-economic status, while the jobs locally available are often of a run of the mill kind — school teaching and work in shops. This may lead to local jobs being scorned by local residents — a situation which will be further discussed in Chapter 6.

In summary, we can conclude that response will be high if there is a local surplus of jobs, if the region is physically isolated, and if the local job mix balances with the local population.

The Response to Local Employment Opportunities by Local Area

Not only are there broad regional differences in the response to local employment opportunities; there are differences within regions. These are brought out in Maps 9 and 10, the first showing the proportion of jobs in each census zone taken by persons living within three straight-line kilometres, and the second showing the proportion of the workers living in each census zone who work locally.

In areas with job deficits, the proportion of jobs taken by locals is closely equivalent to the proportion of those actually working locally to those who could do so. High response rates in the deficit regions of Table 4.1 thus correlate on Map 9 with high proportions of available jobs taken by locals. On the other hand, in areas with surplus jobs the response rate to local opportunity can be high even though the proportion of jobs actually held by locals is low. Thus on Map 9 the city centre, Auburn and much of South Sydney draw less than 15 per cent of their workforce from among people living locally. Two other areas also appear on the map as obtaining most of their workforce from afar: these are the industrial area east of Liverpool and that at Kurnell. In both cases these are areas of extensive industrial development with very small resident populations. Too few workers live locally to take many of the jobs; the rest have to come from more than three kilometres away.

The areas shown on Map 9 as having a high proportion of available jobs taken by locals seem to have two characteristics: they all lack local employment in the sense that the number of jobs locally available is much less than the number of resident workers, and secondly many of them are fringe areas, like coastal Warringah, the eastern suburbs, Sutherland and the shores of the Georges River. If an area has only a few jobs, then residents who place a high value on a short journey to work will compete strongly for them. Again, in fringe areas there will tend to be less competition for jobs from people living outside the area than in places better connected to the rest of the metropolitan area. This has already been mentioned in explanation of the high response rates in Manly/Warringah and Sutherland, and it should not be surprising that it also applies in the fringe parts of other regions.

Overall, the conclusion which might be drawn from this analysis is that people appreciate local employment at least to the extent that in areas where there is very little of it available, the few such jobs are taken mainly by local people. Perhaps if more were made available, they would be similarly sought. On the other hand, the low proportion of jobs in Parramatta/Auburn taken by locals gives pause for thought. This is the major decentralised employment zone, and is often cited as a success: the largest concentration of office jobs outside the city centre, and a major industrial area as well. But few of these jobs are taken by nearby residents, and the median journey to work of 6.8 straight-line kilometres is well above local distance. It may be that here we have an example of the kind of decentralisation that is costly in terms of cross traffic; of roadbuilding expenses and maybe even of captive public transport users denied access to work.

Map 10 is based on the same data as Map 9, with the difference that persons working locally are now shown by place of residence rather than by place of work. The result is a pattern which in broad outline is the inverse of Map 9. In areas with few local jobs, even though those jobs be almost wholly taken by residents, the proportion of the population working locally is generally low. Conversely, in areas with plentiful local employment the proportion of residents who work locally is always high, even though the proportion of jobs taken by locals may be quite low. As usual, this is at its extreme in the city centre, where fewer than 15 per cent of the jobs are taken by locals, but well over 60 per cent of the rather few residents work locally. Something of the same applies to Parramatta/Auburn. However, the two maps are not a complete mirror image. In areas of job deficits but high response rates — Warringah, Sutherland except Kurnell, the Eastern suburbs and perhaps a few other places like Campbelltown and Riverstone — both the proportion of jobs taken by locals and the proportion of the population working locally are relatively high.

There are special reasons why high proportions of residents are shown as working locally in certain zones of Map 10. The proportions are high on each of the heads of the harbour, due to defence installations and a Catholic seminary. The other obvious special case is a zone in Auburn, which includes the Rookwood cemetery and the Lidcombe State Hospital and Home. Virtually the only employed residents of this zone both live and work in the hospital. Apart from such special cases, most of the employment zones of Map 5 are recognisable on Map 10, their outline a little blurred to the limit of three kilometres each way.

Readers of *Sydney at the Census, 1971* (Davis & Spearritt, 1974) or of *Ideas for Australian Cities* (Stretton, 1975) will probably have been disappointed not to recognise a close relationship between travel distances and the socio-economic status of the different suburbs of Sydney. True, much of the high status fringe lacks local employment, but much the same is true of the low status west. This pattern is repeated in the map of persons working locally: the areas with very high proportions working locally are mostly of fairly low status, but those close to the city centre include several of Sydney's most exclusive residential areas. At the other extreme, the new executive belt stretching north west from Ku-ring-gai and the Housing Commission estates beyond Blacktown and Liverpool are alike in that under 15 per cent of the residents work locally. It may be argued that this is no hardship in the higher status areas, for high

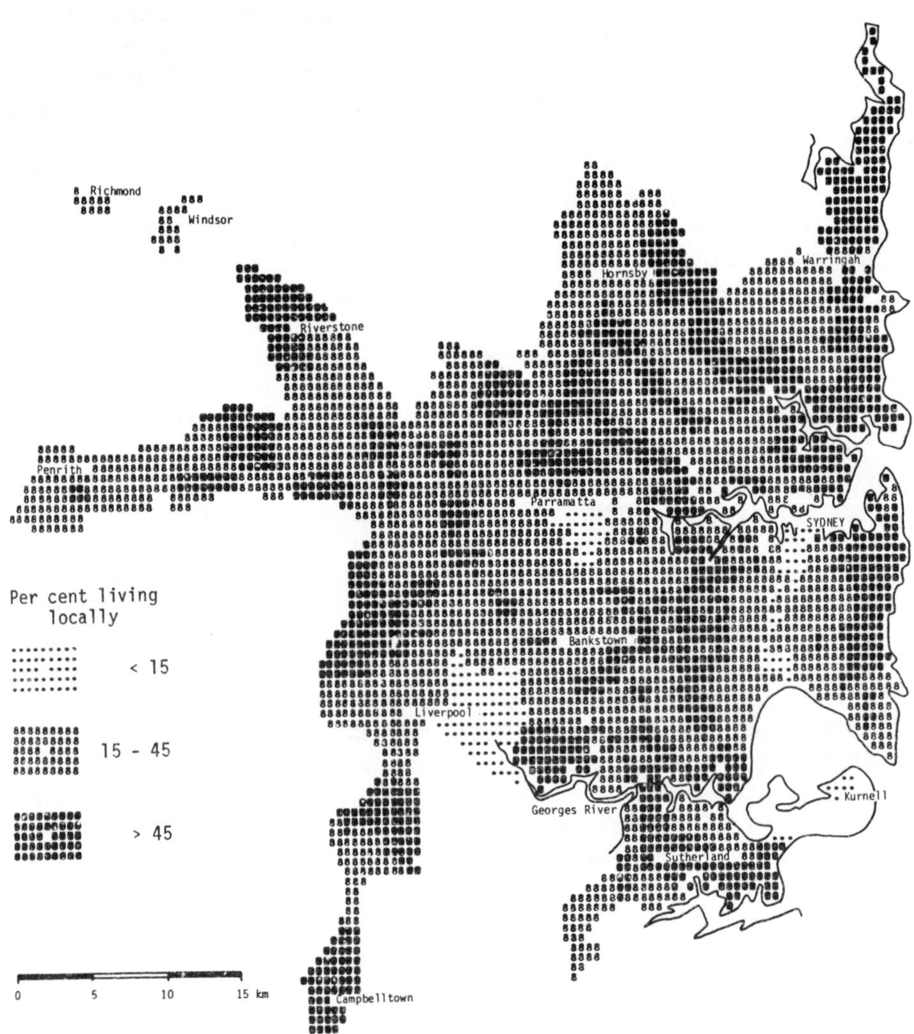

MAP 9. Percentage of the Workforce Living Locally by Employment Zone, Sydney, Census 1971 (see text, page 68). Comparing this map with Map 5, it can be seen that the major employment areas draw a low proportion of their workforce from suburbs within three kilometres, whereas in areas of low employment density it is usual for over 45 per cent of the jobs to be taken by people who live locally.

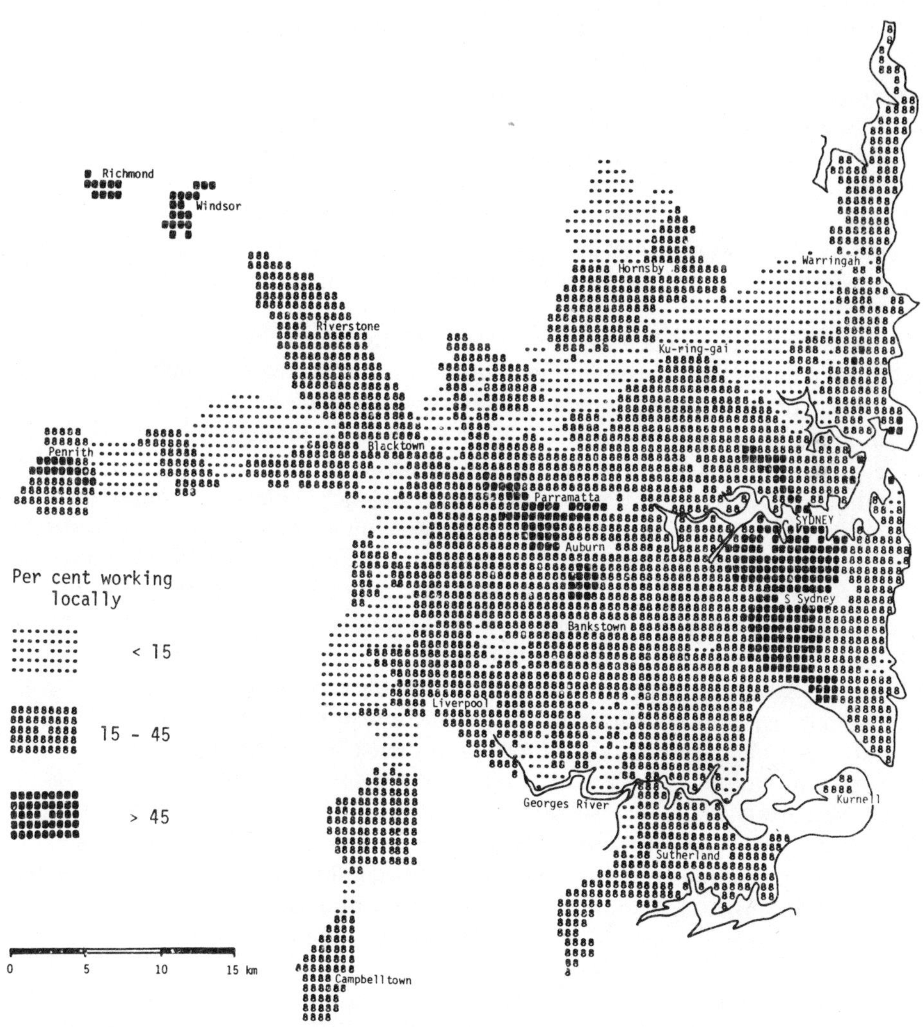

MAP 10. Percentage of Resident Workers Working Locally by Residential Area, Sydney, Census 1971 (see text, page 69). In the major employment areas most residents work within three kilometres of home, while in the outer suburbs a shortage of local jobs means that few residents can work near home — even though a high proportion of such jobs as are available is taken by locals (cf Map 9).

income people can more easily afford fast transport, but the fact remains that local jobs are no more easily obtained in Ku-ring-gai than in Blacktown.

In addition to these outer suburban tracts, a few other areas have a low proportion of residents in local employment. Most of these are coastal or river fringes with very few jobs available.

In summary, Maps 9 and 10 indicate that local jobs are taken by locals, especially when, as in Manly/Warringah, venturing further afield is troublesome. In areas where jobs are numerous compared to the population, a high proportion of the residents work locally, but fill only a low proportion of the available workplaces. By contrast, in areas deficient in employment, such jobs as there are will be taken by locals, but few residents will be able to work locally.

On the basis of this data it is not easy to answer the question as to whether further dispersion of employment would lead to increased numbers working locally, or to increased unmanageable cross-traffic. Certainly in areas deficient in local jobs an increased supply would generate a favourable local response, especially in isolated areas like Manly/Warringah. On the other hand, as the number of jobs in any area approaches balance with the population, and particularly if an attempt to retain the economies of co-location of various activities leads to the building up of suburban concentrations, the likelihood of cross-traffic is much greater. The only suburban location where jobs available roughly balance with the population is Parramatta/Auburn, and it is not an encouraging example — though two thirds of those few who live in the midst of the industrial zone work locally, over the whole area within three kilometres of the employment concentration the proportion working locally is only about a third — which represents a rather low response to the opportunities available (see also Graph 3.4). Part of the reason for this is doubtless that locals in Parramatta/Auburn are subject to competition from the job-deficient areas further out, so that if these areas were better supplied with work, Parramatta people might find it easier to obtain local employment. However, as things stand, Parramatta/Auburn is the destination of a large number of long and unmanageable journeys to work. The position will be further discussed in Chapter 8.

The tentative conclusion so far is that up to a point further dispersion of employment, especially into areas presently deficient, would be of benefit in enabling more people to work locally, but that the building up of major suburban concentrations might have transport consequences much more difficult to manage. However, this is not the last word on the subject; more can be learnt by considering employment patterns differentiated by sex and occupation.

CHAPTER 5

Men and Women in Local Employment

So far this study has followed the convention that sex does not matter in analysing travel patterns. Indeed, in some ways it truly does not: a car takes up the same amount of roadspace whether its driver be male or female. However, the convention hides the fact that the travel patterns of men and women are remarkably different, which means that any complete account of the journey to work should treat men and women separately. Accordingly the tables and maps in this chapter repeat those of Chapters 3 and 4, differentiating men and women.

The Location of Employment by Sex

As shown on Maps 11 and 12, the pattern of job locations for women is broadly similar to that for men. However, on closer inspection two main differences emerge. First, women's jobs are relatively much less important in the major manufacturing areas — South Sydney and Parramatta/Auburn. Though women comprise 36 per cent of the labour force in the metropolitan area[1] they hold only 23 per cent of the jobs in South Sydney/Botany and 31 per cent in Parramatta/Auburn, this latter despite the shops and offices of Parramatta itself (Table 5.1). Several other factory areas are also male territory, especially some of those in the Bankstown municipality. However, manufacturing employment is not necessarily masculine. In some factory areas the sexes are represented more or less in the same ratio as in total employment (this is broadly true of the inner western suburbs) and in some like Meadowbank and St Marys there is a higher proportion of women's jobs.

1. This figure, like most others in this chapter, is derived from the census journey to work tables, and is subject to the drawbacks mentioned in Chapter 1. It overstates the proportion of women in the workforce because women less frequently failed to name a destination, and so less frequently excluded themselves from the journey to work data. For this reason the lower estimates from the Sydney Area Transportation Study shown in Table 5.1 may be more accurate. However, from census information covering the whole population including those who failed to name a workplace, the true proportion of women in the workforce in Sydney is (1971) 34 per cent, which is closer to the census (journey to work) estimate of 36 per cent than to the SATS estimate of 31 per cent.

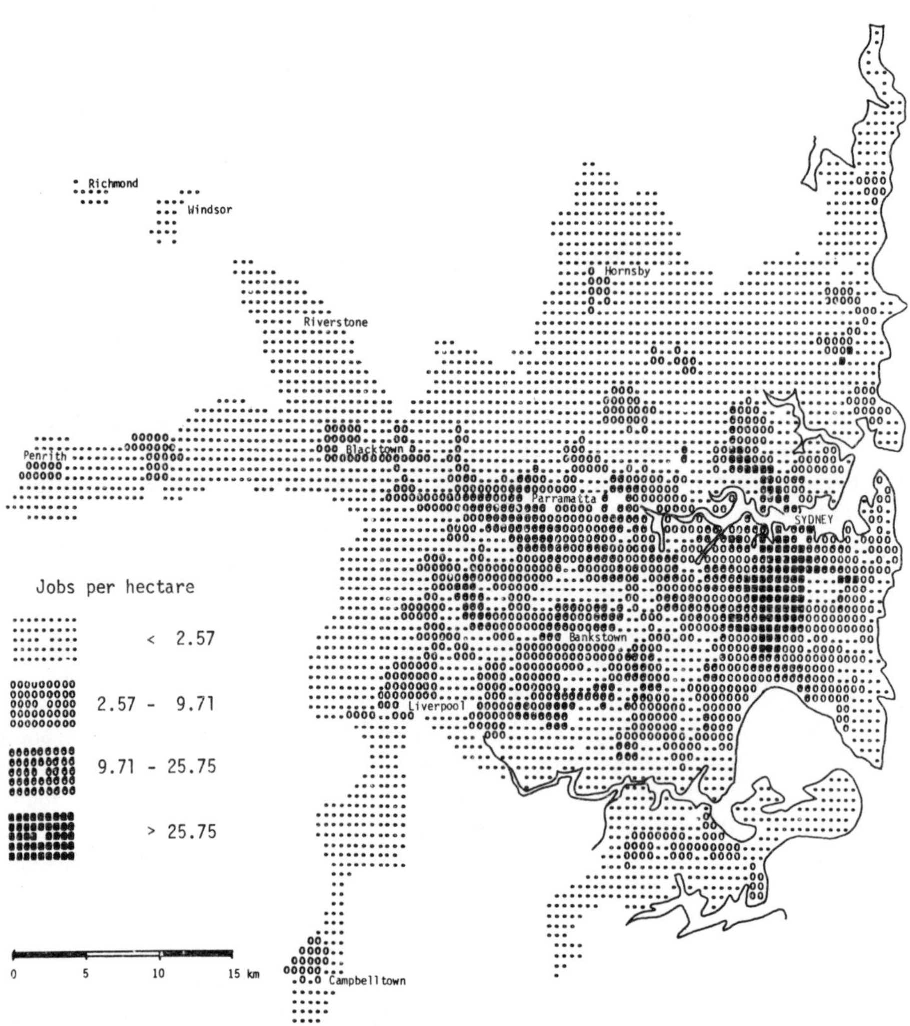

MAP 11. The Location of Men's Jobs, Sydney, Census 1971 (see text, page 73). Men comprise 64 per cent of the total workforce, so it is not surprising that the locational pattern of their jobs is similar to that for the workforce as a whole (Map 5). Even so, there are differences of detail, e.g. the relatively greater importance of industrial areas near Bankstown and Parramatta.

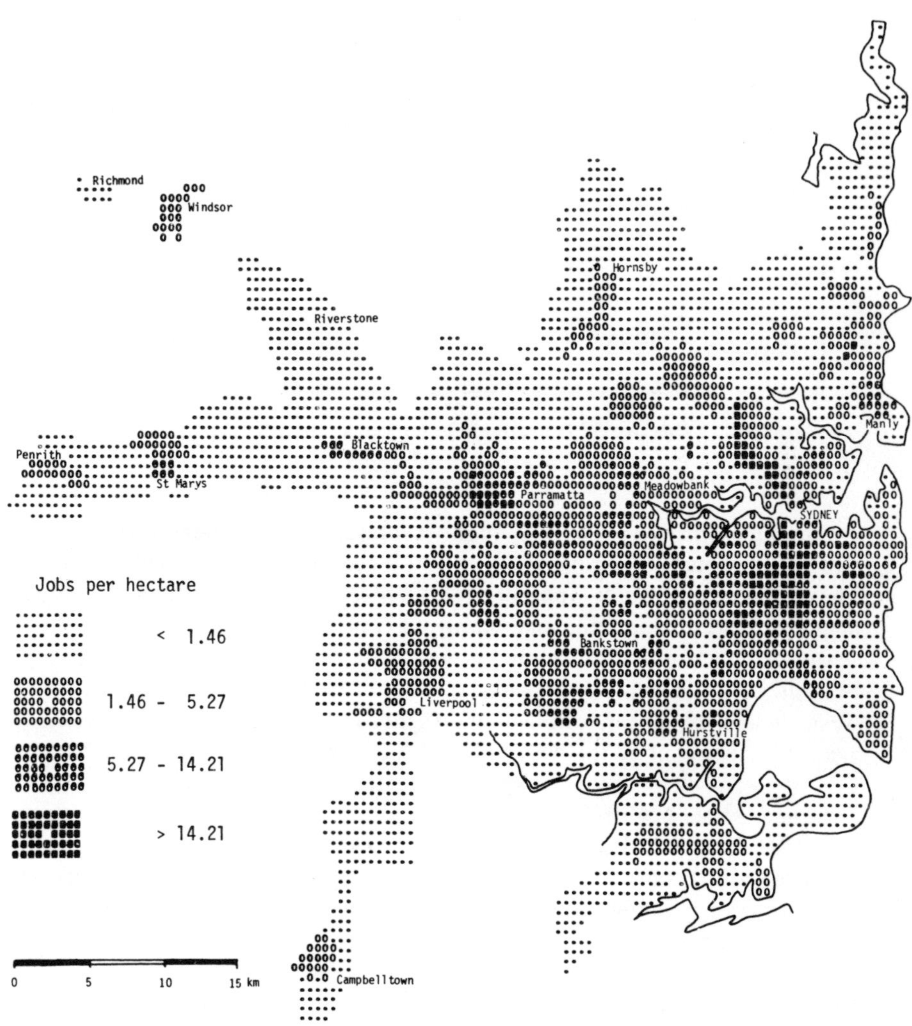

MAP 12. The Location of Women's Jobs, Sydney, Census 1971 (see text, page 73). As compared with men, women more frequently work in the commercial and retailing areas, and less often in the major industrial zones. Overall, women's jobs are about as widespread as men's, and the sexes have a similar degree of opportunity to work locally.

TABLE 5.1 *Percentage of Jobs in the Major Employment Areas Held by Women. Sydney, 1971.*

Employment Area	Census estimate	SATS estimate
City of Sydney	40	36
South Sydney/Botany	23	21
North Sydney/Willoughby	38	33
Parramatta/Auburn	31	27
Other	37	31
Total	36	31

Source: Census 1971, Journey to work tapes.
SATS tapes.

Second, women are relatively highly represented in commerce and retailing, and in consequence commercial and retail centres are prominent on Map 12. The difference is readily apparent for such centres as Blacktown, Parramatta business district, Hurstville and Manly. It is not quite so apparent that the city centre is slightly more important for women's jobs than men's — the density of both is so high that it appears in the highest class on both the maps. Nevertheless, 29 per cent of the women's jobs in Sydney are in the city centre, as against 25 per cent of the men's (Table 5.2). Forty per cent of the jobs in the City of Sydney are held by women, as against 36 per cent in the metropolitan area as a whole (Table 5.1).

Judged thus by their degree of concentration in the City of Sydney, women's jobs are slightly more centralised than men's. However, the lower proportion in the two major manufacturing areas offsets this, such that half the jobs for each sex are scattered round the metropolitan area outside the main concentrations of employment (Table 5.2). In some locations men are better off than women for local employment, and in others worse off, but the overriding impression from the two maps is that such differences more or less cancel out over the whole of Sydney (Black, 1977 p.27). This equal dispersion means that overall the two sexes have roughly the same opportunities to work locally.

This visual impression of equal opportunity is confirmed by Table 5.3 which, in a manner analagous to Table 4.1, shows the proportion of men and women able to work locally if each took the nearest job available to a person of that sex. Over all Sydney, a slightly higher proportion of women can work locally than men (72 per cent as against 68 — which given the roughness of the figures is not a very significant difference). While it is true that the major factory areas have a less than average proportion of women in their workforce, this does not

TABLE 5.2 *The Location of Jobs in Sydney by Sex. Census 1971.*

Employment Area	Men's Jobs per cent	Women's Jobs per cent
City of Sydney	25	29
South Sydney/Botany	12	6
North Sydney/Willoughby	9	7
Parramatta/Auburn	5	6
All Other	49	52
All Sydney	100	100

Source: Census 1971, Journey to work tapes.

affect the proportion of women able to work locally — such major employment areas have surplus jobs for men and women alike. If there are places where the presence of manufacturing adversely affects women's opportunity to work locally, these (from Table 5.3) would seem to be Bankstown and the Middle Western municipalities of Ashfield/Burwood/Strathfield/Concord. By contrast, in several regions women's opportunity to work locally is better than men's. These are the outer suburbs of high socio-economic status — Ku-ring-gai and Baulkham Hills/Hornsby. The reason lies not so much in a high proportion of women's jobs in such suburbs as in the low workforce participation rate of high status women.

The question of workforce participation casts some doubt on the impression of equality of opportunity for men and women gained from the maps and from Table 5.3. If, as will be argued later, women value a short journey to work more highly than men, two things will tend to happen in areas short of women's jobs. First, women may take jobs which in other parts of the metropolitan area would be held by men. This is particularly likely in clerical and sales work, and will tend to improve the local balance between women and work. Second, women who cannot obtain a local job may drop out of the workforce. It is very difficult to guess the extent of this disguised imbalance. Women's workforce participation rates, which decline from the inner areas towards the urban fringe, are consistent with the thesis that many women need a local job in order to work (local balance between jobs and workers generally worsens with distance from the city centre) but it must be remembered that many women in the outer suburbs have young children and may have given up work voluntarily to look after them. Similarly the high women's workforce participation rates in some of the inner suburbs may be due to young single women who have deliberately moved into such areas to be close to the employment opportunities of the city centre.

TABLE 5.3 *The Local Balance Between Workers and Jobs, by Sex. Sydney, Census 1971.*

REGION (See Map 8)	MEN		WOMEN	
	Resident workers '000	% able to work locally	Resident workers '000	% able to work locally
Penrith	12	95	6	94
Blacktown	35	42	16	48
Outer South West	70	59	33	63
Parramatta/Auburn	40	95	21	95
Baulkham Hills/Hornsby	34	39	16	58
Ryde/Hunters Hill	26	64	15	73
Middle West	40	85	24	75
Bankstown	44	86	22	74
Sutherland	38	45	18	56
St.George/Canterbury	86	59	47	62
Marrickville/Leichhardt	39	95	23	92
South Sydney/Botany	20	100	11	100
Eastern suburbs	62	73	43	65
City of Sydney	14	100	9	100
Ku-ring-gai	23	33	11	60
Inner North	42	89	31	90
Manly/Warringah	45	45	25	63
All Sydney	667	68	371	72

Source: Census 1971, Journey to work tapes, calculations using amalgamated zones.

Journey Length by Sex

Despite the apparent similarity in the overall availability of local employment for men and women, the travel patterns of the two sexes are quite different. In general, women travel much shorter distances. The median straight-line journey to work for women is but two-thirds of that for men (4.8 as against 7.5 kilometres) while the average is about three-quarters (7.4 as against 10.1 kilometres) (Table 5.4). In all employment zones the women workers come from closer at hand — at the extreme, the median journey for women working in Marrickville/Leichhardt is less than half that for men. Only among workers

TABLE 5.4 *Median Length of the Journey to Work in Selected Employment Areas, by Sex. Sydney, Census 1971.*

Employment concentration	Men - km	Women - km
City of Sydney	10.9	8.7
South Sydney/Botany	8.6	5.5
North Sydney/Willoughby	8.1	4.3
Parramatta/Auburn	7.7	4.8
Strathfield/Concord/Burwood	7.8	4.7
Marrickville/Leichhardt	7.0	3.2
Bankstown	6.8	3.8
All other	5.0	2.9
All Sydney - median	7.5	4.8
All Sydney - average	10.1	7.4

Source: Census 1971, Journey to work tapes.

in the city centre does the length of women's journey to work approach men's, and even then a difference of about 20 per cent remains between the medians. (Table 5.4. The differences may be observed in detail in Table 5.14.)

From the census data it is not possible to distinguish persons who work at home from those who merely 'work locally'. However, on an all-Australia basis it seems that about the same proportion of men work at home as women (ABS Journey to Work 1974). The difference between the proportions of men and women working locally is therefore not to be explained by women being in jobs where housing is provided.

Not only do women's travel habits differ from men's; there are considerable differences between married and unmarried women. Unfortunately the census journey to work data does not distinguish women by marital status, but it is possible to fill the gap with statistics from the Sydney Area Transportation Study home interview survey. Being based on a sample, these figures are less reliable than the census (see Chapters 1 and 9) but they have the merit of having been collected at approximately the same time — 1971. Because of the different methods of collection, SATS estimates generally differ from census figures — note, for example, the difference between the census estimate of the average straight-line journey to work for men in Sydney (10.1 kilometres — Table 5.4) and the corresponding SATS estimate (9.2 kilometres — Table 5.5). However, the SATS estimates are internally consistent, and there is no doubt that the differences they show between married and single women reflect behaviour in the real world. Men make the longest journeys to work, followed by single

TABLE 5.5 *Average Length of the Journey to Work in Major Employment Areas, by Men and by Single and Married Women. Sydney Area Transportation Study, 1971.*

Employment area	Men km	Single women km	Married Women km
City of Sydney	12.7	11.9	10.7
South Sydney/Botany	10.7	7.6	6.9
North Sydney/Willoughby	8.9	5.4	6.3
Parramatta/Auburn	8.6	6.3	6.8
Other	7.6	5.4	4.8
Total	9.2	8.1	6.3

Source: SATS Home interview survey tapes. Unlike the Census figures, these exclude persons who worked at home.

women, with married women generally making the shortest trips (Table 5.5). Allied to this difference between single and married women is the fact that unmarried women much more commonly work in the city centre, with concomitant longer work journeys. Thirty-nine per cent of all single female workers in the metropolitan area work in the City of Sydney, as against only 19 per cent of the married women. This results in two-thirds of the female workforce in the City of Sydney being single, in complete contrast to all other parts of the metropolitan area except North Sydney (Table 5.6).

Marriage perhaps makes a dramatic difference in a woman's estate, but the arrival of the first child makes the greatest difference to workforce

TABLE 5.6 *Percentage of Married Women in the Female Workforce of the Major Employment Areas of Sydney. SATS, 1971.*

Employment area	Single Women	Married Women	All Women
City of Sydney	65	35	100
South Sydney/Botany	44	56	100
North Sydney/Willoughby	56	44	100
Parramatta/Auburn	41	59	100
Other	39	61	100
Total	48	52	100

Source: SATS home interview survey tapes.

TABLE 5.7 *Percentage of Total Travel to Major Employment Areas in Sydney by Sex. Census and SATS, 1971.*

Employment Area	Proportion of total passenger-kms			
	Men	All Women	Single Women	Married Women
City of Sydney	64	36	24	12
South Sydney/Botany	83	17	8	9
North Sydney/Willoughby	71	29	15	14
Parramatta/Auburn	76	24	10	14
All other	73	27	11	16
All Sydney	71	29	16	13

Source: Columns 1 & 2: Census 1971, Journey to work tapes.
Columns 3 & 4: Column 2 apportioned in accordance with SATS data, from tapes.

participation. Were it possible to distinguish childless women from those with children, even sharper differences of journey length might emerge than those between single and married women. However, not even the SATS data permits this distinction to be made with any ease.

Two main reasons may be given for the shorter work journeys of women. The first is their lower income compared with men, which means they are less able to pay for travel, particularly speedy travel. Over all Australia in 1968/9 the income of working men was on average double that of working women (ABS Income Distribution 1968/9 Ref. No. 17.17). If this ratio applied in Sydney in 1971, or indeed any ratio approaching it, it is not surprising that there are differences between the sexes in travel habits. However, this is not the only factor at work. In 1968/9 single women had lower average incomes than married women, yet their work journeys were longer — indeed, not very far short of the men's. This suggests that the second factor operating was a shortage of time. A married woman holding down a paid job in addition to that of housewife and mother cannot afford to waste time travelling.

The shorter work journeys of women result in their making relatively less demand on the transport facilities of Sydney. Though women as a whole hold 36 per cent of the jobs, they travel only 29 per cent of total worker-kilometres (Table 5.7). This disproportion is even more acute if only married women be considered — with 19 per cent of the jobs, they travel 13 per cent of worker-kilometres. Once again, consonant with the higher proportion of single women working in the City of Sydney, the difference between the sexes is less marked for city centre travel than for other employment areas. Women hold 40 per cent of the jobs in the City of Sydney (Table 5.1), and because many of them are single and travel almost as far as the men (Table 5.5) they endure 36 per cent of total travel by city centre workers (Table 5.7). In Parramatta/Auburn the corresponding figures are 31 per cent of the jobs, and 24 per cent of the kilometres of travel, while among workers in dispersed locations women hold 37 per cent of the jobs but perform only 27 per cent of the travel. Roadworks built to help long-distance travellers to suburban workplaces are thus much more than average to the benefit of men rather than women.

The fact that men's and women's journey patterns are most similar for city centre travel is again demonstrated in Tables 5.8 and 5.9. The proportion of

TABLE 5.8 *Men by Distance Travelled on the Journey to Work in Sydney. Census 1971.*

Employment Area	Distance Travelled (per cent)				
	0<3km	3<6km	6<10km	10km and over	Total
City of Sydney	9	15	20	56	100
South Sydney/Botany	16	20	20	44	100
North Sydney/Willoughby	23	16	20	40	100
Parramatta/Auburn	20	20	23	37	100
All other	33	20	17	30	100
All Sydney	23	18	19	39	100

Source: Census 1971, Journey to work tapes.

TABLE 5.9 *Women by Distance Travelled on the Journey to Work in Sydney. Census 1971.*

Employment Area	Distance Travelled (per cent)				
	0<3km	3<6km	6<10km	10km and over	Total
City of Sydney	13	19	22	46	100
South Sydney/Botany	30	24	19	27	100
North Sydney/Willoughby	40	21	17	22	100
Parramatta/Auburn	34	24	20	22	100
All other	50	33	13	14	100
All Sydney	36	22	17	25	100

Source: Census 1971, Journey to work tapes.

women working in the City of Sydney with long journeys of over ten straight-line kilometres (46 per cent) is not far short of the proportion of men (56 per cent); likewise the proportion of women who live locally (13 per cent) is not far in advance of the proportion of men (9 per cent). This may be compared with the position over the rest of the metropolitan area, outside the major employment concentrations. Here only 14 per cent of the women have journeys of over ten kilometres, whereas the proportion for men is more than double, 30 per cent. Similarly, half the women live locally, as against a third of the men. The difference between men's and women's behaviour is strongest where

TABLE 5.10 *Destinations of Men Travelling Different Distances to Work in Sydney. Census 1971.*

Employment Area	Distance Travelled (per cent)				
	0<3km	3<6km	6<10km	10km and over	Total
City of Sydney	9	20	27	36	25
South Sydney/Botany	8	12	12	13	12
North Sydney/Willoughby	5	5	6	6	5
Parramatta/Auburn	8	10	11	9	9
All Other	70	53	44	37	49
All Sydney	100	100	100	100	100

Source: Census 1971, Journey to work tapes.

TABLE 5.11 *Destinations of Women Travelling Different Distances to Work in Sydney. Census 1971.*

Employment Area	Distance Travelled (per cent)				
	0<3km	3<6km	6<10km	10km and over	Total
City of Sydney	10	26	38	53	29
South Sydney/Botany	5	7	7	6	6
North Sydney/Willoughby	7	6	6	5	6
Parramatta/Auburn	7	8	8	6	7
All Other	71	54	40	29	52
All Sydney	100	100	100	100	100

Source: Census 1971, Journey to work tapes.

TABLE 5.12 *Percentage of Women Among Workers Travelling Different Distances to Major Employment Areas. Sydney, Census 1971.*

Employment Area	Distance Travelled				
	0<3km	3<6km	6<10km	10km and over	Total
City of Sydney	49	46	42	35	40
South Sydney/Botany	36	26	22	15	23
North Sydney/Willoughby	51	44	34	26	38
Parramatta/Auburn	43	34	27	20	30
All Other	47	40	31	22	37
All Sydney	46	40	33	27	36

Source: Census 1971, Journey to work tapes.

journeys are shortest; women, particularly married women, take more advantage of local employment.

Since women who work in dispersed employment areas tend to have short journeys to work, and only those who travel to the city centre have journey distances approaching those of men, more than half the long journeys (over ten kilometres) undertaken by women have the City of Sydney as their destination (Table 5.11). Among men, the City is the destination of a little more than a third of such long journeys. Almost a third of the men's long journeys are to the other major employment concentrations, leaving a third with dispersed destinations (Table 5.10). As a result, all long distance passenger flows except those to the city centre are highly masculine (Table 5.12). Only 15 per cent of those who travel more than ten kilometres to South Sydney/Botany are women, and in most other areas the proportion is little higher than 20 per cent. Even in the City of Sydney the proportion goes no higher than 35 per cent — that is, no higher than the proportion of women in the workforce as a whole. Once again it can be seen that capital works and subsidies to speed the long distance commuter, particularly the long distance crosstown traveller, benefit men disproportionately.

The other side of the coin is that women are strongly represented among the shorter distance travellers. Thirty-six per cent of them work locally, as against 23 per cent of the men (Tables 5.8 and 5.9). Nearly half the workers with local journeys (under three kilometres) are women, compared with only a quarter of those travelling long distances (Table 5.12). The proportion of female travellers reduces with distance whatever the destination, the difference being most marked where the destination is dispersed employment (47 per cent women for local trips, 22 per cent for long journeys.) In the industrial areas the difference is also considerable but where the destination is the city centre or North Sydney/Willoughby it is rather less.

TABLE 5.13 *The Response to Local Job Opportunities, by Sex. Sydney, Census 1971.*

REGION (See Map 8)	MEN			WOMEN		
	% able to work locally	% actually working locally	Response rate (Col.2/Col.1) %	% able to work locally	% actually working locally	Response rate (Col.5/Col.4) %
	1	2	3	4	5	6
Penrith	95	29	31	94	39	41
Blacktown	42	12	29	48	21	44
Outer South West	59	21	36	63	32	51
Parramatta/Auburn	95	27	28	95	36	38
Baulkham Hills/Hornsby	39	11	28	58	25	43
Ryde/Hunters Hill	64	19	30	73	34	47
Middle West	85	25	29	75	34	45
Bankstown	86	23	27	74	33	45
Sutherland	45	18	40	56	30	54
St.George/Canterbury	59	19	32	62	30	48
Marrickville/Leichhardt	95	44	46	92	54	59
South Sydney/Botany	100	55	55	100	64	64
Eastern Suburbs	73	31	42	65	39	60
City of Sydney	100	65	65	100	78	78
Ku-ring-gai	33	9	27	60	25	42
Inner North	89	27	30	90	38	42
Manly/Warringah	45	21	47	63	39	62
All Sydney	68	24	35	72	36	50

Source: Census 1971, Journey to work tapes.
Columns 1, 2, 4 and 5 calculated using amalgamated zones.

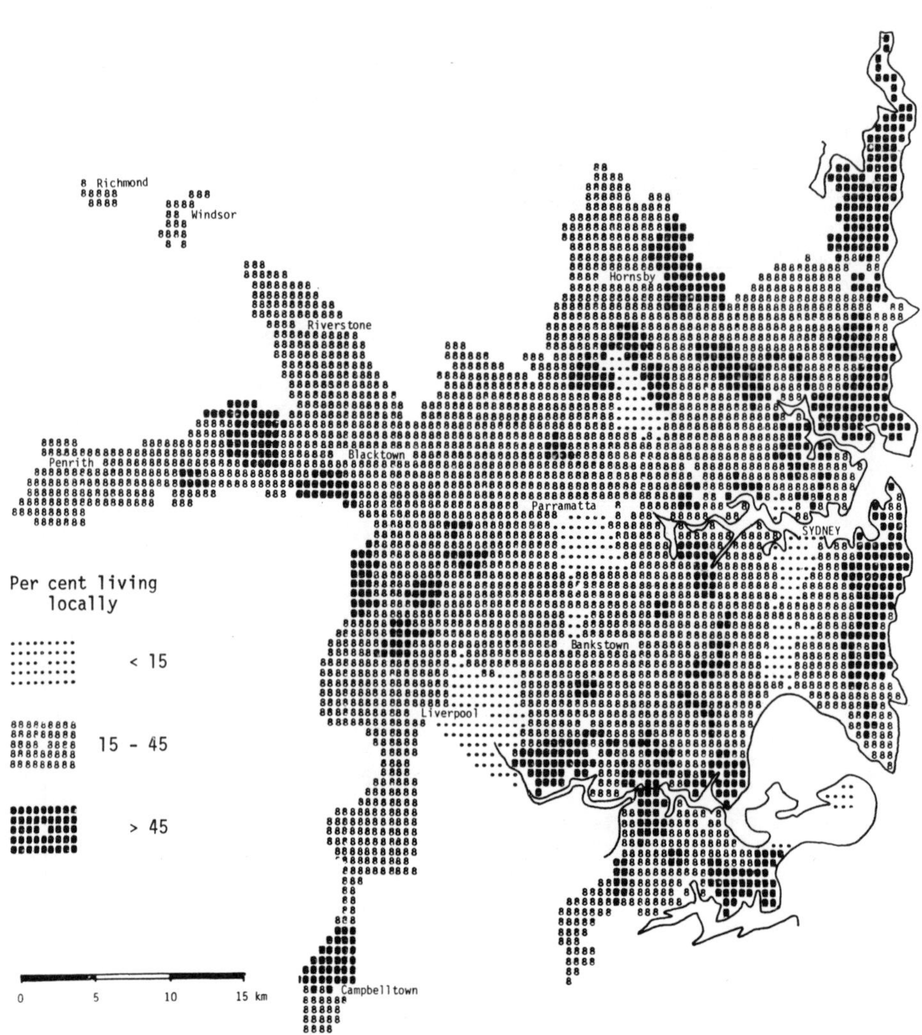

MAP 13. Percentage of Male Workers Living Locally by Employment Zone, Sydney, Census 1971 (see text, page 90). The major employment zones draw a low proportion of their male workforce from suburbs within three kilometres, as do several less important areas of extensive industrial development situated away from residential areas (e.g. the area east of Liverpool and south of Hornsby.) As on Map 9, where jobs are few they tend to be taken by locals.

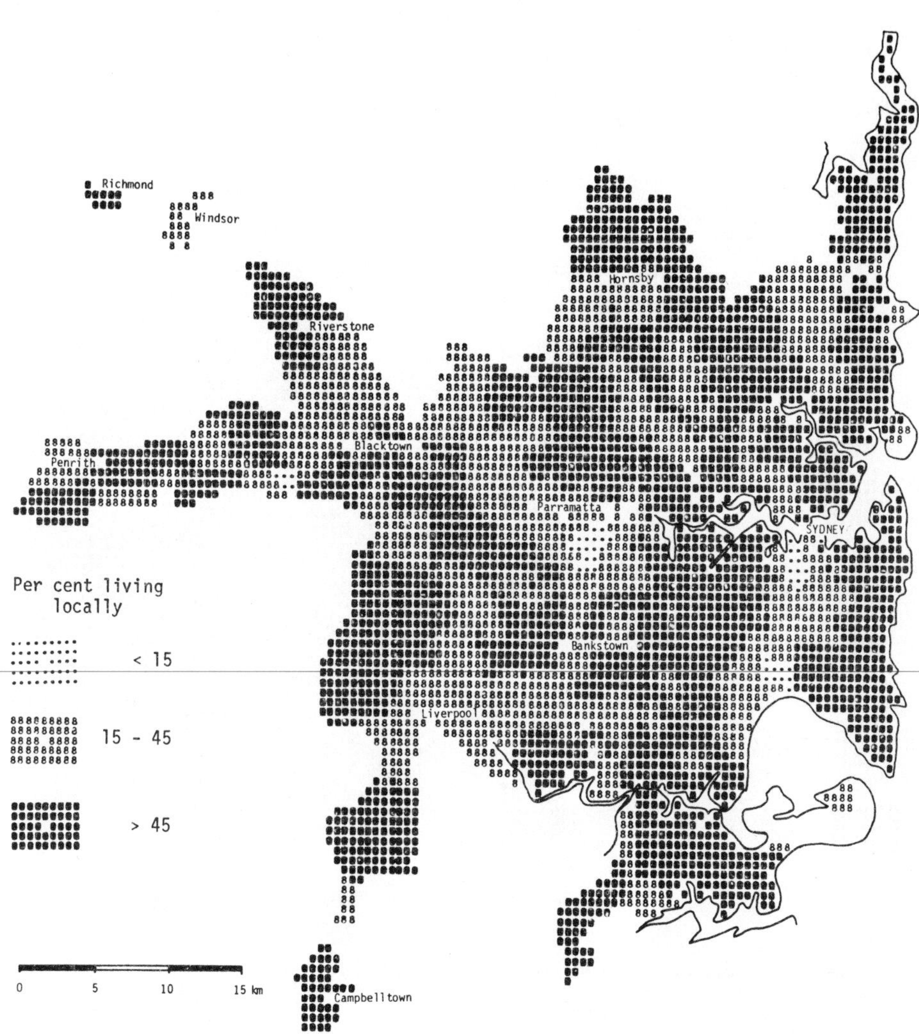

MAP 14. Percentage of Female Workers Living Locally by Employment Zone, Sydney, Census 1971 (see text, page 90). Women much more often work locally than men, hence the darker shading of this map compared with Map 13. With this proviso, the patterns are similar. The areas of high employment density (Map 12) draw a low proportion of their workforce from nearby suburbs, while most women who work in areas of low employment density live locally.

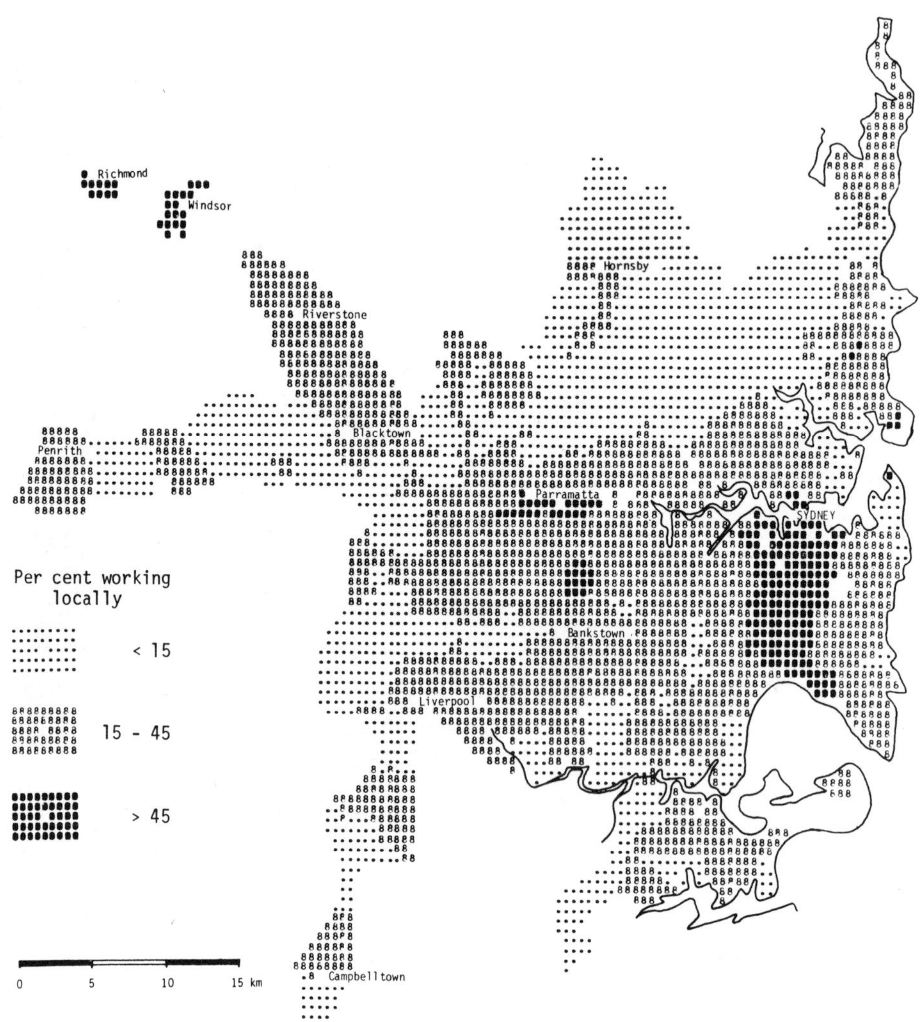

MAP 15. Men Working Locally by Residential Area, Sydney, Census 1971 (see text, page 90). Men who live in the major employment areas — and also those living in the relatively self-contained country towns of Windsor and Richmond — tend to work within three kilometres of home, while those who live in the outer suburbs often have long journeys to work.

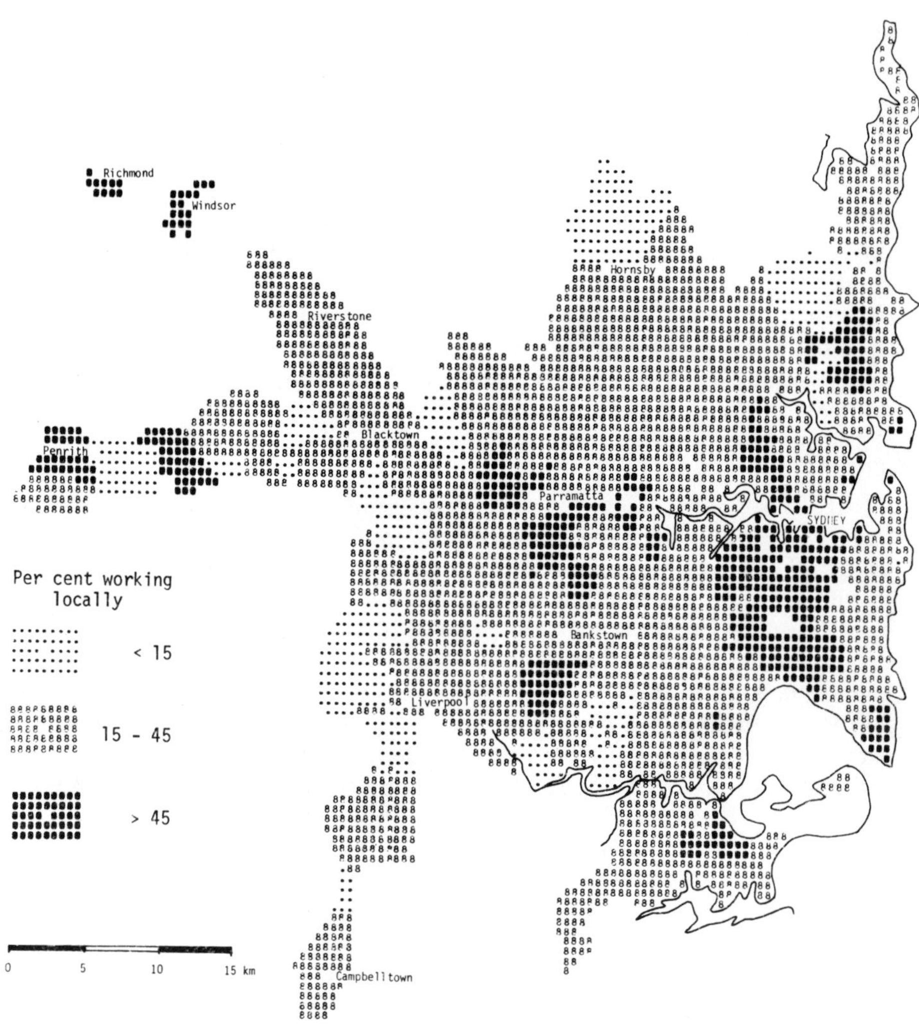

MAP 16. Women Working Locally by Residential Area, Sydney, Census 1971 (see text, page 90). With allowance for the fact that women much more often work locally than men, this map repeats the pattern of Maps 15 and 10. In only a few fringe suburbs does the proportion of women working locally fall below 15 per cent, while it is over 45 per cent in all the major employment areas, and in Penrith and several other minor suburban employment areas in addition to Richmond and Windsor.

Given that a lower proportion of men work locally than women, the geographic pattern of local trip-making is similar for the two sexes. This is shown to be true both on maps by workplace and by place of residence, and is confirmed by the regional response rates to local employment opportunities given in Table 5.13. The pattern of Map 9 (persons working locally, by workplace) is repeated on Maps 13 (men) and 14 (women), save that the proportion of women working locally is generally 10 to 30 per cent above the proportion of men. Similarly, Maps 15 (men) and 16 (women) repeat the pattern of Map 10 (persons working locally, by place of residence) with differences in the intensity of shading. In all the regions given in Table 5.13 women's response rates to local employment are higher than men's, the difference being particularly strong in Bankstown and the Middle Western suburbs, where to some extent it compensates for a contrary difference in the availability of local jobs by sex. Men's response rates are relatively close to women's in the City of Sydney and in South Sydney/Botany, both areas of considerable job surplus, and in some of the fringe regions where transport is difficult.

The consistently higher response of women to local employment opportunities, and their consistently shorter journeys, implies that they choose nearer jobs than men at some sacrifice of range of choice. For married women, though not for single, this choice is associated with an effort to reduce the time spent travelling, while for both married and single women it is associated with the greater use of walking and bus travel — both of them slow but cheap. All this will be fully treated in Chapter 9. For the moment we may conclude that job decentralisation for women would be more appreciated than for men, particularly in the work-deficient outer western suburbs. A high proportion of any women's jobs decentralised to the outer parts of Blacktown municipality, for example, would be taken by locals, avoiding any adverse growth of cross traffic. Given full employment, the extra jobs would enable many women to enter the workforce who at present are prevented from doing so by lack of local opportunities, while they would benefit others by enabling them to spend less time and money travelling. However, the differences between men and women are not so marked that large numbers of women's jobs can safely be decentralised to any one place without giving rise to significant numbers of long journeys. The proportion of women's jobs in Parramatta/Auburn taken by locals is a little higher than men's, but it is still under a third. Again, a fifth of the women workers there (as against 37 per cent of the men) come from over ten kilometres away. Any further jobs in such an area, even if they be filled by women, would attract people from quite long distances away.

APPENDIX TO CHAPTER 5: Table 5.14

Table 5.14 is included here for the benefit of those who find the interpretation of a detailed set of figures more rewarding than the examination of maps. It gives average and median airline distances for the journey to work, for each sex, by both local government area of residence and workplace. It is supported by Table 5.15 which provides correlation coefficients. Many features of the journey to work noticeable on the maps appear also in these tables, including the following:

1. As explained in Chapter 3, distributions of journey length by local government area of residence are quite variable in shape, being to different degrees skewed and generally bimodal. The relationship between the average and the median length of journeys is therefore far from constant, as reflected in correlation coefficients of between 0.73 and 0.9. The median is generally less than the average (the distributions are positively skewed), but this is not always the case — e.g. journeys by men from Ku-ring-gai. In such cases with the median close to or greater than the mean the distribution is likely to be strongly bimodal. This happens when a high proportion of residents work either locally or in the city centre. The degree of skewness (that is, the degree to which a majority have short journeys but a minority relatively long) is greater for women than for men, reflecting the fact that women tend to work either locally or in the city centre.
2. Women's travel distances are consistently shorter than those for men. This is true of both averages and medians, and for all local government areas. The correlation coefficients are high, particularly for the average length of journey (0.97 by residence, 0.93 by workplace), the relationship being that a kilometre increase in men's average distances is generally accompanied by a 750 to 840 metre increase in women's. Because of the differences in skewness already mentioned, the relationship between the medians is less close (the coefficient of correlation is 0.89 in each case). The difference in degree of skewness tends to increase as distances lengthen: as the men's median distance increases a kilometre, the women's tends to go up by around 480 to 640 metres.
3. Average journey lengths increase steadily with the distance of residence from the city centre (correlation coefficient 0.94 for men, 0.95 for women), the increase being roughly 310 metres per kilometre for men, and 230 metres per kilometre for women. The rate of increase of the median journey length is slower (260 metres per kilometre for men, 110 metres per kilometre for women) and the degree of correlation is lower. The skewness of the distributions thus increases with distance from the city centre (the difference between the local workers and the long-travelling minority increases) (Black 1977, p.48).
4. Average journey lengths by workplace are not, according to the correlation coefficients, related either to distance from the city centre, or to

TABLE 5.14 *Average and Median Journeys to Work: Sydney Municipalities — Kilometres. Census 1971.*

LOCAL GOVERNMENT AREA	JOURNEYS BY RESIDENTS				JOURNEYS BY WORKERS			
	MEN		WOMEN		MEN		WOMEN	
	Average	Median	Average	Median	Average	Median	Average	Median
City of Sydney	4.7	2.2	4.0	1.4	13.3	11.3	11.5	9.0
South Sydney	3.7	2.5	2.5	1.8	11.6	9.1	8.5	6.0
Woolahra	5.3	4.2	3.9	3.3	7.2	3.7	3.9	2.2
Waverley	6.7	6.2	5.3	5.6	5.9	2.4	2.9	1.7
Randwick	6.3	5.7	5.2	5.1	8.1	4.5	4.3	2.4
Botany	4.5	3.3	3.6	2.7	9.9	7.8	5.9	4.3
Marrickville	5.0	4.2	3.8	3.3	9.4	7.9	6.1	3.6
Leichhardt	4.2	3.2	3.0	2.4	8.8	6.4	5.3	2.7
Drummoyne	5.9	5.7	4.8	4.8	7.3	4.5	4.3	2.1
Ashfield	6.5	6.7	5.3	5.7	8.3	5.1	5.5	2.6
Burwood	7.2	7.7	6.2	6.3	9.2	7.0	6.7	3.9
Concord	7.0	7.3	5.9	4.6	9.7	7.6	6.8	4.8
Rockdale	8.2	8.2	6.9	6.4	7.6	6.0	5.1	3.4
Kogarah	10.2	10.9	8.5	8.5	6.1	4.2	4.3	2.9
Hurstville	10.4	11.2	8.8	7.7	6.7	4.9	4.6	3.1
Canterbury	8.3	8.2	7.3	6.6	7.3	5.0	4.6	3.0
Sutherland	13.3	14.4	10.3	7.6	6.6	4.7	4.1	2.5
Strathfield	7.9	8.2	7.3	6.8	10.1	8.2	7.3	5.3
Bankstown	10.2	8.7	8.7	5.8	8.8	6.8	5.4	3.8
Holroyd	10.9	9.0	9.2	5.8	8.1	5.4	5.2	3.4
Fairfield	11.6	9.6	10.3	6.5	7.6	5.2	5.3	3.2
Auburn	7.6	6.2	6.9	4.2	10.1	8.4	7.4	5.7
Parramatta	9.0	6.6	7.2	4.3	9.4	7.0	6.5	4.4
Ryde	8.6	8.9	6.4	5.0	8.7	6.4	5.1	3.3
Hunter's Hill	6.6	6.4	5.1	5.3	7.3	5.1	4.0	2.1
North Sydney	5.0	3.9	3.8	3.2	10.5	8.7	7.0	4.6
Mosman	6.2	5.4	4.8	4.7	6.5	4.1	4.2	1.8
Lane Cove	6.4	5.9	4.8	3.7	8.8	6.9	5.6	3.6
Willoughby	6.8	6.7	4.9	3.9	9.3	7.2	6.0	4.0
Ku-ring-gai	12.5	13.1	8.4	7.8	9.0	5.9	5.5	3.3
Hornsby	13.5	15.0	9.2	7.0	10.3	4.9	6.0	3.0
Manly	8.2	8.6	6.1	5.6	5.4	3.2	3.7	2.3
Warringah	11.5	11.2	7.6	5.1	5.9	3.6	4.4	2.9
Baulkham Hills	11.8	10.3	8.4	6.0	6.5	3.6	4.5	2.7
Blacktown	16.2	14.5	13.0	9.4	9.0	5.2	6.5	3.0
Penrith	17.1	8.3	11.9	3.3	13.2	4.2	9.8	3.2
Liverpool	12.8	11.2	10.3	6.5	7.4	4.2	6.0	3.9
Campbelltown	18.7	18.8	15.1	10.5	8.9	2.9	5.7	1.4
TOTAL	10.0	7.5	7.4	4.8	10.0	7.5	7.4	4.8

Source: Census 1971. Journey to work tapes.

TABLE 5.15 *Correlation Coefficients Between Measures of the Length of the Journey to Work. Sydney, 38 L.G.A.'s, 1971.*

Correlation	Correlation coefficient	Increase in median for a 1 km increase in average. km.
Average length to median length		
by residence, for men	.90	.91
by residence, for women	.78	.55
by workplace, for men	.73	.77
by workplace, for women	.82	.69
Men's distances to women's		Increase in women's distance for a 1 km increase in men's.
by residence, average	.97	.75
by residence, median	.89	.48
by workplace, average	.93	.84
by workplace, median	.89	.64
Distances by residence to those by workplace		
for men, average	-.06	-
for men, median	-.53	-
for women, average	-.00	-
for women, median	-.48	-
Distances travelled, to distance of the L.G.A. from the City Centre		Increase in distance for a 1 km increase in distance from the city centre.
LGA of residence, for men, average	.94	.31
LGA of residence, for men, median	.76	.26
LGA of residence, for women, average	.95	.23
LGA of residence, for women, median	.58	.11
LGA of workplace, for men, average	.04	-
LGA of workplace, for men, median	-.47	-
LGA of workplace, for women, average	-.11	-
LGA of workplace, for women, median	-.24	-

average distances covered by the residents of the same local government area. In fact this apparent lack of relationship conceals something of a U-shaped distribution, by which average distances are long for journeys to jobs in the city centre and to those in some of the far outer suburbs, but more generally short in between. In a number of the outer suburbs concerned, the distribution of workers' journeys is highly skewed (the average very much more than the median) such that median distances do not increase in these areas even though averages do. There is thus a mild but consistent tendency for the median length of the journey to work to decline as the distance of the workplace from the city centre increases.

So much for the interrelationships between different measures of distance. Several other questions might be addressed to the figures, including:

1. Is there an observable relationship between the distances travelled to work in a local government area and the composition of its workforce? Journeys tend to be long when there are many clerks in the workforce (correlation coefficients range from 0.55 to 0.75); they also increase when there are numerous metal tradesmen, though not so strongly (coefficients of between 0.15 and 0.26 — these increase when multiple correlation is performed which includes the proportion of clerks). Journey lengths tend to be shorter to areas where women are a high proportion of the workforce (correlation coefficients of -0.37 to -0.47). In other words, Table 5.14 reflects the obvious fact that journeys to the city centre and major industrial areas tend to be longer than average, while those to local employment (which is more highly feminine than most) tend to be shorter. The variation of journey lengths with occupation is treated more fully in Chapter 6.
2. Is there any relationship between the distances travelled by the residents of different suburbs and the socio-economic status of those suburbs? In terms of simple correlation there is virtually no such relationship (correlation coefficients range from -0.08 to 0.17 where socio-economic status is measured by the proportion of employers in the workforce). However, once adjustment is made for distance from the city centre a low but significant degree of correlation emerges: distances travelled tend to increase with the socio-economic status of the suburb. This again is no surprise: high status jobs tend to be in the city centre, and hence to engender long travel. Again, not surprisingly to those who have studied the maps in Chapter 5, the socio-economic status of the suburb of residence is more closely related to work journeys for men than for women.

CHAPTER 6

Local Employment in Different Occupations

The benefits of any policy of job decentralisation depend strongly on the kinds of work decentralised, and on the places to which jobs are shifted. On the evidence so far presented transferring men's jobs from the city centre to places like Auburn might cause a costly increase in crosstown commuting, whereas providing more work for women in outer suburbs at present short of women's jobs would enable many to work locally who would like to do so and currently cannot. The response to changes in the location of jobs will depend, however, not only on the gender of the jobs and on the suburbs in which new jobs are provided, but on the occupations involved. Further decentralisation of employment in occupations where jobs are already widespread is prima facie less likely to reduce work travel than the dispersal of jobs in highly concentrated occupations. Again, it might be that the decentralisation of jobs in low income occupations would be more appreciated than the dispersal of those which pay high wages, since low income people perhaps give a higher priority to limiting travel expenses by keeping their work journeys short.

To pursue these questions it is necessary to take up once more the discussion in Chapter 2. There, occupations were classified into those centralised in the City of Sydney, those concentrated elsewhere in the metropolitan area, and those dispersed throughout it. How do these differences in locational pattern affect local employment opportunities, and how do people respond to such differences in opportunity? In this chapter these two questions are discussed in turn.

The Balance between Homes and Workplaces, by Occupation

In Chapter 1 it was predicted that differences in journey lengths between occupations would depend first on the wages paid in each occupation and second on its degree of concentration. Journey lengths should be shorter in the more widespread occupations, and in those where incomes are low. These predictions can be confirmed by comparing occupations of different degrees of dispersion and different average incomes. For this comparison the 67 occupations listed in Chapter 2 were reduced to 18 by omitting occupations where a high proportion of workers gave no workplace address, and amalgamating many of the remaining occupations where jobs are similar both in socio-economic status and geographic pattern. The several professions were not amalgamated because they show considerable differences of geographic pattern and because a person with professional qualifications does not usually consider working in jobs outside his profession. Men's and women's jobs were considered separately according to the sex of their current incumbent, without any special regard for work which might be carried out by persons of either sex. The complete definitions of the occupational groupings are given in the appendix to this chapter (p.188).

In Table 6.1 the 18 selected occupations are listed in descending order of average income. These income estimates are for all Australia and date from a survey a few years before the 1971 census, but still give a rough indication of relative earnings in Sydney in the early 1970s. Income figures were not available for several small occupations, which were therefore slotted into the table alongside similar occupations for which figures were known. It can be seen immediately that the incomes of men working full time all the year, both overall and in any occupation, average roughly 80 per cent greater than those of full year, full time female workers. For each sex the range of average incomes is considerable, and should provide evidence on the predicted association of journey length with income. The occupations also range from those concentrated in the city centre to those dispersed throughout the metropolitan area.

Before the effect of income on journey length can be assessed, it is necessary to measure and allow for the degree of geographic concentration and dispersal of jobs in the different occupations. One way of doing this would be to use the classification developed in Chapter 2, and shown for the selected occupations in the first column of Table 6.1. However, this classification, for all its virtues in providing a simple mathematical way of identifying concentrated and dispersed occupations, is not as useful for present purposes as the measure developed in Chapter 4: the proportion of the workforce that would be able to work locally (i.e. within roughly three kilometres) if all obeyed a set of rules designed to minimise journey lengths. Calculation of these estimates was by hand, and even using amalgamated zones (as explained in Chapter 4) was laborious — hence the restriction of the analysis to 18 occupational groupings, rather than the 67 distinguished in the census.

In Chapter 4, the proportion able to work locally was calculated by balancing the number of jobs available against the local workforce. The obvious adaptation of this indicator to individual occupations offsets the number of jobs in each occupation and the resident workforce in that occupation. The resulting all-Sydney estimate of the proportion able to work locally is affected both by the distribution of jobs in the occupation, and by the residential distribution of its workers. Differences in the estimates for different

TABLE 6.1 *Selected Occupations by Degree of Concentration and Average Income. Sydney, 1971.*

		MEN		WOMEN	
	Classi-fication	Number (1971) '000	Average Income (1968/9) $ '000	Number (1971) '000	Average Income (1968/9) $ '000
Doctor	2b	4	13	1	n.a.
Lawyer	3c	3	11		
Engineer	2b	5	8		
Scientist	2b	3	n.a.		
Manager	2b	73	6	10	3.7
Official	2c	1	n.a.		
Teacher	2a	11	4.7	17	3.6
Technician	2b	25	4		
Clerk	3c	67	3.8	81	2.2
Typist	3c			52	2.2
Nurse	2b			17	2.2
Clergy	1b	2	n.a.		
Metal trades	2a	109	3.5		
Cleaner	2b			32	1.9
Sales	2b	30	3.1	38	1.8
Process worker	2a	57	3.1	29	1.7
Clothing worker	2a			22	1.7
Storeman/labourer	2b	55	2.8		
All Other		222		73	
All occupations		667	3.8	371	2.2

n.a. Not available.

Key to classification (see Table 2.2).

1b. Occupations of low concentration with 15 to 45 per cent of total jobs in the City of Sydney.

2a. Occupations of moderate concentration with less than 15 per cent of total jobs in the City of Sydney.

2b. Occupations of moderate concentration with 15 to 45 per cent of total jobs in the City of Sydney.

2c. Occupations of moderate concentration with over 44 per cent of total jobs in the City of Sydney.

3c. Occupations of high concentration with over 44 per cent of total jobs in the City of Sydney.

Source: Classification: See Table 2.2.
Number: Census 1971, Journey to work tapes.
Income: ABS, Income Distribution 1968/9.
Average income is for full-year full-time workers.

occupations reflect the extent to which their job locations are more or less concentrated than average, and also the extent to which there is compensating variation in the suburbs in which their workers live. Through the workings of socio-economic status, Sydney exhibits a considerable degree of residential segregation, with workers in high status occupations living in snob suburbs and those in other occupations elsewhere (Davis and Spearritt, 1974 Map 48). This segregation effect may counteract or exaggerate the impact of the degree of dispersion on the local availability of jobs. In order to compare the degree of dispersion between occupations it is therefore necessary to calculate the proportion of the population which could work locally in the absence of residential segregation. This can be done by assuming that the workforce in each occupation is distributed residentially in the same pattern as the working population as a whole — that is, as a constant proportion of the resident workers in each suburb. This estimate depends on the degree of dispersal of jobs in the occupation in relation to the population as a whole, and is not affected by any compensating variation in the social composition of the suburbs. Comparison of this figure with the proportion actually able to work locally (i.e. the balance for each occupation of jobs and actual numbers of resident workers) then gives an indication of the way in which the residential segregation of Sydney aids or hinders people in finding local employment.

As reflected in columns 1 and 3 of Table 6.2, the degree of dispersion of jobs in different occupations varies widely, from strongly concentrated (lawyers and clerks) to highly dispersed (teachers, cleaners and saleswomen). These estimates broadly reflect the degree of dispersion for different occupations calculated and described in Chapter 2.

Except in the case of doctors, whenever a comparison is possible women's jobs are more dispersed than men's — though the difference in the overall employment situation in favour of women is less, because so many of them work in the centralised clerical occupations. Three reasons may be given for this greater dispersion of women's jobs. First, within occupations, women may be employed in work which is by its nature more spread around. For example, among teachers, men dominate in higher education, which is more concentrated than the primary schools staffed largely by women. From this point of view it is perhaps significant that among doctors, where the kinds of work done by men and women and perhaps even their earnings are fairly similar, the proportion of women able to work locally is very nearly the same as men. Second, in occupations where the same job may equally well be taken by men or women, the latter, because of their unwillingness to travel, may well pre-empt the local work. Finally, women in occupations deficient in local employment may withdraw from the workforce, thus increasing the proportion of the remainder who can find local jobs.

A comparison of column 2 with column 1 of Table 6.2, and of column 4 with column 3, gives an indication of the extent to which residential segregation affects the ability to work locally. Judging from the 'all occupations' estimate at

TABLE 6.2 *The Local Balance Between Workers and Jobs, by Occupation. Sydney, Census 1971.*

	MEN		WOMEN	
Column	% able to work locally - no residential segregation 1	% actually able to work locally 2	% able to work locally - no residential segregation 3	% actually able to work locally 4
Doctor	70	68	71	71
Lawyer	29	29		
Engineer	45	48		
Scientist	55	48		
Manager	68	62	75	77
Official	48	43		
Teacher	77	71	88	86
Technician	57	54		
Clerk	44	43	60	57
Typist			56	55
Nurse			73	86
Clergy	78	89		
Metal Trades	72	71		
Cleaner			76	84
Sales	73	73	81	80
Process worker	69	73	76	81
Clothing worker			66	75
Storeman/labourer	67	79		
All other	69	70	73	75
All occupations	66	67	69	71

Source: Census 1971, Journey to work tapes, calculated using amalgamated zones.

the bottom of the table, it has very little aggregate effect. However, this overall outcome balances occupations in which the workers tend to live near their kind of work (even if they do not actually work locally) against those where they tend to live well away. Residential segregation noticeably increases the mismatch between jobs and dwellings only among men, and then only for certain occupations; teachers, scientists, managers and government officials. These are all high status occupations where many of the jobs are in low status suburbs, in which their holders decline to live. The best example is that of the teachers, who tend to live in the less pricy suburbs north of the Harbour, but whose jobs are concentrated (so far as this can be said of so dispersed a pattern) in the low income western suburbs. Similarly the managers of factories in South Sydney/Botany and Parramatta/Auburn tend to live in Ku-ring-gai. Such people put living in an area of the correct status above the convenience of their journey to work and, being highly paid, are able to bear the extra transport costs. They are perhaps also able to arrange their hours of work to avoid peak-period travel. However, high status and high pay do not always result in a residential pattern divorced from employment opportunities. The engineers live in high status suburbs and, by locating their consulting offices in North Sydney, succeed in working there as well. On the other hand, many doctors work in low status suburbs, and resist the temptation to live in a huddle in the high status areas even though they could well afford to do so. Two other professional groups where the actual balance between jobs and residents is more favourable than the unsegregated balance are the clergy and nurses. In these two cases a tradition of being 'on call' is assisted by the provision of housing along with the job.

The other occupations where residential segregation brings people closer to their work are all low in status and income: cleaners, storemen, labourers and process workers, of either sex. To some extent this may be due to industrial blight: those areas, particularly in the inner suburbs, where there are many factory jobs are not particularly pleasant places to live, and are therefore left to low status residents. Also, jobs may be more easily substituted within and between low income occupations, leading people to take whatever is locally available. For example, 13 per cent of the women living in the eastern suburbs, in Sutherland and in Manly/Warringah work either as cleaners/domestics or as process workers. The eastern suburbs are relatively well supplied with domestic jobs and undersupplied with process work. (If the population were distributed on an all-Sydney basis they could provide 45 per cent of their process workers with local jobs, as against 80 per cent of the domestics. The ratios in Manly/Warringah are 66/68 and Sutherland 97/80.) As a result, three per cent of the women workers in the eastern suburbs are process workers and ten per cent domestics, as against six and seven per cent in the other two regions.

The abiding impression from Table 6.2 is similar to that from the equivalent table in Chapter 4 (Table 4.1): that a remarkably high proportion of the workers of Sydney could work locally if all were to obey a few stringent but simple rules. In no women's occupation is the proportion less than half, and among men only the exceptionally concentrated legal profession records a proportion of less than 40 per cent. Even so, there is considerable variation between occupations in the proportion of the workforce which could work locally. The proportion tends to be higher in the more lowly paid occupations, both because jobs in these occupations are more widespread than average, and because such workers tend to live closer than average to their kind of work. However, several of the highly paid professions (including medicine, the most highly paid of them all) also have a favourable local balance of jobs and residents.

The scope for the decentralisation of employment is obviously greatest in the concentrated occupations, but action directed at decentralising such jobs may not be the most effective way of increasing local employment opportunities. For example, town planning regulations which encourage neighborhood shopping centres at the expense of regional centres are more likely to increase local employment opportunities than efforts to shift clerical jobs from the city centre to Parramatta. In the same way the development of outer suburban industrial estates directly encourages the continuing decentralisation of manufacturing employment. In other words, it might be easiest to provide local employment opportunities by further dispersion of already widespread occupations. Such a policy assumes that people who want local work are willing to take whatever jobs are available; that it is enough that those who want to work near home should be able to obtain a local job of some kind or other. Yet why should people with clerical skills be forced so often to choose between exercising their skills and working locally? A sense of fairness might demand that jobs of all kinds should be spread around more evenly. If this is indeed the people's demand then such jobs as are available locally in the more concentrated occupations should be taken by locals; in the jargon of Chapter 4, they should show high response rates. We now turn to see whether this is so.

The Response to Local Employment Opportunities, by Occupation

Table 6.3 continues from Table 6.2, showing the proportion of workers in each occupation able to work locally, the proportion who actually do, and the response rate — the ratio of those actually working locally to those who could. The table shows that the proportion actually working locally indeed varies with the proportion able to do so — more people work locally in the more widespread occupations ($r = .86$). Contrary to expectation, response rates are if anything higher in the dispersed occupations. (On average, the proportion actually working locally increases by more than 1 per cent for a 1 per cent increase in the proportion able to work locally.) Prima facie, workers in the

TABLE 6.3 *The Response to Local Employment Opportunities by Occupation. Sydney, Census 1971.*

	MEN			WOMEN		
Column	% able to work locally 1	% actually working locally 2	Response Rate (Col.2/Col.1) per cent 3	% able to work locally 4	% actually working locally 5	Response Rate (Col.5/Col.4) per cent 6
Doctor	68	35	51	71	35	49
Lawyer	29	12	41			
Engineer	48	13	27			
Scientist	48	15	31			
Manager	62	21	34	77	40	52
Official	43	13	30			
Teacher	71	24	34	86	32	37
Technician	54	14	26			
Clerk	43	13	30	57	26	46
Typist				55	25	45
Nurse				86	50	58
Clergy	89	67	75			
Metal Trades	71	23	32			
Cleaner				84	51	61
Sales	73	31	42	80	45	56
Process worker	73	28	38	81	43	53
Clothing worker				75	46	61
Storeman/labourer	79	33	42			
All other	70	27	39	75	36	48
All occupations	67	24	36	71	36	51

Source: Census 1971. Journey to work tapes, calculated using amalgamated zones.

concentrated occupations do not seem to be jostling one another in competition for the limited supply of local jobs. The only case where this might be so — where a concentrated occupation turns in a high response rate — is that of the lawyers, and here there is an alternative explanation. Legal employment is so highly concentrated in the city centre that most of the lawyers who are able to work locally live within the City of Sydney, and, not surprisingly, work there. The resulting high response rate is more a result of where these lawyers live than of the shortage of local work in their profession.

This legal case raises the question as to whether the variation in response rates between occupations generally can be explained by their peculiarities of location; that is, whether it is due to the inter-regional variation described in Chapter 4. However, an attempt to predict the occupational response rate from the regional distribution of the workforce failed for all occupations except the legal profession. The most that can be said is that people working in low income occupations who happen to live in high income suburbs often work locally, and similarly people with high income occupations living in low income suburbs. The few process and service workers living north of the harbour have an above average response rate, and similarly professional people and managers living in the western suburbs. In each case the supply of local people into the labour market is relatively small, and those who are on the spot therefore find it relatively easy to get a local job. Indeed, they may be living where they are solely because of the job. Overall, however, such people comprise a minority of their trade or profession, and do not much affect its response rates. Differences between occupations in response rates are therefore almost completely independent of differences between regions, and have different causes.

The first of these causes is not far to seek: that women have a lower willingness to spend time travelling, and a lower financial ability to pay for travel. Table 6.3 confirms the analysis of Chapter 5, in that female response rates are higher than male rates overall, and for all occupations except doctors. The apparent equality of women doctors with men perhaps indicates that feminine distinctiveness disappears once one gets high up enough on the income scale — or perhaps that the woman doctor's willingness to travel is truly lower than the man's, but is counter-balanced by something else, such as a lower propensity to invest in general practices with house attached.

The doctors' high response rates can perhaps be put down to a tradition of local service. Having found that they live near their jobs (Table 6.2) it is not surprising to find that they actually work where they live (Table 6.3). The clergy and nurses are once again similar. A contrasting case is that of the teachers, who are subjected to transfer by their employer, but who, unlike the clergy, do not have to shift house at the same time. This shifting about appears to affect female teachers quite severely (their response to local employment opportunities is way below that for any other women's occupation) but even in this case the women's response rate is above that for men in the same profession, and above men such as metal tradesmen who have the same average income.

Apart from cases like these, there is a general correlation between the response to local employment opportunities and average incomes. Low income occupations (for men, storemen/labourers, process workers and salesmen) have relatively high response rates, while jobs a cut above (metal tradesmen) have lower, and jobs above that (technicians) lower again — though here the series stops, for of all men the technicians have the lowest response rates. At least to this extent — that is, at least amongst occupations of low to middling average income — the prediction of Chapter 1 holds good, and workers in higher income occupations have longer journeys to work. This also explains the association of low response rates with concentrated occupations: both are related to high income. Response tends to be higher, and the local balance between jobs and residents more even, in low income occupations.

TABLE 6.4 *The Length of the Journey to Work, by Occupational Group. Sydney, Census 1971.*

Occupational Group	Average distance		Median distance		Proportion Travelling:				TOTAL
	Men km	Women km	Men km	Women km	1<3 km %	3<6 km %	6<9 km %	10km and over %	persons '000
Male clerks, etc.	12.1		10.4		12	16	21	51	95
Male lawyers, scientists, engineers, technicians	11.5		10.1		13	16	21	50	53
Female clerks and typists		8.8		6.4	26	21	19	34	159
Female process workers		6.1		3.8	42	25	16	17	60
Male process workers	8.3		5.8		28	23	19	30	67
Metal trades etc.	10.0		7.9		20	20	20	40	125
Saleswomen		5.7		3.4	47	22	15	16	38
Female doctors, nurses and teachers		6.7		4.6	38	20	17	25	49
Male doctors, clergy and teachers	8.5		6.4		32	17	18	33	20
Male managers	10.2		8.6		22	15	19	44	73
Salesmen, storemen, care-takers, waiters etc.	8.4		5.0		31	20	19	30	91
Female cleaners, waitresses etc.		5.7		3.2	48	21	14	17	53
All men	9.7		7.4		24	19	19	38	655
All women		7.3		4.8	36	22	17	25	367
All people	8.8		6.4		28	20	18	34	1022

Minor disagreements with Table 6.3 are due to differences of classification of occupations and to the use of census rather than amalgamated zones.

Source: Census 1971, journey to work tapes. Straight-line distances calculated using census zones.

Any prediction as to how a general increase in incomes might affect response rates can be little more than speculation. However, insofar as the high response rates in the lower income occupations and among women are due to lack of money for transport expenses (particularly lack of a car) increasing income is likely to reduce response and increase road congestion. On the other hand, if it be true that response rates bottom out at 30 per cent (for men) future increases in income might not have quite the same traffic-generating consequences as those over the past three decades.

This analysis of response rates has not produced any evidence that there is a strong demand for the decentralisation of employment among male clerks or the members of the men's concentrated professions. Shifting such jobs from the city centre to major suburban concentrations of employment, or even to neighborhood centres, would not encourage many more people to work locally. Any reduction of journey lengths would come through the substitution of middle length, quite possibly crosstown trips for previous long journeys. If any action is to be taken to promote the dispersal of employment it would therefore seem more urgent to ensure that jobs in the traditionally widespread occupations — low income work and women's work of all kinds — are balanced with the population in all and not merely most suburbs.

So far the discussion of this chapter has concentrated on the response to employment opportunities as measured by the proportion of workers in each occupation working locally. For the sake of completeness Table 6.4 gives the proportion travelling long distances, and the average and median distances, for occupations grouped according to the classification of Chapter 2. By and large these figures add little to the discussion, since the measures of distance are closely related. For all the groups of occupations the average distance travelled is roughly two kilometres greater than the median, and both are closely related to the proportion working locally. The only deviations from this relationship are that the median is unexpectedly low for male process workers, given the proportion working locally, and unexpectedly high for men's dispersed professions (doctors, clergy and teachers) — indicating in the former case a relatively high proportion of workers travelling the intermediate distances, and in the latter a relatively long tail of long journeys.

Such, then, are the journey to work patterns of those who work locally — those who put very little strain on the transport system, and who could at a pinch walk to work. But what of the remaining three-quarters of the population? The most readily identifiable are those who work in the city centre — a further quarter of the labour force, and the one most given to long distance travel. These are the subject of the next chapter.

CHAPTER 7

The City Centre

The city centre has always had the most intense concentration of employment in Sydney. Of late its dominance of the employment pattern has been declining, but it still accounts for between a fifth and a quarter of all jobs in the urban area. (The vagueness of the estimate is due to the difficulty of defining the city area — the looser the definition, the greater the proportion.) No other part of the metropolitan area has jobs at such density, a fact which can be readily appreciated from Graphs 3.2 to 3.6.

Though very few people actually live there, the city centre automatically comes to mind when people think about 'Sydney'. Aesthetic descriptions of the city concentrate on the view of the Opera House from the Bridge, and the exhilaration of Sydney's prosperity seems — or seemed — reflected in the tall buildings rather than in the spreading suburbs. Much that is said about the city centre therefore concentrates on its appearance, and not on the way it works. This is as well for the good spirits of all concerned, since when attention is diverted to the way the city centre interacts with the rest of the metropolitan area the ground for exhilaration disappears (Sandercock 1975 p.196).

One of the chief interactions is the daily flow of workers in and out. Concentrating a quarter of all employment in Sydney in a small area, harbourside and off-centre, of necessity condemns people to long journeys to work. There simply is not room for them all to live close by at Australian residential densities, or even at Singapore densities. This is specially serious for those working in occupations where a majority of the jobs are in the city centre, for these people may have little choice of job location. Those most adversely affected are the clerks and some kinds of professional men. One result of the office building boom of the 1960s has been that the concentration of these occupations in the city centre has been maintained, while other kinds of employment have ebbed away (Neutze 1977 p.97). In most lines of work the proportion of total jobs in the city centre is much less than half, which means that a non-central alternative should be available to most workers if they want it.

The long journeys of those who work in the city centre should be kept in perspective. It is true that very few city centre jobs are taken by locals (Map 9), but this does not mean that everybody commutes from the outermost fringes of the metropolitan area. The median straight-line length of journeys to work in the city centre in 1971 was 10.5 kilometres, which would represent an actual distance of about 13 kilometres. This may be compared with the straight-line median for Sydney as a whole of 6.4 kilometres — a significant but not enormous difference (Table 3.3). Slightly over half the workers in the City of Sydney travelled more than ten kilometres, as against a third of those who worked elsewhere in the urban area (Table 3.2), but since jobs elsewhere were far more numerous this third represented the majority of workers who travel long distances. Indeed, 60 per cent of those who travelled more than ten kilometres had their destinations outside the city centre (Table 3.5). It seems, therefore, that the city centre is not the only generator of long journeys to work in Sydney, even if it is the most significant. Why is it, therefore, that city centre journeys seem to bring forth more complaints than the numerous long trips in other parts of the urban area?

One reason is that the trip for most workers has to be made relatively slowly, by public transport, and is therefore more time-consuming than its geographic length would indicate. At present prices and incomes the preferred means of transport, to work or anywhere else, for most Australians is the private car. It is the fastest and most comfortable. The trouble is that cars require space for parking and land for multi-laned roads. In most parts of the metropolitan area such space and land can be found, but not in the city centre; the concentration of jobs is such that if every worker brought his car the whole area would be layered several deep before they could all be parked. As a result many city workers are obliged to travel by means of transport which are more economical both of line haul and terminal space — by ferry, train or bus. Those who do come by car find that they (or their employers) have to pay heavily for parking space. They also encounter an unpleasant amount of traffic congestion; their motoring speed is far less than on the open road. Public transport speeds are likewise slower than those of an unfettered private car. Until the recent introduction of transit lanes speeds by bus were of necessity less than by car — there was little hope of line haul speeds faster than motoring, and to this time for stopping for passengers should be added, and for walking and waiting. Line haul speeds by train may be faster, but usually they are not fast enough to make up for the time taken getting to the station and waiting (Chapter 9).

All in all, a journey to the city centre by whatever means of transport is likely to be slower than a trip of similar length made elsewhere in the metropolitan area by car. On the other hand, because of greater frequency of service and more direct routing, trips by public transport to the city centre are likely to be faster than trips of similar length made by public transport in other parts of the metropolitan area. He — or more likely she — who has no choice but to go to work by public transport is therefore likely to be relatively well disposed towards city centre employment.

Travel to and from the city centre is costly not only in terms of time, but in public expenditure on transport facilities. Recent attempts to speed motorists on their way to the city centre have included the Warringah Expressway, an exceedingly expensive piece of road. Some would claim that each motorist using it daily should pay an annual toll of at least $50 in addition to other motoring taxes, and that without such a toll he is grossly subsidised (Ravallion 1974 p.72). Nor is the situation with public transport much better. The notorious losses of Sydney public transport services are incurred in large part in carrying workers to and from the city centre. Such work journeys comprise about a quarter of total public transport patronage (SATS 1974 vol.1 Tables 6.9 and 6.4) but are more costly to haul than most, being longer and occurring mainly during peak periods. No simple figure can be given for the subsidy to each city centre worker travelling by public transport, but it would be of a similar order to the Warringah Expressway motorists.

These are good reasons for concern about the city centre. At the least they are arguments for the prevention of further expansion of employment in the city centre, for this would require prohibitive transport investments, and condemn yet more people to time-consuming journeys. On the other hand, they are less certainly arguments for the transfer of existing office activities into the suburbs. A wholehearted policy of job dispersion, even assuming that there were means available to implement it, would not necessarily provide faster or even cheaper journeys. If jobs were more dispersed, some people would take the opportunity to work locally, but many would not, and a considerable proportion would surely switch from public to private transport in the process. It is even possible that widespread job decentralisation could lead to road congestion and to demands for roadbuilding in the suburbs that would be more costly than maintaining subsidies to public transport carrying people to work in the city centre. The long daily journeys, not to speak of the social anomie and violence of Detroit and Los Angeles may in part be blamed on such policies, and their consequence, a virtually centreless city (Thomson 1977 ch.3).

Unlike Detroit, Sydney still has a strong city centre. What can be learned from the travel patterns of those who work there?

Defining the City Centre

Discussion of the journey to work in the city centre presumes a definition of the central district. This is difficult. People in Sydney would not be hard put to name the centre of the centre — some such point as the general post office — but the boundaries of the centre give greater trouble. Job densities decline more or less with the skyline, which gives a clear break at the harbour and where offices abut onto parklands, but this line does not form a complete boundary. One tradition defines the city centre — the central business district — so as to enclose only the higher offices and bigger department stores. On this definition the central business district of Sydney extends from the Quay to the Railway,

TABLE 7.1 *The Composition of Employment in the City of Sydney. Census 1971.*

	Percentage of total jobs			
	All Sydney	Central Business District	Rest of City of Sydney	Total - City of Sydney
Male lawyers, scientists, engineers, technicians	5	10	6	9
Male doctors, clergy and teachers	2	1	3	1
Male clerks etc.	10	16	6	15
Male managers	7	10	7	9
Metal trades etc.	13	5	9	6
Male process workers	7	3	6	4
Salesmen, storemen, caretakers, waiters etc.	9	8	14	9
TOTAL MEN	64	60	62	61
Female doctors, nurses and teachers	5	3	9	4
Female clerks and typists	16	27	14	24
Female process workers	6	3	6	4
Saleswomen	4	3	2	3
Female cleaners, waitresses etc.	5	3	5	3
TOTAL WOMEN	36	40	38	39

Note: Includes only those who nominated their workplace.

Source: Census 1971, Journey to work tapes.

and from Darling Harbour to the Domain (see map, P.E.C. 1976 p.14). It has the advantage of including only those areas where the most typically city centre activities are carried on — the head offices and lawyers' chambers. The composition of employment is distinctively different from the rest of Sydney, with a far higher proportion of lawyers, managers and clerks, and a low proportion of industrial workers (Table 7.1).

Around the central business district the activities are less exclusively central, but many of the establishments still serve the entire metropolitan area and beyond. This is obviously true of Sydney University and the major hospitals, and of the entertainments of Kings Cross; less obviously, but more important for employment, it is also true of the warehouses of Ultimo and the small businesses of East Sydney. It can be argued that these activities should also be included in the city centre.

Rather than spend further time arguing the merits of different definitions, that adopted here is political — the City of Sydney as delimited since 1968. In that year the boundaries of the City were redrawn with the specific purpose of including 'central' functions and excluding as much as possible of everything else. Spreadeagled on the map, this City of Sydney looks like a bird with broken wings. The body contains the central business district, while one wing extends to include the University of Sydney and several major hospitals. The other wing consists mainly of parkland, including the Royal Agricultural Society's showgrounds, and is not at all important from an employment point of view. The northern boundary is Port Jackson, with the single connection by bridge to North Sydney; to the east lies a superior residential area, while to the west and south the City merges with areas of old lower-status housing intermixed with factories and warehouses. The City is six kilometres across on its longest diagonal, and has an area of 1340 hectares.

In 1971 the City of Sydney had a resident population of 62470 of whom 35167 reported themselves as being in the workforce. However, only 24130 actually stated a workplace: as recorded in Chapter 1 the rest are excluded from the journey to work data. Similarly the recorded total of 273000 jobs within the City is an underestimate, probably by about 15 per cent (Neutze 1977 p.97). However, despite the roughness of the figures, it is easy to see that the City is not primarily a residential area. The whole of it, apart from Moore Park, comes out in the highest levels of shading on the map of job densities (Maps 5 and 6).

The 273000 jobs recorded in the City of Sydney comprise about 26 per cent of the metropolitan total. Of them, about 210000 (20 per cent of the metropolitan total) are in the central business district. As compared with the central business district, other parts of the City include a higher proportion of educational and health personnel, many more service workers and a few more industrial workers. On the other hand, the political City has a slightly lower proportion of clerks and of lawyers, engineers and technicians than the narrowly-defined central business district. Despite this, the proportion of these groups in total employment in the City is still well above that for the rest of the metropolitan area (Table 7.1).

In Chapter 6 it was found that, given the pattern of employment opportunities, men with higher incomes (including professional men and tradesmen) will tend to have longer journeys to work than women, or men in lower status occupations. The occupational structure of the City thus predisposes its workers to long journeys, though the slightly higher proportion of women offsets this. However, the effects of occupational structure are difficult to disentangle from the much stronger effects of the high concentration of employment in the City. Such concentrations cause long journeys whatever the composition of their workforce.

The Journey to Work in the City of Sydney

Two generalisations may immediately be made about the pattern of travel to the city centre, applicable to both sexes, and thus illustrated on Maps 17 and 18. First, the proportion of the resident workforce working in the City is highest within the City itself, and generally declines towards the fringe of the metropolitan area — a natural result of distance (Table 3.1 and Graph 7.1). The rate of decline is slow but steady, but still takes the percentage from a peak of over 60 per cent in the areas local to the central business district down to fringe values more of the order of 10 per cent. Over wide areas of the middle suburbs the proportion of the workforce working in the City is around a quarter — similar to the proportion of total jobs in the city centre.

The second generalisation is that few residents of the major manufacturing areas work in the city centre. Rather, they work locally. This applies even in South Sydney/Botany, an area contiguous with the City itself. Similarly most people work locally, and few in the city centre, in zones dominated by institutional hostels — the Lidcombe State Hospital and Home, and the defence and educational establishments on the heads of the harbour.

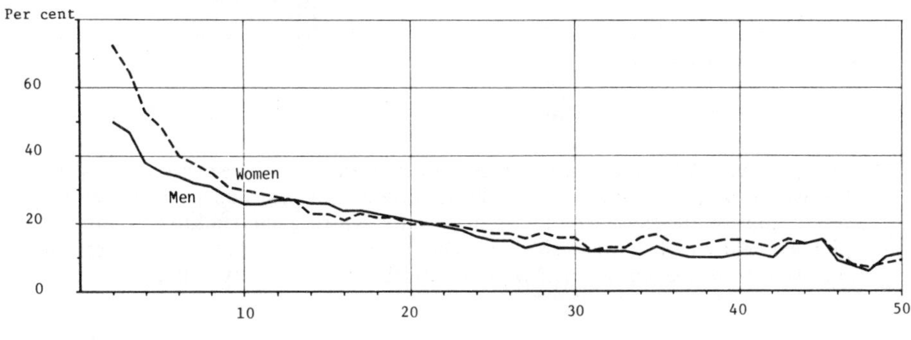

GRAPH 7.1 *Percentage of the Resident Workforce Working in the City of Sydney, by Distance from the City Centre, Census, 1971.*

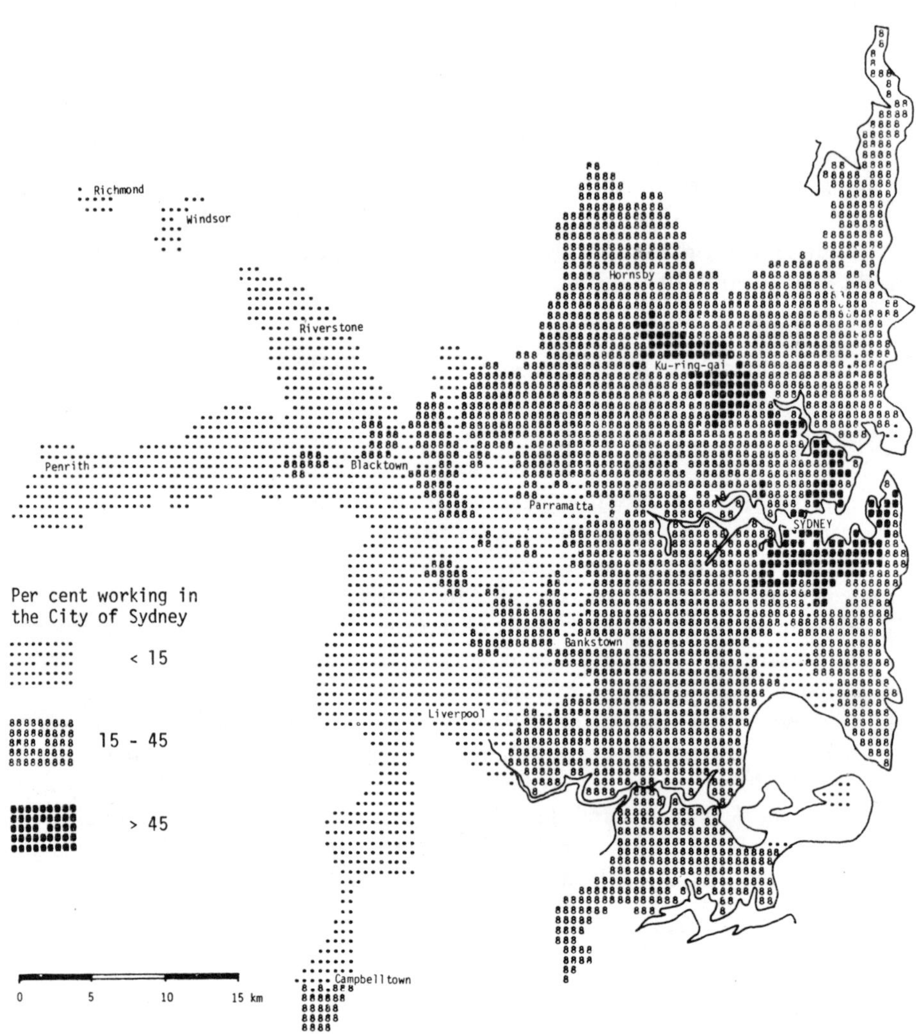

MAP 17. Men Working in the City of Sydney, Census 1971 (see text, page 111). Men who live in the high status harbourside suburbs to the east and north of the City of Sydney, and equally those who live in high status Ku-ring-gai, tend to work in the City, which has many high status men's jobs. On the other hand, less than 15 per cent of the male residents of the typical outer western suburb work in the city centre.

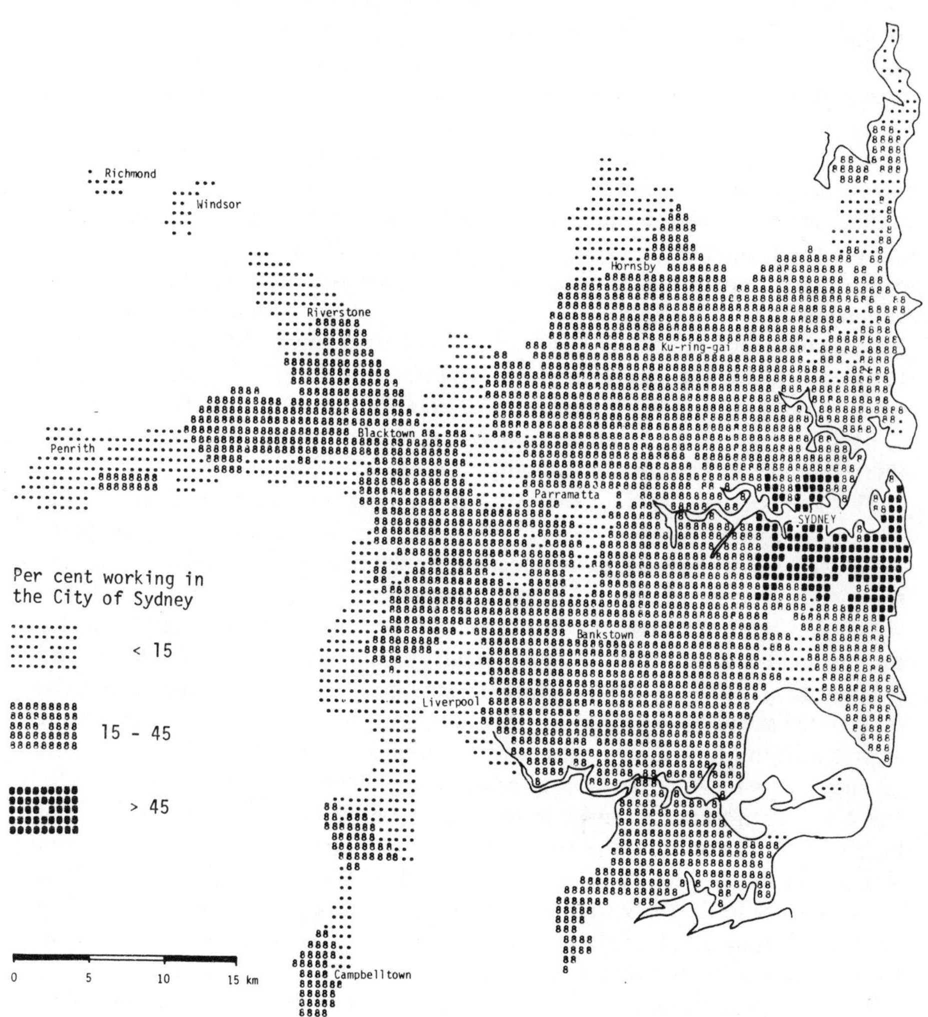

MAP 18. Women Working in the City of Sydney, Census 1971 (see text, page 111). Women's jobs in the City of Sydney are not as high status as the men's. Accordingly women who live in the high status harbourside suburbs and in Ku-ring-gai work in the City less often than male residents of these suburbs, while women who live in the western outer suburbs more often work in the City (compare this map with Map 17).

The workforce in the City is slightly more feminine than average, such that 29 per cent of the female workers in the metropolitan area have jobs in the City, as against 25 per cent of the men. One would thus expect slightly higher proportions on Map 18 (women) than on Map 17 (men), and this is indeed the case in most suburbs. However, true to form, women working in the City have shorter journeys to work than men, their median travel distance being 8.7 kilometres (straight-line) as against 10.9 kilometres (Table 5.4). This means that the proportion of women working in the city centre tends to be higher than men in the inner areas, and should decline more rapidly with distance. In fact it does so only up to a point. In suburbs between 10 and 25 kilometres from the city centre the proportion of men and women working in the city centre is overall very similar (Graph 7.1), and beyond 25 kilometres the proportion of women is once again greater. This is because most of the suburbs between 25 and 42 kilometres from the city centre are of low socio-economic status. In such suburbs most women work locally, but a minority travel to the city centre — a minority proportionately greater than that of men, whose long journeys take them to work in various manufacturing areas.

This status effect provides the outstanding difference between Maps 17 and 18. Socio-economic status strongly influences the sources of male workers for the city centre, while not greatly affecting the women. Male occupations of high socio-economic status tend to be concentrated in the city centre; women's less so. Professional women tend to be nurses or teachers, occupations of moderate dispersion. The high proportions of men from high status residential areas who journey daily to the city are therefore not unexpected, but the importance of the high status suburbs as sources of male workers for the city centre can best be appreciated in Map 17. The areas with the highest proportions of male workers journeying to the city centre are the eastern and northern waterside suburbs, and the 'North Shore' suburbs in the Ku-ring-gai municipality — all areas of high status. By contrast, the suburbs with the highest proportions of women working in the city centre lie to the east, and on the North Sydney side of the harbour close to the ferry wharves. The higher status parts of the North Shore do not show at all strongly on the women's map — workers coming from Ku-ring-gai are predominantly men. On the other hand, in most of the western suburbs the proportion of women working in the city centre is higher than that of men; the men work crosstown, in manufacturing, while the women take clerical or sales jobs in the City, or work locally.

On both maps, but particularly that for women, one can see the shadow of the suburban railway routes. In the southern and western suburbs particularly this appears as a high proportion of travellers to the City, as would be expected given the easier transport.

Maps 17 and 18 thus show significant differences in the pattern of city centre travel by sex. Similar maps can be constructed to see whether there are differences by occupational groups. None are included here, however, for the different patterns are not very interesting. They can be accounted for almost wholly by differences in sex, in the residential distribution of the workers, and in the proportion working in the city centre. In other words, the map of city centre workers for each occupation looks much like that for any occupation of that sex, with differences in the levels of shading according to the proportion of workers journeying to the city centre. For all occupations the City draws on the whole metropolitan area.

The fact that the city centre draws workers from a wide range of areas of different social status raises doubts about the extent to which job decentralisation would increase the number engaged in local employment. Many of the enterprises in the city centre, particularly government offices and the head offices of private firms, employ a variety of people of differing status. Given that the social geography of Sydney is not likely to change dramatically, any move to shift the enterprises toward the north would reduce journeys for the average executive, but increase them for clerical and cleaning staff. Similarly, a shift to the south or west would improve local employment opportunities for junior staff, but lead to long journeys and grumbling by those living in the northern suburbs. However, if a large office development were to take place at Penrith, it could be predicted that within a few decades the executives who worked there would be living in the Blue Mountains and the clerks and cleaners on the plains below.

In considering the role of the city centre, it should also be remembered that most of the women who work there are single (Table 5.6). Whether or not this combination of unmarried women and high-status men in a single workforce contributes to social mobility by marriage, it is certain that young single women are more attracted to the bright lights, and less put off by long travelling, than married women. This again reduces the urgency of decentralisation policies.

In summary, the city centre draws its workers from all over the metropolitan area, but particularly (for men) from the high status areas, and (for both sexes) from nearby. This is as the theory of Chapter 1 would predict. But what of the other main concentrations of employment?

CHAPTER 8

The Major Suburban Concentrations of Employment

What contribution do the major suburban concentrations of employment make to shortening journeys to work in Sydney? Much is sometimes expected of them, particularly of Parramatta, which on some accounts is to become a second city centre for the west. In 1971 these ambitions were far from realised, but an examination of the journey to work patterns for the suburban centres in that year at least has the virtue of setting a base mark from which developments can be charted.

For convenience, the three major suburban concentrations of employment were defined in Chapter 3 in terms of local government boundaries. Each consists of two municipalities, South Sydney/Botany, North Sydney/Willoughby and Parramatta/Auburn. These definitions will also be used in this chapter, for the advantages of ready-made boundaries outweigh the consequent inclusion of areas which are residential rather than manufacturing or commercial, and which add considerably to the area without contributing many jobs. If the interest of this study lay in job densities such definitions would be indefensible, but as it is they merely dilute the employment figures for the major concentrations with a small minority of jobs more properly considered of local interest.

Two of the major concentrations are adjacent to the City of Sydney. South Sydney and Botany occupy the low lying land between the City and Botany Bay, separating the eastern and western residential suburbs with an almost continuous belt of warehouses, manufacturing plants and transport installations. The employment concentration of North Sydney/Willoughby, on the other hand, consists of a discontinuous strip starting on the harbour foreshore opposite the city centre, and following the ridge line (and the Pacific Highway and the North Shore railway) for eight kilometres north-west to Chatswood. By further contrast, the employment zone in Parramatta/Auburn lies mainly on reclaimed swamps at the polluted limit to navigation on the Parramatta River, between 15 and 25 kilometres west of the city centre.

As defined by local government boundaries, each of these major

TABLE 8.1 *The Composition of Employment in the Major Suburban Employment Areas of Sydney. Census 1971.*

	PERCENTAGE OF TOTAL JOBS							
	All Sydney	S. Sydney/ Botany	N Sydney/Willoughby			Parramatta/Auburn		
			North Sydney	Willoughby	Total	Factory District	Business District	Total
Male lawyers, scientists, engineers, technicians	5	4	14	7	11	4	4	4
Male doctors, clergy, teachers	2	0	1	1	1	1	3	2
Male clerks etc.	10	7	13	10	11	8	7	8
Male managers	7	6	7	4	5	4	5	4
Metal trades etc.	13	18	6	15	11	17	10	16
Male process workers	7	10	2	6	4	11	5	10
Salesmen, storemen, caretakers, waiters etc.	9	7	10	8	9	9	11	9
TOTAL MEN	64	77	63	63	63	73	58	70
Female doctors, nurses, teachers	5	1	6	7	6	3	7	3
Female clerks and typists	16	10	23	16	20	11	17	12
Female process workers	6	7	2	5	4	8	4	7
Saleswomen	4	1	3	5	4	2	8	3
Female cleaners, waitresses etc.	5	2	4	4	4	3	6	4
TOTAL WOMEN	36	23	37	37	37	27	42	30

Note: Excludes jobs held by people who failed to state the address of their workplace.

Source: Census 1971, Journey to work tapes.

concentrations of employment has a much larger area than the City of Sydney. However, each provides fewer jobs — their combined total is a little short of the City (Table 3.3). None of them contain areas of more than a few contiguous hectares developed to central business district densities. In employment composition only North Sydney is remotely like the City itself, with a high proportion of clerks and a particularly high proportion of men in the more concentrated professions — engineers, architects and technicians particularly (cf Table 7.1 and Table 8.1). However, Willoughby is less strongly given to offices and has a little light manufacturing, so that the composition of their combined workforce is not unlike that for Sydney as a whole. Only the concentrated professions still stand out.

South Sydney/Botany is basically a manufacturing area, with a low proportion of jobs for women. It has few workers in the professions, and not very many in sales or services either. The factory workers include more tradesmen than process workers, and the area has its bare quota of clerks and managers (Table 8.1).

Parramatta/Auburn may be divided into an industrial part and the business district of Parramatta. The former provides three-quarters of the total employment in the area, with an occupational composition very similar to South Sydney/Botany. The remaining quarter of the jobs lie in the commercial area. Despite its bold appearance on Map 1 (the location of office employment) this Parramatta business district is far from being a second city centre. Even on a generous definition of its boundaries (P.E.C. 1976 p.16) it had in 1971 but 12000 jobs, as against the 208000 in the central business district. Not only this, but the work involved was less obviously of the kind that occurs in a city centre. The proportions of male clerks and of men in the concentrated professions (engineers, technicians etc) were actually below metropolitan average, and the proportion of female clerks was nothing unusual (Table 8.1). Indeed, the area is more notable for shops than for offices, and in any case it is quite small compared with the adjacent manufacturing zone. Taken as a whole, Parramatta/Auburn emerges as a manufacturing area with a leavening of shops and offices.

The composition of employment in these three concentrations does not lead to any strong predictions concerning the length of journeys to work in them. The greater proportion of women working in North Sydney/Willoughby presages shorter journeys, but these are likely to be counterbalanced by the long journeys of male professional and clerical workers employed in the same offices. Similarly the shorter trips of the process workers employed in the manufacturing areas are likely to be offset by the longer journeys of the tradesmen.

Rather more may be predicted from the location of the employment concentrations. Two of them are adjacent to the City of Sydney. According to the discussion in Chapter 1 they should draw the greater part of their workforce from further out in the same sector of the metropolitan area — anybody coming from the other direction would have to cross the city centre, putting up with the congestion and bypassing the numerous employment opportunities available there. Within the sector the general rule that the proportion of the population working in a given centre declines with distance from that centre should apply, just as it does for city centre workers. Difficulties of prediction arise, however, when it is asked how the attractions of a city centre satellite as a workplace interact with those of the city centre itself. The presence of the satellite reduces the number of people who go that little further to the city centre, but does it otherwise affect the fall-off in worker proportions with distance? One possibility is that jobs in the secondary centre are staffed by locals, and bypassed by city centre workers who come from further out. Alternatively, the centre and its satellite may draw from the same suburbs in the sector, each more or less in proportion to its size. The latter is more likely if jobs in the secondary centre are similar to those in the city centre, while the former may result if the jobs are in some way different, and closely match the occupations of the local residents. Prima facie, the first case may be represented by North Sydney/Willoughby, and the second by South Sydney/Botany.

Parramatta/Auburn, on the other hand, lies at a distance from the city centre, though embedded well inside the metropolitan area. Were it the work-centre of a freestanding country town, then with its present complement of jobs the town would be perhaps five kilometres in diameter, and journeys to work within it would be mostly local. As it is, it is but one of several employment centres within range of a large number of people. It can draw workers from four directions: they can come from further out (in which case they are travelling with the city centre flow); they can travel crosstown north or south, while those who live in the direction of the city centre can come to work against the main flow of traffic. According to the discussion in Chapter 1 those who do this should be relatively uncommon — people living between two centres of employment should be attracted to that which provides the wider range of job opportunities. To a lesser degree this should also be true of crosstown travel. Accordingly Parramatta/Auburn should draw its labour force from its own local area, and from further out. The distances travelled will be longer than they would were it an independent country town, how much longer depending on the interaction of Parramatta/Auburn with other suburban labour markets, and with the influence of the city centre.

Average and median travel distances are given in Table 8.2. As explained in Chapter 3, the distributions of journey distances to workplaces are such that the average is fairly consistently greater than the median. Such is the case with the major employment areas. Again, as discussed in Chapter 5, women's journey distances tend to be shorter than men's. As regards the difference between married and single women, there is, however, some divergence between the areas. Over the whole metropolitan area single women tend to have longer journeys than married women. However, the average length of journey for single women working in North Sydney/Willoughby and in

Parramatta/Auburn is less than for married women (Table 5.5). In North Sydney at least this may partly be explained by the high proportion of single women living in flats nearby. Again, such is the strength of the attraction of the city centre to single women that those who work in the suburban concentrations may be those with a strong desire for local work. Married women, by contrast, are less attracted to the bright lights and more grateful for any reduction in their length of journey, be it even quite small. The resulting paradox is that both North Sydney/Willoughby and Parramatta/Auburn draw married women from further afield than single women.

Both average and median length of journeys to work in the four major employment concentrations are related to the number of jobs in the centre (Tables 3.3 and 8.2). However, the relationship is far from proportional. The workforce in the largest centre (the City of Sydney) is four times that in the smallest (North Sydney/Willoughby) but the median journey to work is only a little more than one and a half times the distance. Further, while women's average and median journey lengths rank in the same order as the numbers employed in each centre (the city centre with the longest journeys, followed by South Sydney/Botany, Parramatta/Auburn and North Sydney/Willoughby) this is not strictly true for men. Men's average and median journeys to North Sydney/Willoughby are longer than for Parramatta/Auburn. This may be due to the one being a city centre satellite and the other freestanding — the satellite draws workers from similar places, and hence similar distances, to the city centre, while the freestanding centre to some extent has its own labour catchment. However, a median journey to work of nearly seven kilometres in Parramatta/Auburn compares badly with an estimate of about three kilometres were the area an independent country town.

The places of origin of the workers in the three suburban concentrations can be seen on Maps 19, 20 and 21. In each case the prediction concerning the sources of the area's workforce is confirmed. Workers in South Sydney/Botany rise above 15 per cent of the resident workforce only in the suburbs around Botany Bay; those in North Sydney/Willoughby only on the North Shore. Most workers in Parramatta/Auburn are locals or come from points west, mainly Blacktown. This is not to say that reverse or crosstown journeys to work are few in number. Though only a few people in any suburb may engage in such travel, added together they form an appreciable part of the labour supply to each suburban employment concentration. As shown on Table 8.2, a quarter of the men working in North Sydney/Willoughby come from across the harbour, paying an average penalty of four kilometres' travel over and above the distance to the city centre. (The three-quarters who come from north of the harbour travel on average five kilometres less than their fellow residents working in the city centre.) Again, 10 per cent of male workers in South Sydney/Botany cross the bridge. Women are much less prone to such difficult travel. Often the people so travelling are minorities in the workforce of the employment area. North Shore residents working in South Sydney tend to be

TABLE 8.2 *Work Journey Patterns to Major Employment Areas. Sydney, Census 1971.*

Employment area	Sector of journey origin	Percentage of workers coming from sector		Average distance km		Median distance km	
		Men	Women	Men	Women	Men	Women
SOUTH SYDNEY/BOTANY	North of the Harbour	10	4	14.6	11.8		
	South of the Harbour *	90	96	10.9	8.2		
	TOTAL	100	100	11.2	8.4	8.6	5.5
NORTH SYDNEY/WILLOUGHBY	South of the Harbour	24	12	16.9	15.1		
	North of the Harbour *	76	88	7.3	5.5		
	TOTAL	100	100	9.9	6.8	8.1	4.3
PARRAMATTA/AUBURN	Strathfield and points East	8	5	15.3	14.2		
	Bankstown and points South-East	11	6	12.9	10.6		
	Ryde and points North East	11	7	13.2	10.7		
	Auburn and points West *	70	82	7.9	6.5		
	TOTAL	100	100	9.7	7.4	7.7	4.8
CITY OF SYDNEY	North of the Harbour	27	20	12.1	9.9		
	South of the Harbour *	73	80	13.2	9.5		
	TOTAL	100	100	12.9	11.4	10.9	8.7

* includes local journeys.

Source: Census 1971, Journey to work tapes.

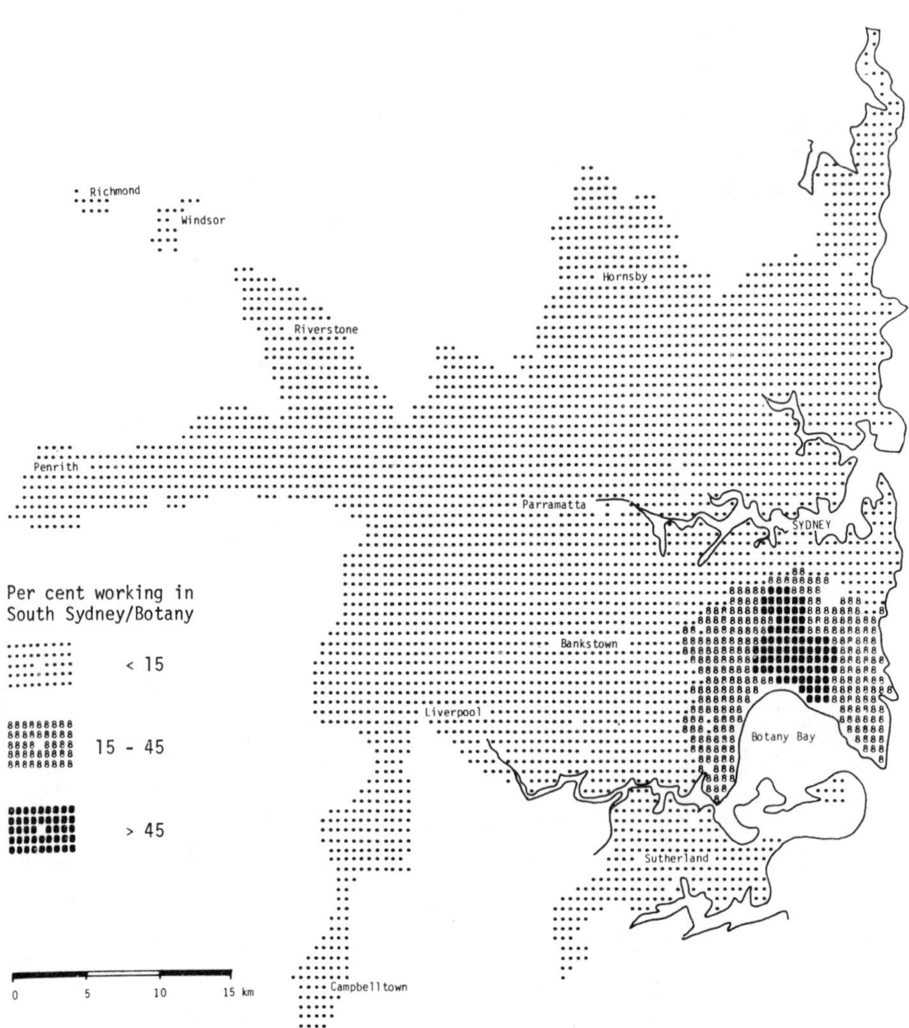

MAP 19. Workers Working in South Sydney/Botany, Census 1971 (see text, page 120). The proportion of residents working in South Sydney/Botany rises above 45 per cent only in the industrial area itself, and above 15 per cent only in the adjacent areas away from the City of Sydney.

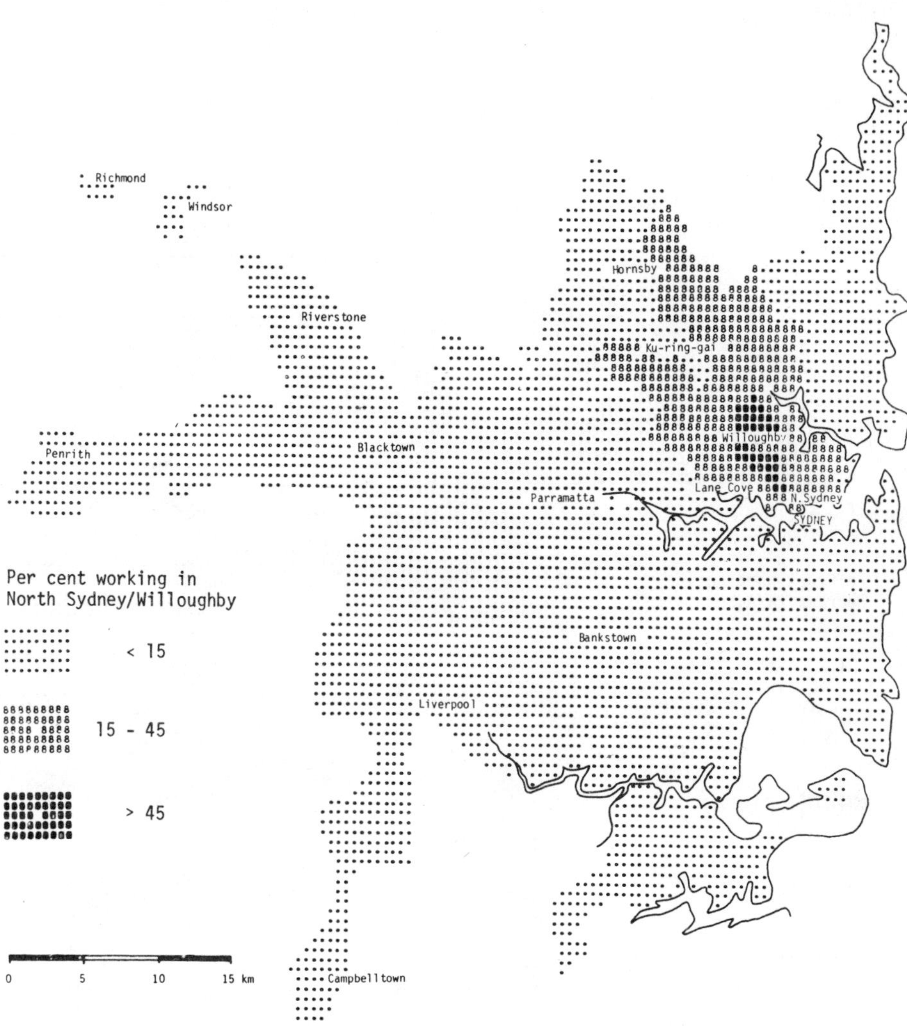

MAP 20. Workers Working in North Sydney/Willoughby, Census 1971 (see text, page 120). The proportion of residents working in North Sydney/Willoughby rises above 45 per cent in parts of these two municipalities, and is above 15 per cent in suburbs radially outwards from them — particularly the newer parts of Ku-ring-gai away from the railway line from Sydney to Hornsby.

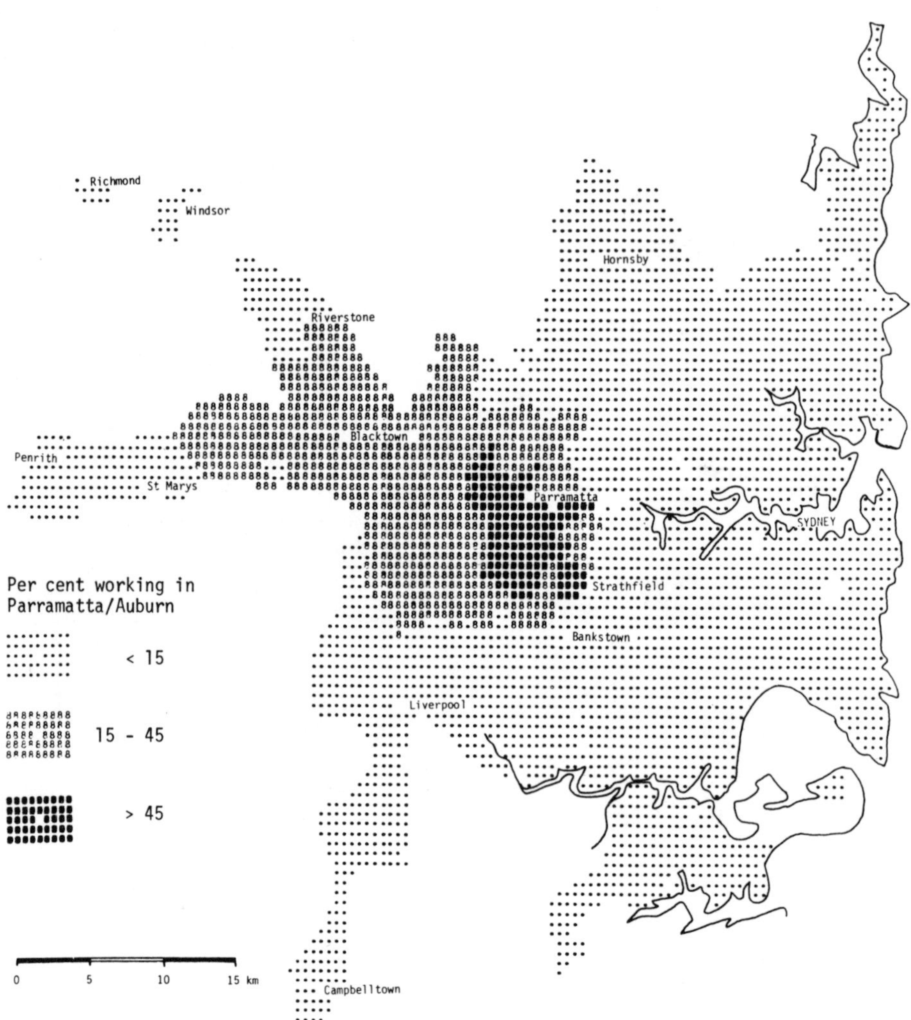

MAP 21. Workers Working in Parramatta/Auburn, Census 1971 (see text, page 120). The proportion of residents working in Parramatta/Auburn is high in the area itself, and in suburbs radially outwards. Towards the city centre, however, the proportion declines abruptly to less than 15 per cent.

managers, while those making the reverse trip to Willoughby tend to be tradesmen or process workers.

Returning to the maps, the proportion of the resident population working in a suburban concentration tends to be high only within the area itself, where it may reach or surpass 45 per cent. Most of these people are working locally as defined in Chapter 4, and indeed a third of the women employed in the manufacturing areas, and 40 per cent of those in North Sydney/Willoughby, are locals (Table 5.9). The proportions for men are around a fifth (Table 5.8). In a Cityward direction from the employment area the proportion falls off rapidly — only 10 per cent of the employed population of Strathfield work in Parramatta/Auburn. Crosstown — north and south from Parramatta/Auburn, east and west from the other two — the falling away is fairly rapid, such that within five kilometres of the zone boundary the proportion of workers travelling to the zone is generally less than 15 per cent. On the other hand, radially outwards the area sending over 15 per cent of its resident workers to the suburban concentration may extend for quite some distance — in the case of Parramatta/Auburn, as far as St Marys (Map 21). In such areas, particularly in the outer suburbs, the proportion travelling to the suburban centre may be of the same order as that travelling to the city centre. Significantly the labour catchment of Parramatta/Auburn does not extend diagonally outwards towards Liverpool, even though transport from this direction is quite convenient. The habit of radial travel in a city like Sydney is still strong.

The pattern of radial travel is somewhat distorted for South Sydney/Botany by the fact that outwards from Botany there is strictly nothing but Botany Bay. The transport routes southwards from the city centre bypass South Sydney, so that travellers to the manufacturing area must diverge from the main flow, and often find themselves in conflict with it. Perhaps this explains one peculiar feature of Graph 8.1. Within the manufacturing area itself the proportion of the workforce working locally is very high, but to the south east (across Cooks River) the proportion working in South Sydney/Botany falls suddenly, to stabilise at between 15 and 20 per cent of the male workforce resident over a wide section from Bankstown to Sutherland. The proportion of the female workforce is much less, such that the proportion of the total workforce is generally under 15 per cent, which means that the areas do not show on Map 19, yet taken as a whole, they supply the greater part of the male labour force of South Sydney/Botany. This accounts for the distances travelled being not far short of those to the city centre, and also causes a great deal of traffic congestion and conflict.

By contrast, the employment areas in North Sydney/Willoughby lie astride the road and the railway line to the city centre. The pattern of travel shown on Map 20 is therefore broadly as expected, with a relatively high proportion of the population working locally in the area itself, and with gradually diminishing proportions of workers coming in from further out. However, the

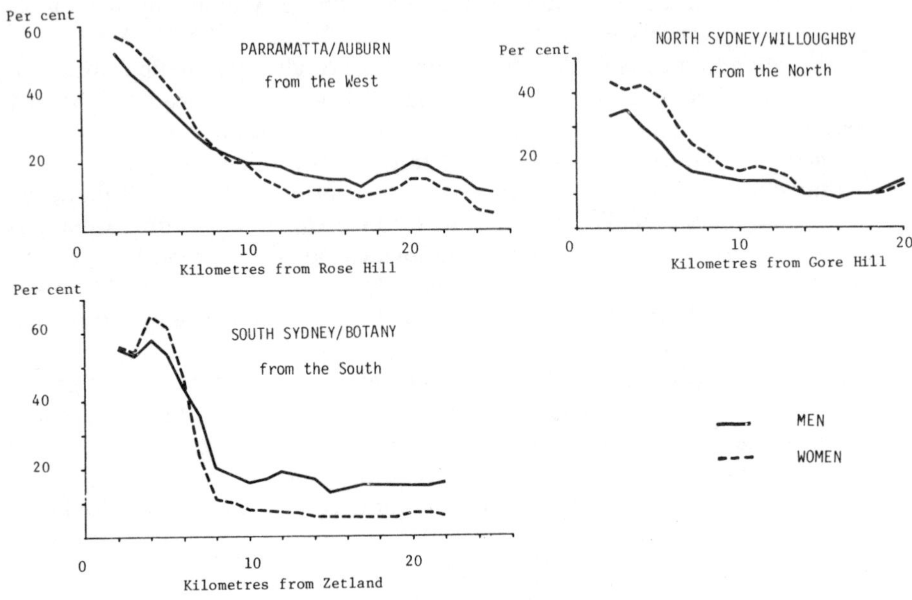

GRAPH 8.1 *Percentage of the Resident Workforce Working in Major Centres of Employment, by Distance and Direction from the Centre. Census, 1971.*

detail of the pattern is peculiar in that the areas near the railway line in North Sydney itself have high proportions working in the area (i.e. locally) but further out in Ku-ring-gai the areas near the railway tend to send their workers to the city centre rather than to North Sydney. The high proportions along the railway within North Sydney/Willoughby can be explained, for these are the areas where local employment is most convenient. Those who dwell on the fringes of Willoughby and Lane Cove tend to be high status city centre executives. The low proportions along the railway in Ku-ring-gai, and higher proportions further away from it, may be explained in two ways. First, the office developments in North Sydney are relatively recent, and may be staffed with workers who bought their houses in the correspondingly newer parts of Ku-ring-gai. Second, if one lives near the railway line and finds it convenient to travel by train, one might as well go the extra few kilometres to the city centre, while a job in North Sydney would be relatively attractive to those who live far from the station and prefer to drive to work.

From the figures already given for the differences between men and women workers in the three areas, and from the maps, it is possible to imagine the separate maps for men and women travelling to the areas. In each case the men's map is more dispersed, while the women's reaches a higher peak of local travel within the area itself, but falls away much more rapidly. The situation is summarised in Graph 8.1 which shows how the proportion of the workforce travelling to the suburban centres declines with distance from them, even in the outwards direction. In each case the proportion of women declines faster than men — in South Sydney/Botany very much so, for nearly all the rather restricted number of women's jobs in that area are taken by locals. By contrast the decline in the proportion of women working in North Sydney/Willoughby is fairly slow as one proceeds up the North Shore line. There are more women's jobs in North Sydney/Willoughby than can be taken by locals, especially since many locally resident women are attracted to a job in the nearby city centre.

Graph 8.2 provides a means of assessing the effect of suburban employment concentrations on travel to the city centre. First, South Sydney/Botany absorbs most of the labour living locally, but attracts fairly low proportions from a wide area outside. As can be seen from Graph 8.1, over half the people living within the area work there, but once outside the proportion drops quite suddenly to 15 to 20 per cent for men and under 10 per cent for women. This has its effect on travel to the city centre from the south. Graph 8.2 shows that

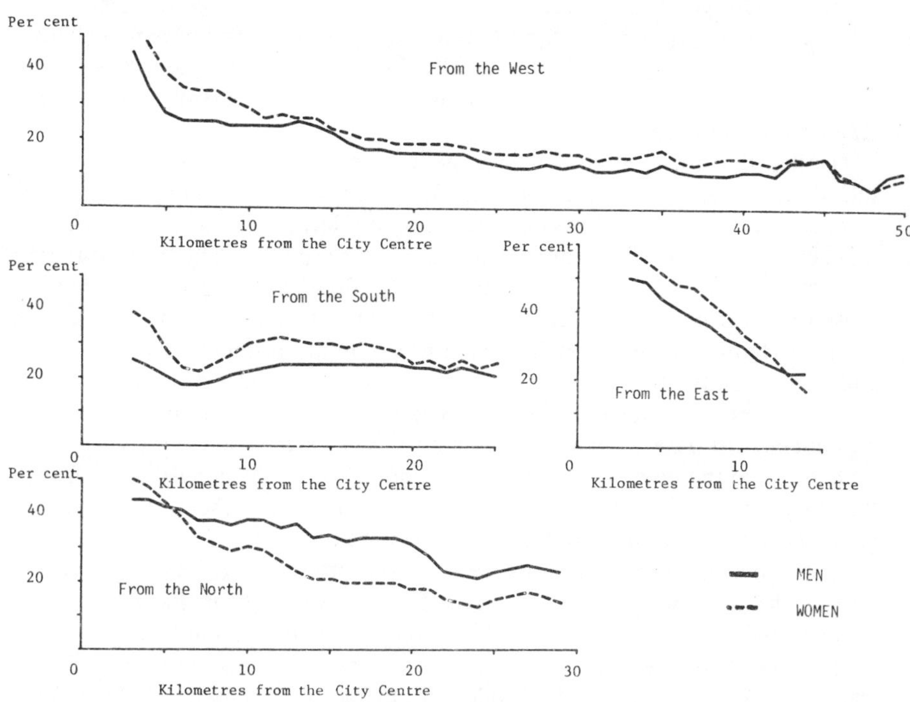

GRAPH 8.2 *Percentage of the Resident Workforce Working in the City of Sydney by Distance and Direction from the City. Census 1971.*

the proportion of workers living at about five kilometres south of the city centre who work in the City is relatively low, but that beyond nine kilometres the proportion picks up again and indeed is remarkably constant to the end of the suburbs in Sutherland. South Sydney/Botany also affects city centre travel from the east, and the high proportion of the population in the southern part of Randwick municipality which works in Botany accounts for the rapid fall in the city centre proportion as distance increases east and south east from the City.

Travel to Parramatta/Auburn and North Sydney/Willoughby falls away much more evenly with distance (Graph 8.1). It starts from a lower peak (less than half the residents of these suburbs work in their local employment concentration) and tails away more evenly — indeed, 20 kilometres west of the centroid of the area the proportion working in Parramatta/Auburn rises a little with distance, this being due to lack of any local employment in the newer housing estates north and west of Blacktown. The result is that the impact of these two employment concentrations on the pattern of city centre travel is rather harder to discern. Even so, the proportion of the western workforce working in the city centre declines perceptibly at over 15 kilometres from the City, this being the beginning of Auburn. The effect of North Sydney/Willoughby is best seen in the much lower proportion of North Shore women travelling to work in the city centre as against North Shore men. This is partly due to the women working locally, but is also partly due to the greater proportion working in North Sydney/Willoughby, at least from points within Ku-ring-gai municipality.

The fact that the median and average distances covered by travellers to the suburban concentrations are not much less than to the city centre, at least for men, may lead one to doubt the effectiveness of large-scale decentralisation in reducing the burden of the journey to work. This is particularly the case for the inner suburban concentrations, where traffic flows are largely additional to those to and from the city centre. The important difference, as will be seen in the next chapter, is that they include a much higher proportion of motorists, and correspondingly lower proportion of public transport travellers. The benefit of decentralising work to a city centre satellite lies therefore not so much in reducing distances as enabling people to use a faster means of transport — perhaps up to the point where its speed is cancelled out by congestion. Though there may be private benefits in terms of time saved, the public costs of increased inner suburban motoring are considerable.

In Parramatta/Auburn the problem is of a different kind. Twenty-two per cent of the male workers journey crosstown to work (from Bankstown and beyond, and Ryde and beyond) which increases potential conflict with other traffic flows (Table 8.2) and worsens the competitive disadvantage of public transport. On the other hand, people journeying to Parramatta/Auburn from further out are separated in time of travel from those using the same roads and railways to get to the city centre, thus spreading the peak and reducing the average costs of travel. Again, were it not for Parramatta/Auburn, these people would have to travel even longer distances. On the other hand, if there were more jobs further out, in places like Blacktown, they would not have to travel as far as at present. Long journeys are costly whatever their direction, and many of the employees in the suburban concentrations have long journeys.

It is sometimes argued that Parramatta is ideally placed to become a second city centre, because it lies not far from the boundary between the high status sector of Sydney and the low. If this is to come true, however, substantial investments will have to be made in improved transport routes from the north and north east. The distance from most of Ku-ring-gai to Parramatta is in any case similar to the distance thence to the city centre, and high status workers have little to gain by the change.

The conclusion of this chapter must be tentative. As against a more centralised pattern of employment, the suburban concentrations have reduced travel distances, but as against a more dispersed pattern they have increased them. And they generate substantial crosstown traffic, and generally encourage motoring as against public transport, all of which tends to counteract their otherwise beneficial effect on the transport system. The effects of different travel patterns on this system require closer examination, to which we now turn.

CHAPTER 9

The Means of Transport

Throughout this study the case has been argued that shorter journeys to work would be desirable in Sydney. There was, however, some doubt about the priority the people of Sydney themselves gave to shorter journeys, for even with the existing pattern of job locations it seems possible for many more people to work locally than actually do. On the other hand, there is no doubt that the present pattern of work travel strains the transport system, and leads to demands for public expenditure to alleviate this strain. In terms of government spending, there are two main areas of concern, first public transport deficits and second road congestion, which leads to the demand for costly roadbuilding and to the vocal opposition of various resident action groups to the building of particular roads.

It is sometimes suggested that these two could be dealt with at once if only more people would walk or use public transport. They would then leave their cars at home, relieving the roads, while their patronage, through economies of scale, would allow the public transport system to break even. This could perhaps be accomplished by penalties against the use of the motor car, but such being unlikely, various other measures have been suggested. One of them is that the city should be designed for ease of travel on foot and by public transport. Different patterns of job location have different consequences for the decision whether to walk, ride or drive, and at the very least these should be taken into account in planning where jobs shall be.

Walking is admirably cheap but unfortunately slow and tiring as a means of transport. It is only practicable for short distances: few Australians nowdays are willing to walk more than a kilometre or so regularly on any trip, though in times past three kilometres was an acceptable walk. Accordingly only people who work locally can walk to work. A policy of job decentralisation would lead to increased numbers working locally, and hence to more walking, but the increase may be so slight that the policy is not worth pursuing.

Public transport is at its best in carrying large flows of passengers from a common origin to a common destination. When the buses and trains are kept full the costs of running them can be spread over a large number of travellers.

Costs per passenger trip begin to rise when the loading develops a peak/off peak pattern, for equipment has to be provided to handle the peak, and much of it is unused the rest of the time. They rise further as the traffic to be handled drops away, for then both fixed costs and the costs of vehicle operation have to be covered by fewer passengers. This usually results in a worsening service as operators try to group the few intending travellers into economic loads. Eventually there is a limit where taxis are the only economic public transport service. Here the wages of the driver must be borne at the most by five travellers at a time, with correspondingly high costs per passenger-kilometre.

In theory a city layout in which large numbers of people wish to make similar trips will encourage the use of public transport. This implies that the city be built at a high density, both to increase the number of potential travellers, and to reduce the distances they have to walk to and from bus stops and railway stations. A high density can be achieved by the concentration of economic activity (no expansive industrial estates), by minimising the amount of open space, street space and vacant land near public transport routes, and by building housing in the form of flats and terraces. None of this sounds like Sydney. Only the old inner areas, built in times when journeys to work were on foot as much as by public transport, seem friendly to train and bus travel, while the new outer suburbs are hostile in almost every respect. The rebuilding of Sydney to encourage a high level of public transport patronage would be quite an undertaking.

By contrast, the private car as a means of transport works best in low density situations. This is primarily because it requires a great deal of land, both for parking and for roads and interchanges. Again, air pollution is not so bad if there is plenty of room for it to blow away. Journey destinations have to be dispersed, otherwise car parks become enormous and walking distances within them excessive. This limits the size of office and commercial centres. However, within these limitations a city could be designed which would work very well for everybody able and willing to drive long distances daily. (The distances could be driven at high speed, so time is not quite the constraint it is with walking or bus travel.)

The different means of travel thus work best in quite different circumstances. Much of the trouble with Sydney, as with most other cities, is that it was originally built for walking and public transport, and has only recently been converted for reliance on the motor car. Those who argue for a return to public transport have the design of the old areas on their side, but they are otherwise battling against the trend of the times. Even so, despite increasing car ownership and use, walking and public transport are still significant means of getting to work in Sydney, and an account of their present role may give some indication of their role in the future. The present chapter consists of two sections: first of some general statistics on the relative importance of public and private transport, and second of a discussion of the differences between men and women in the choice of means of transport for the journey to work. It is followed by a further chapter, which covers the means of transport used for particular traffic flows, and the consequences of this for the duration of journeys.

The Sydney Area Transportation Study

Unfortunately the 1971 census, on which the bulk of this study is based, did not ask people how they travelled to work. (Such a question was asked in 1976, but it will be some time before the results are available.) However, over a period of months in 1971 — that is, more or less at the same time as the census — the Sydney Area Transportation Study (SATS) conducted a home interview survey which, inter alia, asked the means of transport people used for the journey to work. Interviewers contacted 20 347 households (2.47 per cent of the total number of households in Sydney, and covering a similar percentage of the population). (SATS 1974 vol.1 ch. 5.) This sample was certainly large enough for reasonably accurate estimates to be made of the modal choices of the whole population of Sydney, or of large parts of it — estimates such as those presented in Tables 9.2 to 10.10. However, some doubts as to the accuracy of these estimates arise from possible inadequacies in the sampling procedure and in the collection and processing of the data. The following discussion is based on information from the SATS personnel and from Richard Davis.

The first cause for doubt lies in the survey's non-response rate of 20 per cent. By checking the SATS interview population with the census it seems that elderly people were under-represented, and also young people in their 20s. This is fairly normal for such surveys: the elderly are reluctant to be interviewed, and young adults are so often away from home as to be difficult to contact. The relative lack of elderly respondents is perhaps of little account — they are likely to be people not in the workforce — but the shortage of young people is worrying, especially since their travel habits may be different from average (e.g. they may not yet have saved up to buy a car).

Second, the SATS sample was selected using a variable sampling fraction. The fraction was high in areas of low population density (outer suburbs) and lower in the inner parts of the metropolitan area. Each observation was weighted inversely to its probability of selection to enable accurate population estimates to be obtained. The estimates so calculated in fact vary very little from those deriving from the crude sample, and the SATS tables in this chapter derive directly from the latter.

Third, the origin and destination zones used in SATS differed from those in the census journey to work data. Since both respected local government boundaries, the major employment areas can be defined similarly in both sources. However, differences in the boundary of the urban area may have lead to slight discrepancies between the two.

Confidence in the SATS estimates is increased by the fact that they are broadly consonant with the results of two smaller sample surveys of the journey to work in Sydney carried out by the Australian Bureau of Statistics in 1970 and 1974 (Neutze 1977 p.125, also Table 9.1). Again, the estimates were checked against returns of public transport passengers for the period, and stood up reasonably well (SATS vol.1 ch.5). On the other hand, the sample was not of such size as to make accurate estimates possible for small areas. The maps in Chapter 10 depend on such estimates, and should therefore not be taken as presenting any more than a broad picture. On these maps zones are shown blank if they had less than four respondents in the relevant category.

The Rival Means of Transport

As things stand at present it is possible to get from any place in Sydney to any other by private car, or more slowly by some combination of train, bus, walking and waiting. Few trips mix private and public transport; the two constitute virtually separate and rival transport systems. The rivalry is unequal, and the motor car has been steadily increasing its share of the traffic. In 1974, 62 per cent of the work journeys in Sydney were undertaken by private car (Table 9.1), a very considerable increase over the 53 per cent reported in 1970 (Neutze 1977 p.125). Judging from car sales and returns of public transport passengers, this trend has continued, and all comments in this chapter should be read in the light of it.

According to Table 9.1, trains in 1974 carried 16 per cent of all journeys to work, or 45 per cent of all journeys by walking/public transport. Buses were apparently less important (13 per cent) and walking quite minor (6 per cent). Ferries, with their very limited route network, carried less than one per cent of all work trips. However, these figures understate the importance of walking — all public transport trips involve some walking — and also of buses. Trips which included sections by both train and bus are classified as by train (the 'main travel mode'), a procedure justified in that the rail section of the journey is generally the longer, but which underestimates the role buses play in carrying people to work.

Both the private and public transport systems provide complete coverage of the metropolitan area, and cater to all trips whatever their length. At the SATS survey in 1971 the split between them was roughly 60/40 irrespective of distance, though with some tendency for the motor car to lose out to walking for very short trips, and to the railways for very long — meaning mainly travel to the city centre (Table 9.2). The competitive disadvantage of public transport seemed to be worst for middle-distance travel, for here two-thirds of all trips were by car.

Each of the different modes of public transport and walking tended to cater for its own distance category in the travel market (Table 9.2). Trains are emphatically long-distance transport. Two-thirds of their work-bound passengers had journeys of over ten kilometres (Table 9.3). Walking was even more emphatically short-distance — 93 per cent of all journeys were under

TABLE 9.1 *The Main Travel Mode of All Persons who Travelled to Work in Sydney, 1974.*

Mode	Percentage	
Car driver	51.7	
Car passenger	10.1	
Motor cycle	1.1	
PRIVATE TRANSPORT		62.9
Train passenger	16.3	
Ferry passenger	.7	
Bus passenger	12.6	29.6
Pedestrian		6.3
Other (taxi etc.)		1.0
		100

Note: Where a journey involved more than one means of transport, the main travel mode was whichever came first on the following list: ferry, train, bus, car, walking.

Source: ABS, Journey to Work and Journey to School, August 1974.

TABLE 9.2 *The Main Travel Mode Chosen for Work Journeys of Different Length. Sydney, Typical Weekday, 1971.*

Main Travel Mode	Percentage of all journeys by distance in straight line kilometres			
	Less than 3	3 to 10	Over 10	Total
Car	57	65	58	61
Train/ferry	4	16	38	20
Bus	14	18	4	12
Walk	25	1	0	7
TOTAL	100	100	100	100

Note: For the definition of main travel mode see Table 9.1. 'Car' includes drivers and passengers by car, truck or utility, and motor cyclists. This and subsequent tables from the SATS survey exclude persons who worked at home.

Source: SATS home interview survey tapes.

TABLE 9.3 *The Length of Work Journeys by Each Main Travel Mode. Sydney, Typical Weekday, 1971.*

Main Travel Mode	Percentage by distance straight-line km.			
	Less than 3	3 to 10	Over 10	Total
Car	26	42	32	100
Train/ferry	5	30	65	100
Bus	32	58	10	100
Walk/cycle	93	5	2	100
TOTAL	27	39	34	100

Source: SATS home interview survey tapes.

TABLE 9.4 *Average Work Journey Length, Speed and Duration by Main Travel Mode. Sydney, Typical Weekday, 1971.*

Main Travel Mode	Average distance km	Average speed km/h	Average duration mins.	% of journeys taking more than one hour (a)
Car	8.3	18.7	27	4
Train/ferry	14.3	14.4	60	41
Bus	5.1	7.8	39	10
Walk	1.4	6.1	14	1
TOTAL	8.6	15.3	34	12

(a) Strictly 64 minutes and over.

Source: SATS home interview survey tapes.

three kilometres, with a few longer due probably to the inclusion of bicycle rides in this category. Buses were most used in middle-distance travel — those distances where public transport is least successful in competition with the private car. This provides a first indication that buses are the weak link in the walking/public transport system.

The average length of a journey to work by private transport is very similar to the average by walking/public transport — between eight and nine kilometres in both cases. However, as a result of the division of labour within public transport, train trips average 14 kilometres (Table 9.4), bus trips five kilometres, and walked trips a kilometre or so. This specialisation of the different modes of transport in carrying different lengths of work trip is to be expected, given their different characteristics. In peak hours at least, the railways of all modes have the highest line haul speeds, but they serve a restricted number of routes converging on the city centre. They lack direct routes for cross country travel, while for short journeys the speediness of the train may not compensate for the slowness of getting to and from the station. The railways thus specialise in long distance travel to and from the city centre, in which they excel, and indeed are at a competitive advantage over motor cars hampered by congestion and parking difficulties.

Buses have a much more complete route network than the railways, and time spent walking to the bus stop and waiting there is generally less than for the railway station, but their line haul speed is slow. In most cases they are the only form of public transport available for local or crosstown travel, but except in those few places where car parking is extraordinarily difficult they cannot match the private car for speed or convenience.

Average speeds for the different modes of transport are shown in Table 9.4. The figures must be interpreted with care, since they estimate the speed of travel over the whole of all journeys to work, from door to door in different parts of the metropolitan area, including time spent walking and waiting. The distance over which the speed is estimated is once more the straight-line distance based on zone centroids. The maximum speed reached on most journeys will thus be faster than the speed given in the table. Again, the speeds given in the table average those accomplished by those actually using each means of transport, and whose journeys are presumably reasonably convenient by those means. If people were forced to switch from their present mode to a less convenient mode, the change would drag down the recorded speed for that mode.

Despite these drawbacks, Table 9.4 compares the overall speeds of the different modes reasonably accurately. Car travel is generally fast (though 19 kilometres an hour is no great speed). Trains are reasonably quick when there is a route available, and carry their passengers at overall speeds little short of the car. As expected, walking is slow — the average walking speed of six kilometres an hour given in the table is overstated, mainly because of the inclusion of some bicycle trips. Bus travel is also slow — indeed, it is probably slower today than the legendary Bondi steam tram which used to shoot through 80 and more years ago. If there is any means of transport with potential for speeding up, it is the bus.

Combining distances and speeds, we obtain the average duration of the journey to work. This for all workers in all Sydney is around half an hour each way daily — a fair proportion of each person's total waking time. Journeys by train are the longest, in time as well as in distance — two hours a day to and from work. Bus trips, though relatively short, are so slow as to take an average of nearly 40 minutes each way, while car trips take just under half an hour. Trips by the slowest means of transport, walking, are generally brief, with an average duration of a quarter of an hour.

Average journey durations are perhaps not as good an indication of the impact of work travel on people's lives as the proportion of travellers with very time-consuming journeys. Very few walking or private car trips take more than an hour, but over 40 per cent of those by train, and one in ten of those by bus, do so. Insofar as journey times are causing concern, public transport seems to be the culprit.

Journeys to Work and other Travel

The journey to work provides a major part of the load on the passenger transport system in Sydney. One third of all trips by private transport, and 45 per cent of those by public (train, bus, ferry) were work travel (Table 9.5). Of the rest, most of those by private car were for social/recreational purposes, while the greater number of those by public transport were journeys to school. (Public transport is at a competitive advantage in carrying schoolchildren, because they do not drive; its competitive disadvantage is severe for all travel where the whole family goes in the car at once.)

Work journeys are longer than the average trip for other purposes, and work travel therefore accounts for a greater proportion of the total transport task (measured in passenger kilometres) than of total trips (Table 9.5). It accounted in 1971 for nearly half of total weekday travel by car, and nearly 60 per cent by public transport. Worse, since much of this work travel was during the peak periods (especially public transport work travel — SATS vol. 1 p.vi-4) it imposed a severe strain on the transport system. Work journeys are chiefly responsible for the necessity to make investments in greater road capacity, and for high operating costs on public transport.

Men, Women and Means of Transport

Just as there are considerable differences between men and women as to distances covered on the journey to work (ch. 5), and among women between the single and married, so there are again considerable differences as to choice of means of transport (Table 9.6). More than two thirds of all men travel to work by car, as against under one third of the single women. Married women

TABLE 9.5 *Travellers by Public and Private Transport by Journey Purpose. Sydney, Typical Weekday, 1971.*

Journey Purpose	Percentage of trips		% of passenger-kms	
	Motor-car	Public Transport	Motor-car	Public Transport
Work in the City of Sydney	4	23	8	36
Work in the other major employ.areas	9	9	14	11
Work elsewhere	20	13	25	12
TOTAL WORK TRIPS	33	45	47	59
School	5	29	3	17
Shopping	12	9	7	6
Other	50	17	43	18
TOTAL	100	100	100	100
TOTAL NO.(mill.)	3.5	1.4		
TOTAL PERSON-KMS. (mill.)			33	14

SOURCE: SATS report Vol.1 Tables 6.3 and 6.9, and figures, also SATS home interview survey tapes.

come in between, with around half of them travelling by car. Motoring is thus overwhelmingly a man's means of transport: nearly 80 per cent of all journeys to work by car are made by men. At the opposite extreme, 54 per cent of all travellers to work by bus are women, as are 52 per cent of those who walk. In both cases the proportion of women who travel by these modes is more than double the proportion of men. Walking is the only means of transport which is not subsidised in some way, so women miss out on subsidies for their journey to work more frequently than men.

The railways occupy an intermediate position between cars and buses in that 60 per cent of their work-bound passengers are men, and 40 per cent women. Because railways serve the city centre, and because the female workforce there has a high proportion of unmarried women (ch. 5) the proportion of all single women workers who travel by train is roughly double the proportion of male workers, while the proportion of working married women is little greater than that of men.

TABLE 9.6 *Journeys to Work by Main Travel Mode and Sex. Sydney, Typical Weekday, 1971.*

Main travel Mode	Number (thousand journeys a day)			
	Men	Single Women	Married Women	All Persons
Car	466	47	78	591
Train/ferry	116	47	30	193
Bus	59	38	32	129
Walk	37	18	21	76
TOTAL	678	150	161	989
	Percentages by population group			
Car	69	32	48	60
Train/ferry	17	31	19	20
Bus	9	25	20	13
Walk	5	12	13	8
	100	100	100	100

Note: This table refers to the journey <u>to</u> and not from work; therefore each worker is counted only once.

Source: SATS home interview survey tapes.

TABLE 9.7 *Average Speed on the Journey to Work by Main Travel Mode and Sex. Sydney, Typical Weekday, 1971.*

Population Group	Speed over airline distance (km/h) by main means of travel				
	Car	Train/ ferry	Bus	Walking/ cycle	Weighted Average
Men	19.0	14.6	8.1	6.2	16.2
Single women	16.9	14.4	7.5	5.8	12.9
Married women	17.4	13.8	7.5	5.6	13.0
TOTAL	18.7	14.4	7.8	6.1	15.3

Source: SATS home interview survey tapes.

TABLE 9.8 *Average Length of the Journey to Work by Main Travel Mode and Sex. Sydney, Typical Weekday, 1971.*

Population Group	Main means of travel				
	Car km	Train km	Bus km	Walking km	Weighted Average km
Men	8.8	14.8	5.7	1.5	9.2
Single women	6.7	14.3	4.7	1.3	8.1
Married women	5.9	12.6	4.6	1.2	6.3
TOTAL	8.3	14.3	5.1	1.4	8.6

Note: Train includes ferry, walking includes cycle.

Source: SATS home interview survey tapes.

TABLE 9.9 *Average and Median Duration of the Journey to Work by Main Travel Mode and Sex. Sydney, Typical Weekday, 1971.*

(mins.)

Main Mode of Travel	Men		Single Women		Married Women		TOTAL	
	Average	Median	Average	Median	Average	Median	Average	Median
Car	28	22	24	19	20	17	27	20
Train/ferry	61	59	60	57	55	52	60	57
Bus	42	39	38	37	37	34	39	37
Walk	15	13	13	12	13	11	14	12
TOTAL	34	30	38	34	29	28	34	30
Compare ABS journey to work survey, 1974:							34	30

Source: SATS tapes.

As explained earlier in this chapter, it is possible from the average straight-line distances and average times to estimate the average speed of travel by the different modes. This is again done in Table 9.7, from which it appears, surprisingly, that women travel more slowly than men by any given means of transport. This may be partly because they have shorter journeys (Table 9.8) but may also be due to their walking more slowly. If Table 9.7 is to be believed, men even walk faster (or cycle more often) than single women who in turn walk faster than their married sisters. However, the main reason why men travel faster than women, overall, is that women more often travel by slower means of transport — buses and walking.

In Chapter 5 (Table 5.5) it was noted that men tend to travel further than single women, who in turn travel further than married women. This is not only true overall; it applies to each means of transport taken individually — even walking (Table 9.8). The difference is particularly marked for car travel, where 2.9 kilometres separate the average journeys of men and married women.

Once again, speed and distance give duration of journey. Married women, who on average have the shortest trips, albeit at the slowest speeds, have the briefest journeys (Table 9.9). Men, whose trips are longest, travel faster than women, so that the average duration of their journeys is less than for single women. With an average journey to work of 38 minutes single women have the most time-consuming work journeys of the three population groups.

Table 9.9 gives median durations as well as average. For all modes and population groups the median is less than the average, and for men's car travel this is particularly so. Male motorists seem to be divided into a majority with relatively brief journeys and a minority who travel for long periods.

This series of tables confirms the suggestion made in Chapter 5 that married women are more concerned than others to curtail the time they spend in travel to work. Many married women in effect hold two full-time jobs and cannot spare much time for travel. They therefore try to limit their travel time, both by shortening the length of their journey and (less successfully) by trying to buy speed. However, women as a whole are less able to buy speed than men, because of their lower incomes. It may also be that they are less inclined to do so, in that young men may set their heart and masculinity on a car while their sisters are saving for a house. Taken together, the greater value of their time at home and its lower value at work would explain why married women's journeys are brief compared to men's, yet are not so often undertaken by car.

Single women are inclined towards public transport both because of lack of income and, perhaps, through a lack of other urgent calls on their time, which makes them willing to put up with a lengthy daily journey to the attractions of the city centre (ch. 5). However, despite the high proportion of single women travelling to the city centre, their average length of journey is less than for men (Table 9.8).

It would be desirable to pursue further the relationship of modal choice to income, and indeed the SATS data has enabled other investigators to tabulate the main means of transport for the journey to work against family income (CBR 1975 p.131, repeated in Neutze 1977 p.135). These tables demonstrate that the proportion of trips undertaken by car increases with family income, while the proportion by train stays constant and the proportion by bus decreases. It is not possible to press the investigation much further than this, because the income question in the SATS home interview survey asked only total family income, and gave no means of imputing income to individual trip-makers.

In summary, it would seem that women travel shorter distances than men because they can afford to travel only by slower means of transport, and, in the case of married women, because their time is more valuable. However, the reverse case can be made: that women are less fussy about their jobs than men, and therefore have no incentive to look far afield for work. Having selected a nearby job, they do not incur excessive journey times if they save money by travelling slowly. How often this is true is a matter of judgement. Certainly it does not apply to those women who work in the city centre. But whatever the reason why women more often use public transport than men, one implication of their decision remains obvious: that expenditure on roadworks (specially those like freeways which aid long-distance travel) is largely for the benefit of men, whereas public transport subsidies, particularly those to local buses, are more evenly distributed between the sexes.

Yet perhaps these inferences are premature. This account of modal choice and journey duration has so far made no reference to the differences between suburbs — both suburbs of residence and those of workplace. These differences are considerable and any conclusions must wait till they have been described.

CHAPTER 10

Speeds, Times and Suburbs

Not only do walking and public transport tend to be used in preference to motor cars for short journeys or very long, and to be used by women rather than men; they play quite different roles in bringing people to work in the various employment areas of Sydney. Broadly, the proportion carried by public transport increases with the size of the centre and also with the average length of journey, while the proportion arriving by motor car decreases (Table 10.1 and Map 22). The proportion of workers in the City of Sydney travelling to work by car is less than a third and for the central business district itself the proportion is about a quarter. In the city centre satellites of North Sydney/Willoughby and South Sydney/Botany it rises to nearly two thirds, and elsewhere it approaches and in places is more than three quarters. By contrast, public transport carries two thirds of all workers in the City of Sydney, declining to under 20 per cent for dispersed suburban employment.

TABLE 10.1 *The Main Mode of Travel to Work by Employment Area. Sydney, Typical Weekday, 1971.*

Employment area	Percentage travelling by:				
	Car	Train/ ferry	Bus	Walk	TOTAL
City of Sydney	30	47	19	4	100
South Sydney/Botany	62	19	13	6	100
North Sydney/Willoughby	62	14	11	12	100
Parramatta/Auburn	73	15	7	5	100
Other	72	9	9	9	100
AVERAGE	61	20	12	7	100

Source: SATS home interview survey tapes.

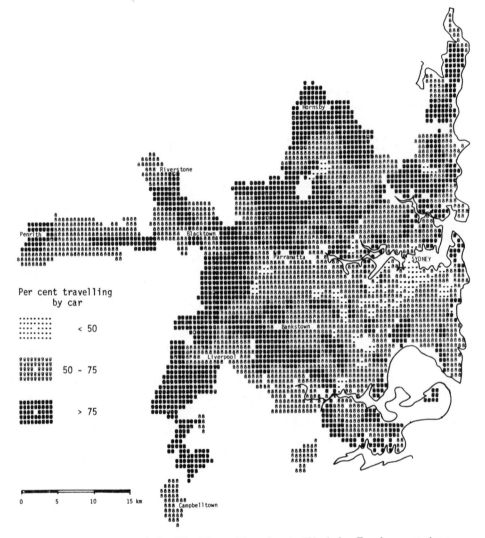

MAP 22. Percentage of the Workforce Motoring to Work by Employment Area, Sydney, Typical Weekday, 1971 (see text, page 143). The great majority of those who work in the suburbs get to work by car. Only in the City of Sydney is there any large area where a majority of the workforce arrives at work by means of transport other than the car — by public transport or on foot.

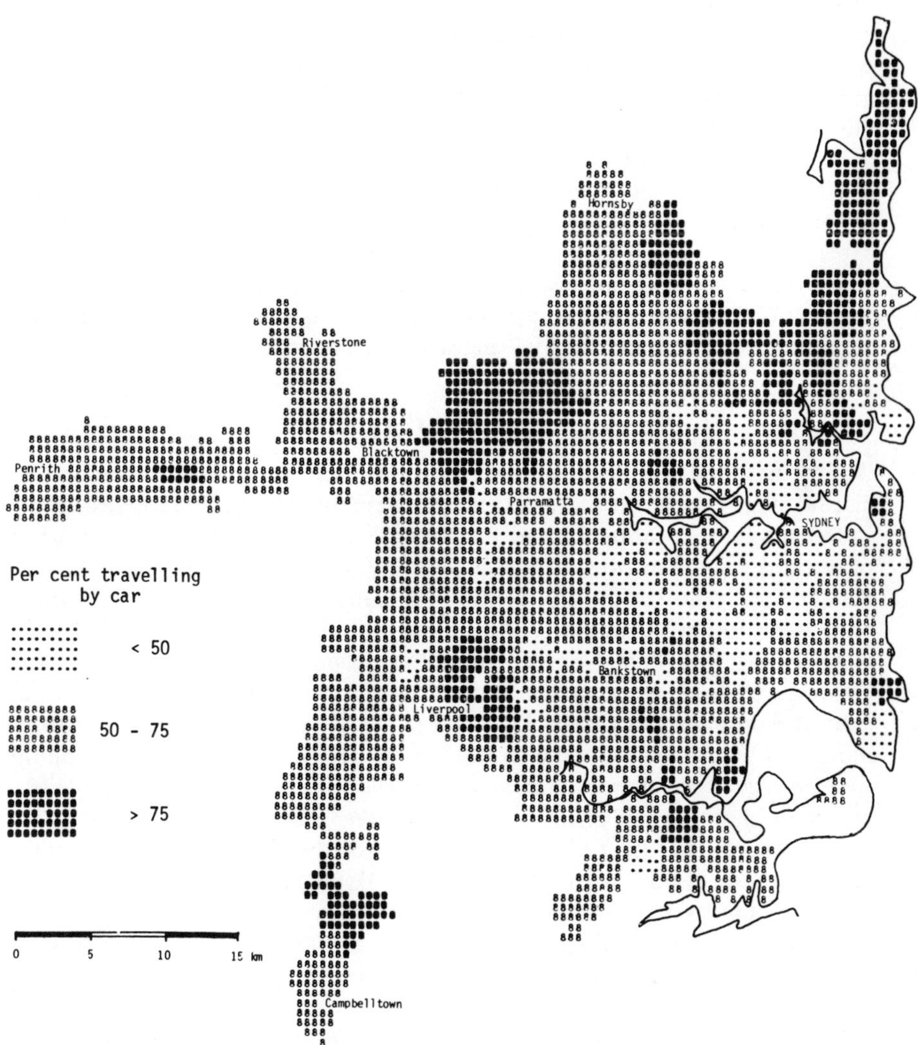

MAP 23. Percentage of Residents Motoring to Work by Residential Area, Sydney, Typical Weekday, 1971 (see text, page 146). The overall density of shading on this map is less than on Map 22, because areas where less than half the workforce arrives by car tend to be areas of high employment density. The inner suburbs are the places where people most commonly walk or take public transport to work, while outer suburban residents, particularly those away from railway lines, travel by car.

The decline is more pronounced for rail passengers than for those who go by bus — trains carry nearly half the workforce of the City of Sydney and only 9 per cent of that in the dispersed areas, the bus proportions being 19 and 9 per cent. This pattern confirms the importance of trains for city centre travel, and of buses as the chief (but not very successful) competitor with the motor car for other traffic flows.

In the dispersed areas a further 9 per cent of the workers walk to work, which is a higher proportion than in the city centre, Parramatta/Auburn or South Sydney/Botany, but lower than in North Sydney/Willoughby. One would expect the proportion of the workforce arriving on foot to be low in major employment areas (relatively few live within walking distance) but North Sydney/Willoughby is an exception to this rule: the location of an employment concentration in an area of high density housing encourages walking.

Transport Modes and Residential Areas

Given that walking and public transport are at a severe competitive disadvantage against the motor car for journeys other than local trips and those to the city centre (Tables 9.2 and 10.1) it may be predicted that the proportion of workers driving to work will be highest in those suburbs where people work neither locally nor in the city centre. The suburbs with a low proportion of residents working locally are predominantly those on the northern and western fringes (Map 10), while the areas with a low proportion working in the City of Sydney are mainly those on the western fringe, particularly those places away from the railway lines (Maps 17 and 18). The prediction is therefore that the motor car will be most commonly used for work travel by people living on the western edge of the metropolitan area. However, as can be seen from Table 10.2 and Map 23, an income effect intervenes between this prediction and actuality. The motor car is at least as commonly used for the journey to work from the outer parts of Manly/Warringah and from Baulkham Hills/Hornsby as it is from the outer western suburbs. In these northern outer areas the proportions working locally and in the city centre are not quite as low as on the western fringe, but the greater income of their inhabitants inclines them towards motoring.

Compared to the areas along the railway line through Ku-ring-gai, those outer northern suburbs where very high proportions of workers travel by car have relatively low numbers working in the city centre, as well as few working locally. This leads one to wonder which came first. Do the residents of such areas use their cars because their work destinations cannot conveniently be reached by public transport, or do they pick their workplaces because public transport in the fringe suburbs is poor and they want to work in a place which can easily be reached by car? And indeed, did they go to live on the fringe because they do not value convenient public transport? The maps and tables raise more questions than they answer.

The inverse prediction, that motor car usage will be low (and walking and public transport travel high) in the inner suburbs, where many people work either locally or in the city centre, is borne out by Map 23 and Table 10.2. In many of the inner suburbs less than half the residents travel to work by car, and many of them walk — up to a third in the City of Sydney (Map 26). However, the City of Sydney supplies such a small proportion of its own workforce that this walking third make up only 4 per cent of the total number of people working in the City (Table 10.1).

The railways cater mainly for city centre traffic, but carry people to intervening work destinations as well. The suburb with the highest proportion

TABLE 10.2 *The Main Mode of Travel to Work by Residential Area. Sydney, Typical Weekday, 1971.*

Residential area	Percentage travelling by:				
	Car	Train	Bus	Walking	TOTAL
Penrith	74	20	3	4	100
Blacktown	67	27	3	3	100
Outer South West	66	23	6	5	100
Parramatta/Auburn	62	23	8	7	100
Baulkham Hills/Hornsby	75	18	4	3	100
Ryde/Hunters Hill	64	14	17	5	100
Middle West	52	26	13	8	100
Bankstown	62	25	7	5	100
Sutherland	68	25	3	4	100
St.George/Canterbury	60	27	7	5	100
Marrickville/Leichhardt	43	17	24	16	100
South Sydney/Botany	47	7	26	20	100
Eastern suburbs	55	2	35	8	100
City of Sydney	29	7	28	36	100
Ku-ring-gai	66	29	2	2	100
Inner North	51	22	15	12	100
Manly/Warringah	71	11	13	4	100
TOTAL	61	20	12	7	100

Note: For boundaries of residential areas see Map 8.
Train includes ferry, walking includes cycle

Source: SATS home interview survey tapes.

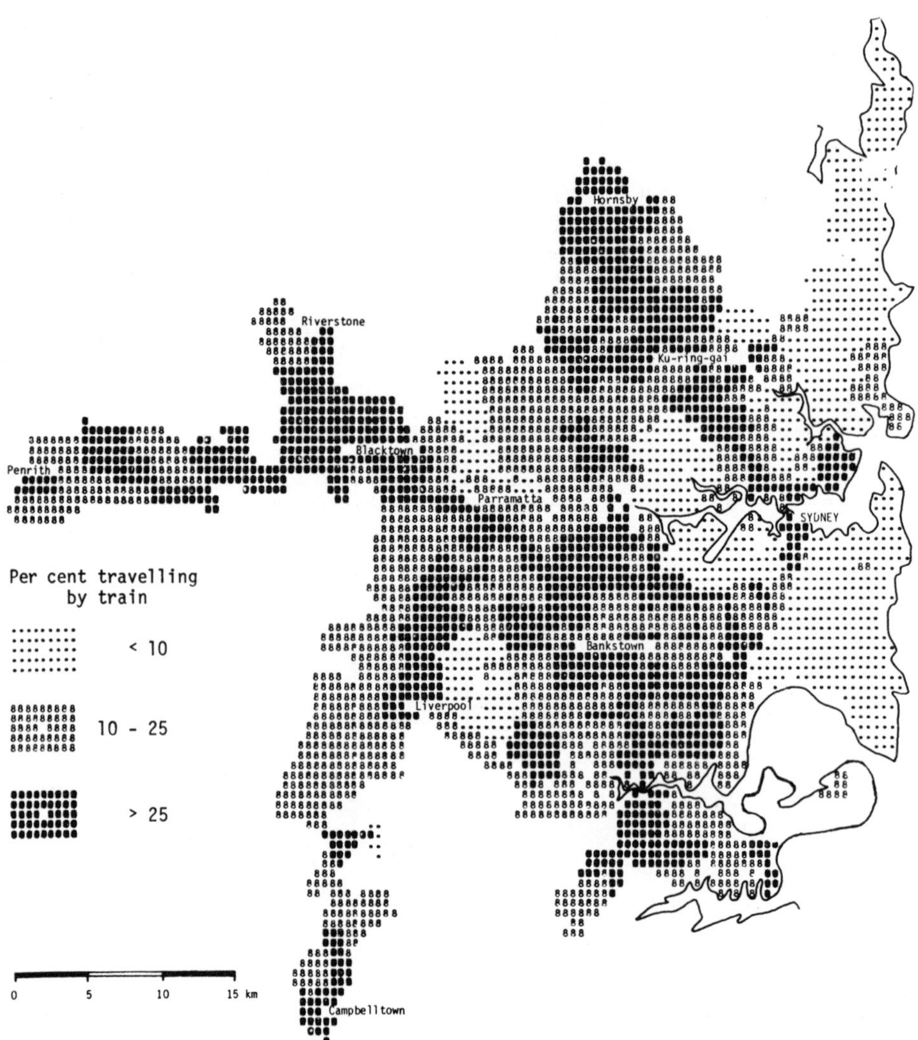

MAP 24. Persons Travelling to Work by Train or Ferry, by Residential Area, Sydney, Typical Weekday, 1971 (see text, page 147). In comparing this map with Maps 22 and 23 note that the levels of shading are different. The train is a relatively popular means of getting to work in all suburbs served by rail.

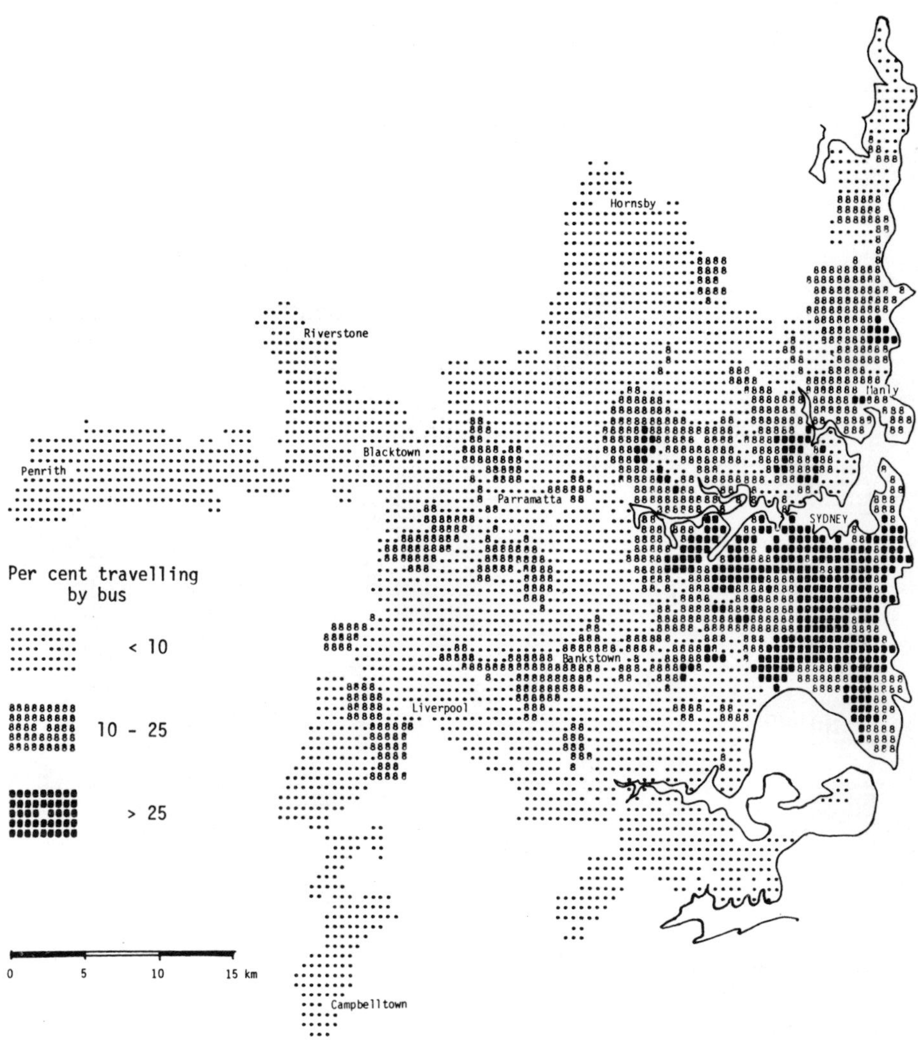

MAP 25. Persons Travelling to Work by Bus by Residential Area, Sydney, Typical Weekday, 1971 (see text, page 151). Buses are a popular means of transport to work only in the inner areas, in the eastern suburbs and a scattering of middle western suburbs not served by rail.

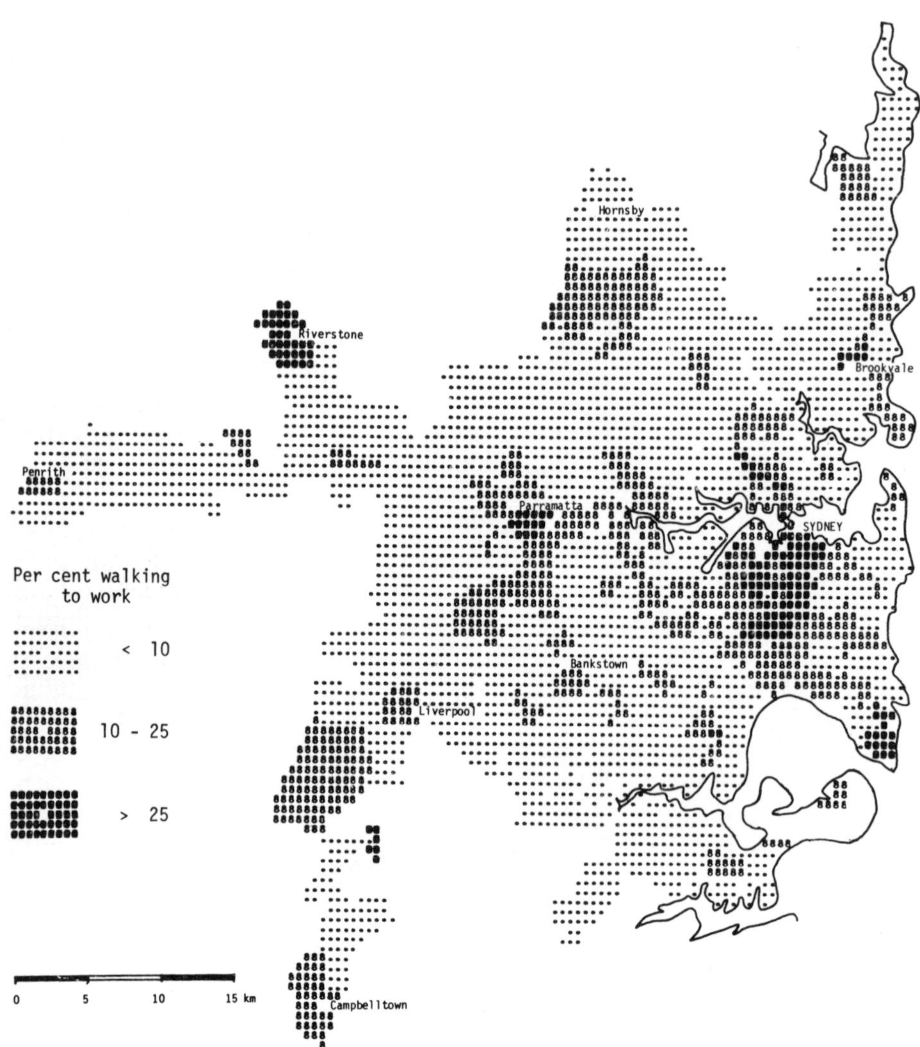

MAP 26. Persons Walking to Work by Residential Area, Sydney, Typical Weekday, 1971 (see text, page 151). This map also includes cyclists, who are few in number in Sydney. Walking and cycling are relatively common in areas of high job density, and also in a few outer suburbs (e.g. Riverstone) where workers live close to their workplace.

of train travellers is Ku-ring-gai, an area with an unusually high proportion of city centre workers (Map 17). Though the typical train journey is a long ride from an outer suburb to the city centre, those inner suburbs with rail and ferry services still make good use of them. As a result, wherever there is a railway line there are train travellers, and the pattern of the lines (and ferry wharves) can be traced on Map 24.

Despite their ubiquity, buses as sole carriers only account for a significant proportion of work journeys in areas without rail service, particularly the eastern suburbs (Map 25, Table 10.2). As already mentioned, this underestimates the role that buses play as rail feeders in the rest of Sydney, but even allowing for this, in all outer areas except Manly/Warringah (which has no railway line; only the ferry to Manly) the proportion travelling by bus is very much less than the proportion by train. The bus offers very little competition to the motor car for the middle-distance work journeys so common in outer suburbs which lack local employment.

Finally, Map 26 (walking and cycling to work) should be compared with Map 10 (the proportion of the resident workforce working locally). The patterns correlate, with a high proportion of walkers in the city centre, North Sydney, South Sydney/Botany and parts of Parramatta/Auburn. Again, such small concentrations of local employment as Riverstone and Brookvale (in Warringah Shire) show up as places where people walk. However, this should not overly encourage hopes that the localisation of employment would lead to any considerable switch from motoring to walking. If a thousand jobs were decentralised to an outer western suburb, it would be a particularly good result if as many as half were taken by locals (Tables 5.13 and 6.3) and if as many as a third of these locals walked to work (Table 9.2). The most that could be expected, therefore, would be that 150 of the thousand jobs would be taken by walkers. On the other hand, many of the remaining journeys would be short, and overall the benefit in terms of reduced journey times and expense might be quite considerable, especially to married women taking the opportunity of a local job.

Journey Distance, Speed and Duration by Suburb

In Chapter 3 journeys to work were classified into journeys to dispersed employment, which on average were short; journeys to the city centre, which were generally long, and those to the other main employment concentrations, on average of middle length (Table 3.3). In Chapter 9 it was observed that train journeys tend to be long, car trips about average in length, bus trips short and walked trips very short (Table 9.4). Table 10.3 puts these two patterns together. They fit very neatly. For all employment areas train journeys are on average the longest, followed by car and bus and finally walking (actual estimates are not given in the table, but all are between one and two kilometres). Further, by each transport mode, journeys to the city centre are the longest, followed by South

TABLE 10.3 *The Average Length of the Journey to Work by Main Travel Mode and Employment Area. Sydney, Typical Weekday, 1971.*

Employment Area	Average distance (km) by:				
	Car	Train/ ferry	Bus	Weighted average (a)	cf.census estimate
City of Sydney	11.4	16.1	6.1	12.3	12.6
South Sydney/Botany	10.3	15.4	4.8	10.0	10.3
North Sydney/Willoughby	8.7	12.8	4.7	7.9	8.6
Parramatta/Auburn	8.4	10.6	4.4	8.1	8.8
All other	7.3	11.0	4.4	6.8	7.1
Average	8.3	14.3	5.1	8.6	9.1

(a) Includes allowance for walking.
Estimates of distance for walked journeys are considered too unreliable to be given for individual areas.
All distances in straight-line kilometres.

Source: SATS home interview survey tapes.
Census estimate: See Table 5.12.

Sydney/Botany, then the other major employment areas, with the shortest journeys being to dispersed employment.

The average journey length from any suburb depends on its distance from the city centre and the other main employment areas, and on the proportion of its residents working locally, in the city centre, and elsewhere. Average journey lengths were not calculated in Chapter 3, because the average was often not representative, falling between the averages for different major destinations. However, average distances do provide a means of comparing journeys by the different transport modes, and are so used in Table 10.4.

Given that the motor car is the majority choice for journeys of whatever length (Table 9.2) it is not surprising to find that the average journey distance by car from any suburb is similar to the average length of all journeys from that suburb (Table 10.4). However, in the outer suburbs car journeys are generally a little shorter than the average by all transport modes, a position which is reversed in the inner areas. In the outer suburbs the chief alternative to a local or middle-distance journey to work by car is a long journey by rail (Table 10.2); this increases the overall average to greater than the average by car. In the inner

TABLE 10.4 *The Average Length of the Journey to Work by Main Travel Mode and Residential Area. Sydney, Typical Weekday, 1971.*

Residential Area	Average distance (km) by:				
	Car	Train/ferry	Bus	Average (a)	cf. census estimate
Penrith	12.1	32.1	*	15.5	15.6
Blacktown	11.8	23.4	*	14.4	14.5
Outer South West	9.4	18.7	5.4	10.9	11.9
Parramatta/Auburn	7.1	13.4	4.4	8.0	8.2
Baulkham Hills/Hornsby	10.5	18.3	*	11.4	11.7
Ryde/Hunters Hill	7.4	10.8	7.5	7.6	7.6
Middle West	6.4	8.4	4.8	6.3	6.5
Bankstown	7.9	15.4	3.7	9.1	9.2
Sutherland	10.1	17.9	*	11.6	12.4
St.George/Canterbury	7.6	11.7	5.5	8.2	8.6
Marrickville/Leichhardt	5.1	5.9	3.7	4.3	4.2
South Sydney/Botany	4.6	*	3.9	3.8	3.8
Eastern Suburbs	5.8	*	5.3	5.3	5.7
City of Sydney	4.5	*	2.5	2.8	4.4
Ku-ring-gai	11.0	13.9	*	11.6	11.5
Inner North	6.3	5.6	4.5	5.3	5.3
Manly/Warringah	9.0	13.2	8.9	9.2	9.7
TOTAL	8.3	14.3	5.1	8.6	9.1

* Less than 50 observations in sample.
(a) Includes an allowance for walking.

Source: SATS home interview survey tapes.
Census 1971, see Table 5.14.

areas, on the other hand, many people walk to work locally or make short journeys by bus, car travel being reserved for a minority of rather longer crosstown trips.

Since so many journeys to work by train are to the city centre, the average length of rail journeys from any residential area closely reflects the distance from that area to the city centre. In other words, the typical train journey from an inner suburb is quite short — five or six kilometres — while the average journey from Penrith is at the other extreme at 32 kilometres. Buses, on the

TABLE 10.5 *Average Spped on the Journey to Work by Main Travel Mode and Residential Area. Sydney, Typical Weekday, 1971.*

Residential area of origin	Speed over straight-line distance (km/h)			
	Car	Train/ ferry	Bus	Weighted average (a)
Penrith	30	23	*	26
Blacktown	23	19	*	21
Outer South West	21	16	9	19
Parramatta/Auburn	18	13	8	15
Baulkham Hills/Hornsby	18	16	*	20
Ryde/Hunters Hill	17	12	9	13
Middle West	15	11	7	12
Bankstown	19	14	7	16
Sutherland	20	15	*	17
St.George/Canterbury	18	13	9	15
Marrickville/Leichhardt	13	8	6	9
South Sydney/Botany	14	*	6	9
Eastern Suburbs	15	*	8	11
City of Sydney	13	*	4	7
Ku-ring-gai	20	16	*	18
Inner North	15	8	7	11
Manly/Warringah	20	11	10	15
TOTAL	18	14	8	15

* Less than 50 observations in sample.
(a) Includes an allowance for walking.

Source: SATS home interview survey tapes.

other hand, are used either as a means of getting to the railway station or for local travel, except in suburbs where there is no railway line. Accordingly in most areas the average bus trip is four or five kilometres long, but for suburbs without rail access to the city centre (particularly Ryde and Warringah) the average bus trip is much longer.

As a general rule speeds by any transport mode are faster on longer journeys. With motor cars this comes about because a greater proportion of the journey is on main roads built for speed, while with public transport it is due to the greater proportion of the total distance covered at line haul (even express)

TABLE 10.6 *Average Speed on the Journey to Work by Main Travel Mode and Employment Area. Sydney, Typical Weekday, 1971.*

Employment area of destination	Speed over straight-line distance (km/h)			
	Car	Train/ ferry	Bus	Weighted average (a)
City of Sydney	19.0	15.6	8.0	14.8
South Sydney/Botany	18.7	15.4	7.0	15.8
North Sydney/Willoughby	18.0	13.2	7.2	14.7
Parramatta/Auburn	19.4	11.8	7.5	15.9
All other	19.0	11.8	7.8	15.5
TOTAL	18.7	14.4	7.8	15.3

(a) Includes an allowance for walking. Estimates of walking speeds for individual employment zones have not been attempted.

Source: SATS home interview survey tapes.

speed, as against walking and waiting. Whether by car, train or bus, the speeds shown in Table 10.5 thus correlate with the average length of journeys in Table 10.4. It is equally the case that the speeds correlate with distance from the city centre, and in the case of road transport at least (particularly the bus speed in the City of Sydney, which averages no more than walking pace) reflect the state of traffic congestion. In several areas the recorded speeds turn on special factors. Train speeds from Sutherland are a little lower than the straight-line distance would warrant, reflecting the roundabout rail route, while the low line haul speed of ferries is reflected in the figures for Manly/Warringah. Despite these aberrations, it is generally the case that higher speeds as well as greater use of the faster means of transport partly compensate for longer journey distances in the outer suburbs.

Though the average speeds accomplished by residents of the different suburbs thus vary considerably, the mix of journeys to each major employment area is such that average speeds vary remarkably little by workplace (Table 10.6). This is particularly true by car and bus. Journeys to the city centre and its two neighboring employment areas include some which are short and very slow, and others long and relatively fast: the resulting average speed is very similar to that for all Sydney. On the other hand, train speeds are clearly higher for city centre travel than for journeys which start and end in the suburbs: the average journey is longer, and trains are not affected by inner area road congestion.

Combining distances (Tables 10.3 and 10.4) and speeds (Tables 10.5 and

TABLE 10.7 *Average Duration of the Journey to Work by Main Travel Mode and Employment Area. Sydney, Typical Weekday, 1971.*

Employment Area	Average duration (mins) by:				
	Car	Train/ ferry	Bus	Walk	Average
City of Sydney	36	62	46	19	50
South Sydney/Botany	33	60	41	16	38
North Sydney/Willoughby	29	58	39	12	32
Parramatta/Auburn	26	54	35	17	31
Other	23	56	34	12	26
TOTAL	27	60	39	14	34

Source: SATS, home interview survey tapes.

10.6) we once again obtain the average duration of the journey to work, this time by journey destination (Table 10.7) and origin (Table 10.8). Two contrasting patterns emerge. When trips are classified by employment area, the average journey duration by train and walking is similar for all areas, while the car and bus durations vary, but when trips are classified by residential area, average journey duration is similar for all areas by car, bus and walking, with considerable variation in average times by rail. The explanation lies in the interplay of journey distance and speed.

Since average speeds by car and bus do not vary much by employment area, average journey durations by these modes to the employment areas reflect average distance. The same is not quite true of train travel, for here speed compensates for differences in average distance, and trips typically take about an hour whatever their destination. Walked trips to the City take on average a little longer than elsewhere: perhaps some are relatively long journeys by cycle.

When journeys are classified by residential area, the general pattern is that distances are longer and speeds faster for trips originating in the outer suburbs. By car the two cancel out, and higher speeds in the outer areas compensate for distances which are generally 50 per cent more than the average. As a result typical journey times even from the fringe suburbs are never more than a few minutes more than the all-Sydney average of 27 minutes. With trains, however, the distance difference is of the order of five times, and even though speeds from the outer suburbs are a great deal faster than for shorter journeys, differences of average journey duration remain, such that 40 minutes is typical in the inner areas and 80 on the western fringe. For buses and walking, distance and speed differences are smaller, and so are differences of typical duration: walked trips average a quarter of an hour everywhere, and bus trips between 30

TABLE 10.8 *Average Duration of the Journey to Work by Main Travel Mode and Residential Area. Sydney, Typical Weekday, 1971.*

Region	Average Duration (mins.) by:				
	Car	Train/ferry	Bus	Walking	Average
Penrith	24	82	*	*	35
Blacktown	31	74	*	*	42
Outer South West	27	68	35	13	35
Parramatta/Auburn	24	62	35	15	33
Baulkham Hills/Hornsby	34	70	*	*	37
Ryde/Hunters Hill	27	55	49	*	34
Middle West	25	46	40	14	31
Bankstown	25	64	33	13	34
Sutherland	30	70	*	*	40
St.George/Canterbury	26	54	37	12	33
Marrickville/Leichhardt	24	44	38	14	29
South Sydney/Botany	20	*	38	15	25
Eastern Suburbs	23	*	41	14	29
City of Sydney	21	*	34	16	25
Ku-ring-gai	33	52	*	*	38
Inner North	25	40	38	13	29
Manly/Warringah	27	69	51	11	36
TOTAL	27	60	39	14	34

* Less than 50 travellers in the sample.

Source: SATS home interview survey tapes.

and 40 minutes everywhere except Ryde and Manly/Warringah, where the use of buses for city centre travel raises the average.

The average duration of the journey to work by all travel modes from any area depends on the average for each individual mode, and the proportion of all workers using each mode. Times in the inner suburbs tend to be brief whatever the mode, and many people walk to work (the mode with the briefest journeys) so overall the average trip time can be as low as 25 minutes (City of Sydney; South Sydney) (Table 10.8). Most outer suburban residents travel to work by car, incurring trip times of about the all-Sydney average, but around one in five travel by train, most of them to the city centre and at a considerable cost in

TABLE 10.9 *Journeys to Work Taking More Than One Hour. Sydney, Typical Weekday, 1971.*

	Percentage of journeys		Total	% of all journeys over an hour *
BY DESTINATION	One hour or less	Over an hour *		
City of Sydney	74	26	100	55
South Sydney/Botany	87	13	100	12
North Sydney/Willoughby	91	9	100	7
Parramatta/Auburn	94	7	100	5
Other	95	6	100	21
TOTAL	88	12	100	100
BY ORIGIN				
Penrith	80	20	100	4
Blacktown	75	25	100	12
Outer South West	82	18	100	21
Parramatta/Auburn	86	14	100	8
Baulkham Hills/Hornsby	82	18	100	7
Ryde/Hunters Hill	89	11	100	3
Middle West	96	4	100	2
Bankstown	85	15	100	7
Sutherland	78	22	100	8
St.George/Canterbury	92	8	100	8
Marrickville/Leichhardt	96	4	100	2
South Sydney/Botany	97	3	100	1
Eastern Suburbs	96	4	100	3
City of Sydney	97	3	100	0
Ku-ring-gai	90	10	100	2
Inner North	96	4	100	2
Manly/Warringah	84	16	100	10
TOTAL	88	12	100	100

* Strictly 64 mins. and over.

Source: SATS home interview survey tapes.

TABLE 10.10 *Average Duration of the Journey to Work by Residential Area and Sex. Sydney, Typical Weekday, 1971.*

Region	Average Duration (mins.) for:			
	Men	Single Women	Married Women	Total
Penrith	36	45	28	35
Blacktown	41	56	33	42
Outer South West	34	46	32	35
Parramatta/Auburn	32	42	30	33
Baulkham Hills/Hornsby	39	42	29	37
Ryde/Hunters Hill	34	37	32	34
Middle West	31	36	27	31
Bankstown	34	44	28	34
Sutherland	41	49	29	40
St.George/Canterbury	33	38	28	33
Marrickville/Leichhardt	30	29	27	29
South Sydney/Botany	25	27	23	25
Eastern Suburbs	29	32	28	29
City of Sydney	26	24	21	25
Ku-ring-gai	40	36	29	38
Inner North	30	29	25	29
Manly/Warringah	37	37	29	36
TOTAL	34	38	29	34

Source: SATS home interview survey tapes.

time. As a result, average journey durations from some of the outer suburbs are 40 minutes or more. Average journey duration thus ranges from 25 minutes in the inner areas to 42 in Blacktown. Though this range is much more compressed than the range of average journey distances (3.8 to 15.5, Table 10.4) outer area residents still have cause for complaint.

Travel to dispersed employment tends to be by car, and the duration of the average trip to such jobs is not very different from that of the average car trip (Table 10.7). At 26 minutes it takes only half as long as the average trip to the city centre. In this case a distance difference of 80 per cent (12.6 kilometres to the city, 7.1 to dispersed employment — Table 10.3) is accentuated because city centre travel is more often by public transport, and is a little slower than average (Table 10.6). Once again the complaints by city centre workers concerning long journey times (ch. 7) seem justified.

Similar conclusions can be reached by counting the proportion of journeys which take a long time — say more than an hour (Table 10.9). Few journeys starting in the inner suburbs, or ending at dispersed workplaces, are long in this sense. On the other hand, a quarter of all journeys to work from such outer suburbs as Blacktown, and a quarter of all journeys to the city centre, take more than an hour. City centre travel is responsible for over half the long journeys to work in the metropolitan area. To the extent that people object to long journeys, while remaining relatively indifferent between trips of short or medium duration, it is obvious that travel to the city centre and from the outer suburbs gives greatest cause for concern and possibility for improvement.

Because single women tend to work in the city centre, they tend more than others to incur long journeys. The average journey times for the male residents of any suburb are very similar to the average times for the residents as a whole (Table 10.10), but journey durations for single women are generally greater, and for married women less. In the inner suburbs these differences are small (e.g. Marrickville/Leichhardt, where married women typically travel for 27 minutes, and single women for 29) but in the outer suburbs they are very marked indeed (e.g. Penrith, where married women on average travel for 28 minutes and single for 45.) Confronted with a lack of local employment in the outer suburbs, it would seem that single women take the train to the city centre, while married women withdraw from the workforce if they cannot obtain a job locally. As explained in Chapter 5, available statistics support this hypothesis, though it is not possible to tell how far the lower workforce participation of married women living in the outer suburbs is due to the lack of local jobs, and how far it is due to their having voluntarily given up work to look after their children.

Transport Effects of Employment Decentralisation

Though the decentralisation of employment from the city centre to the suburbs would be appreciated by many outer suburban residents, its consequences for the transport system might not in the long run be favourable. Much depends on the pattern of decentralisation adopted.

Judging from the transport choices of people presently employed in the major suburban concentrations of employment, the decentralisation of jobs from the city centre to such concentrations would lead to reductions in public transport patronage in favour of motoring. There would be some reductions in distances covered, but quite possibly an increase in private and public costs — these latter in the form of roadbuilding. It would even be possible for the roadbuilding to be carried out to such an extent that the end result of the decentralisation was longer, faster journeys rather than shorter trips, with an increased (but really appreciated?) range of job opportunities.

The effect of such a decentralisation on public transport deficits is difficult to predict. While any reduction in peak loads is prima facie a favourable effect, general reductions in patronage are not — particularly where these affect the railways, where it might be difficult to cut back fixed costs proportionately to the reduction in loadings. Again, when patronage falls minimum services must still be maintained for social service reasons, with attendant subsidies. The alternative is to withdraw all public transport, with unfortunate consequences for those unable to drive.

The decentralisation of employment from the suburban concentrations to local areas would lead to further reductions in journey lengths. The increase in crosstown travel would be less than it would were the same number of city centre jobs added to the major suburban concentrations, but such crosstown travel as did arise would be so diffuse as to origin and destination that public transport could not carry it. On the other hand, the shorter journeys would favour walking, and perhaps also the patronage of local bus services, since short trips are likely to be within the speed and routing constraints of bus services. Much depends on neighborhood design and the skill with which local bus services are adjusted to the potential demand.

The argument in favour of the localisation of employment (remembering that 'local' means 'within three kilometres') has been stated several times in this study. It applies particularly to women's jobs, and other kinds of work with high local response rates. The argument was originally put forward simply on the ground that travel distances could be reduced, but to this may now be added the ground that local employment may potentially be reached by cheaper means of transport — walking, cycling or local bus. At least as compared with the decentralisation of employment to major suburban centres it requires less in the way of roadworks, and at the same time it is more likely to enable a local bus service to be maintained. On the other hand, the localisation of the kinds of employment with low local response rates may have much less favourable effects. Perhaps it is better that the concentration of such activity in the city centre be maintained (Thomson 1977 p.265).

None of these arguments can be stated with any certainty without some idea of the costs of different journeys by the several modes of transport. The assessment of these costs is the subject of the next chapter.

CHAPTER 11

The Costs of the Journey to Work

No account of the journey to work in Sydney would be complete without an estimate of its costs. No accurate total estimate is possible, both through lack of data and because of disagreements as to which costs are rightly included and which left out of account, but some at least of the costs are known, and orders of magnitude can be given for others. The costs may be divided into two kinds: those borne by the traveller himself and those carried by the population in general. The two kinds will be taken in turn.

Private Costs of the Journey to Work

From the point of view of the individual worker, the two main disadvantages of the journey to work are that it takes time and costs money. Both these costs are fairly well documented. In addition, there may be costs in terms of mental or physical strain, but there is little evidence on the extent or significance of these (Liepmann 1944 p.54).

The relative significance of the time and cash costs of the journey to work is disputed. It is accepted that 'the hours spent on the way between home and workplace. . .constitute a loss, for they are lost to sleep or recreation, to family life, education or public activities, in short, to the time at the employed person's own disposal. Travelling, even at its best, cannot be counted as leisure. . . . During the journey concentration is as difficult as relaxation; instead the mind is given to killing time. . . .' (Liepmann 1944 p.53). However, to assess the seriousness of the time in relation to the cash costs of the journey, it is necessary to value the lost time. Various methods of valuation have been suggested.

Were work travel conducted in the employer's time, its time cost would be highly significant. Average award wages in N.S.W. at the end of 1974 were $2.64 an hour for men and $2.35 for women (Year Book 1976 p.275-6). These provide conservative estimates of the extra wages employers would have had to pay had their employees travelled in company time: they take no account of overtime payments that might be required, or of the fact that many workers in

Sydney (particularly managerial and professional staff) are paid at higher than award rates. However, even at this conservative valuation, payment for the average journey to work of 34 minutes each way daily (Table 9.4) would have been a little less than $3 a day. Allowing a 47 week working year, with time off for holidays, sickness and unemployment, the nearly 400 million hours a year which Sydney people spend travelling to and from work would have cost employers around $900 million in wages, an addition of more than 10 per cent to their wages bill. This extra cost would be enough to provide employers with an incentive to locate jobs for the convenience of employees, or to try to influence their employees' housing choices to keep journeys short.

However, work travel is not carried out in the employer's time. Perhaps it should therefore be valued at some rate revealed by the worker himself. One source of such revelations is the choices of people confronted with alternative means of transport for a work journey with a fixed origin and a fixed destination, the one means being fast but expensive and the other slow but cheap. In such circumstances it can be shown that the average traveller will behave as though his time were worth some proportion of his wage rate — usually somewhere between a quarter and a half (Quarmby 1967, Hensher 1976). Taking this as the value to the average individual of time saved by speeding up his present journey, the workers of Sydney would be willing to pay roughly $350 million a year to have their journeys to work made instantaneous. The idea of a nine kilometre journey that takes no time is pure science fiction, but the concept does at least put a rough maximum figure on the 'value of travel time savings' some of which might be captured by investments in speedier transport. To put the estimate in context, the Sydney Area Transportation Study proposed that $6000 million be spent between 1971 and 2000 on works designed to speed traffic and cater for additional demands on the transport system (SATS Vol 3 Ch. 1, updated to 1974-5).

This method of valuing time savings, however, is only strictly valid when journey origins and destinations are fixed, so that the only possible benefit of speedy transport lies in reductions in journey time. When origins and destinations can also vary, speed may alternatively be used to increase trip length, rather than save time. The report on the 1966 United Nations survey of time budgets in different countries concludes:

> By far the most intriguing aspect of the trip to work cross-nationally is the relative constancy of the average time allocated to this purpose across our sites in the face of the most complete variation of commuting technology. There seems to be a distinct preference towards using increased efficiency of transport to spread out in space, and modal distances to the workplace across our sites vary by a factor of fifteen or more, while time allocations remain in the average within an impressively narrow range (Szalai 1972 p.123).

TABLE 11.1 *Transport Expenditure by Sydney Households, 1974/5.*

PER HOUSEHOLD/WEEK				$
Motoring expenses:	vehicle purchase registration and insurance			9.81
	running expenses			11.35
			Total	21.16
Fares -	rail			.94
	bus			1.00
			Total	1.94
Compare:	Food expenditure	33.73		
	Housing expenditure	24.63		
	Clothing and footwear	13.40		
ALL SYDNEY, PER ANNUM				$m
Motoring expenses:	vehicle purchase			326
	" operation			670
				996
Fares				91
AS A PROPORTION OF TOTAL HOUSEHOLD EXPENDITURE				%
Motoring expenses				13
Fares				1
				14

Source: ABS Household Expenditure Survey 1974/75.

If this be true, the benefit of speed most often lies in increased journey range within a conventional allocation of time to the journey to work, and hence in a greater choice of dwellings and workplaces. Payments for speed are not evidence of the value of travel time so much as evidence of the value of choice, and ultimately of the value of low density metropolitan development (Schaeffer and Sclar 1975 ch.4, Stretton 1975 ch.2). It is not surprising that people are willing to pay for all these things roughly in proportion to their income.

Given that the time considered reasonable for a journey to work is as much a matter of social convention as anything else, it is not possible to value time so spent as though it were expenditure in dollars and cents. It can only be said that there is cause for concern when journey times rise much above what appears to be the international convention of half an hour each way, and when this happens for any large number of people there is a case either for speedier transport or a more convenient distribution of employment. Second, there may be population groups for whom the desired conventional journey time is less than the average. Such groups would especially appreciate local employment opportunities and fast transport. From the data in Chapters 5 and 9 it would seem that married women are such a group.

Whether or not time spent travelling to and from work can be valued, the cash expenses to individuals can be estimated relatively accurately. Table 11.1 shows average weekly expenditure on motoring and public transport (excluding air travel) for households in Sydney in 1974/5. Transport expenses came to 14 per cent of average weekly expenditure, and as such were less than average spending on food or housing, but nearly double average spending on clothing and footwear. Total transport expenses of $23 per household per week were divided into motoring, $21, and public transport, $2. This latter figure is a little low; it does not tally with the total public transport revenue as reported by the Public Transport Commission or as calculated from fares reported in the ABS Journey to Work survey, 1974 (Table 11.2). Despite this underestimate of perhaps 50 cents, it can be seen that motoring is the major transport expense of most Sydney households.

The journey to work accounts for only part of this total. It is possible to distinguish fares paid on the way to work from fares paid for other journeys, but much harder to divide motoring expenses between work and other travel. It seems reasonable to divide car running costs between work and other travel in proportion to the mileage run for each journey purpose, but the division of fixed costs is more difficult. Some would argue that a car is an Australian necessity, and its fixed costs (which come to nearly half average spending on motoring — Table 11.1) should be written off against the general household budget; others claim that it is necessary mainly for the journey to work, and should be so charged. The true position doubtless varies from household to household, and for present purposes the fixed costs will be allocated between work and other travel in proportion to car kilometreage, in the same way as the running costs.

On weekdays work travel accounts for 47 per cent of the total passenger kilometreage of motorists in Sydney (Table 9.5). Average car occupancy on the journey to work is about 1.22 persons (CBR 1975 p.104) whereas overall it is 1.41 persons (SATS Vol 1 VI-31), which implies that work travel accounts for 54 per cent of weekday car-kilometreage. On the other hand, a much lower proportion of weekend travel is on work journeys. Judging by times spent (Cities Commission, 1975, Appendixes, Table 10, data collected in Melbourne) average weekend car-kilometreage is probably a little more than weekday. On this basis, work travel would be responsible for about a third of all car-kilometreage run by Sydney residents.

Given total motoring costs of $21 per household per week, this implies that work travel by car cost about $7 per week for all households in Sydney in 1974/5. There being 1.44 workers per household (ABS Expenditure Survey) offset by the fact that only 63 per cent of all workers travelled by car (Table 9.1), the average cost of motoring to work was of the order of $7.70 a week for each car traveller, or $9.40 for each car driver, comprising $4.30 fixed costs and $5.10 running costs. On this basis a solo driver with a journey to work three times as long as the average motorist journey (i.e. 25 straight-line kilometres — Table 9.4) would have been paying close to $20 a week.

The cost of fuel in 1974/5 came on average to 40 per cent of running expenses, which in turn was not much more than half the total motoring costs. Accordingly a doubling of fuel prices would increase motoring costs by about 20 per cent. The magnitude of this increase tends to confirm the Commonwealth Bureau of Roads' prediction that an energy crisis expressed in rising petrol prices, rather than in rationing, will not increase the total costs of motoring enough to persuade many people to give up their cars (CBR 1975 Appendix 3).

Information on public transport fares is available more directly from the survey of the journey to work in August 1974 (ABS Journey to Work 1975). According to this survey average spending on fares by those who travelled to work by train in New South Wales was $4 a week, and by bus travellers $2.95. Most of those who go to work by public transport in New South Wales live in Sydney, and in any case there is little reason to believe that those who travel by bus or train outside Sydney (mainly in Newcastle and Wollongong) pay any less than their metropolitan brethren. Taking these figures as applicable to Sydney, the average cash fare for a journey to work by public transport was around $3.50 a week, about half the average cost of motoring. Few public transport users paid more than $9 a week in fares (ABS Journey to Work 1975) so that the most costly public transport journeys were again roughly half as expensive as the most costly car journeys.

TABLE 11.2 *The Average Cost of Work Travel. Sydney 1974/75.*

Mode	Average straight-line distance (Table 9.4) km	Private Cost per worker/wk. (10 trips) $	Private Cost per worker/ kilometre ¢	Total operating cost per worker/ kilometre ¢
Car	8.3	7.70	4.7 (a)	5
Train	14.3	4.00	1.4	2
Bus	5.1	2.95	2.9	6
Walking	1.4	nil.	nil.	1

Note: (a) Running expenses alone approximately 2.5¢ per km.
Train includes ferry.

Source: See text.

To compare fare levels for the different means of transport it is necessary to adjust for differences in the length of the average journey. This is done in Table 11.2. The table takes figures from several sources: average straight-line distances from SATS (Table 9.4) and costs from the household expenditure survey and journey to work survey. The use of straight-line distances overstates costs per kilometre of actual travel, but this effect applies to all modes, and does not vitiate the comparison. For the present the final column should be ignored.

In total private costs per passenger kilometre motoring is the most expensive way of getting to work. However, when car owners compare the cost of driving against the cost of public transport, they generally consider only the running costs they would incur (Quarmby 1967 p.279). This has the effect of making motoring seem relatively cheap: 2.5 cents a kilometre for the fastest travel in Sydney. Against this, the railways offer very competitive fares: 1.4 cents a kilometre for travel which, for city centre journeys, can be faster than driving. On the other hand, not only is bus travel slow, it is also quite expensive; bus fares being of a similar order to motor running expenses in cents a kilometre. Small wonder that bus travel should be mainly confined to those who cannot afford the capital cost of a car (Paterson 1974 ch. 2).

It seems strange that train fares should be so low. They could be put up enough to cover the rail deficit and still be competitive with driving. However, rail fares must be a noticeable expense for many commuters from the outer suburbs, the Blue Mountains and the Central Coast to the city centre (in 1974 season tickets were around $10 a week) which provides a good political reason for keeping fares down. The lack of long journeys by bus results in average fares being higher in cents a kilometre.

Taking motorists, public transport users and walkers together (and noting that walked travel is free) the journey to work in Sydney in 1974/5 would have cost the average worker about $5.85 a week, or about 5.7 per cent of the expenditure of households where someone worked. In households where people walked to work this proportion would have been zero; in households using public transport typically about 3 per cent, and in motorist households more like 7 per cent. Few workers using public transport paid more than $9 a week in fares, and few earned less than $100 a week (Year Book 1975/6 p.270), so that households spending more than 10 per cent of their income on work fares would have been very uncommon. However, a few motorist households may have spent as much as 20 per cent of their income on the journey to work.

Given that the journey to work is responsible for about a third of all private expenditure on motoring in Sydney, the annual private cost of work travel by car would be of the order of $330 million a year (1974/5 prices). Work travel accounts for 59 per cent of public transport passenger kilometres each weekday (Table 9.5) but, after allowance for weekend travel and the likelihood that workers are carried at cheaper fares than average (they travel longer distances at periodical fares) it may be guessed that work travel provides roughly half public transport revenue, or about $65 million a year. A similar estimate results if the average weekly fare ($3.50) is multiplied by the number of workers using public transport. Total private cash spending on the journey to work in Sydney in 1974/5 would therefore have been about $400 million. This ranks it with spending on clothing.

Because people in the outer suburbs on average travel further to work than others, the expenses of the journey are heavier for them. Before leaving the private costs of work travel it is of interest to assess the extent of this disadvantage.

The Disadvantages of the Outer Suburbs

From the point of view of employment, the chief disadvantage of life in the outer suburbs is that they lack local jobs. For some outer suburban residents this is no drawback; by luck or good management they may obtain a local job that suits them, or maybe they actually enjoy a long journey to work.[1] On the other hand, there are others for whom the lack of local work spells no job at all. In between come those who travel further than they would like and those who accept a less congenial job.

There is no measure available of the extent to which outer suburban residents find their jobs less congenial than others (if it be that they do at all), but it is possible to estimate the extra costs they incur in travelling. The time costs were calculated in Table 10.8, while the distances given in Table 10.4 can be converted into cash costs using the information in the first part of this chapter. The result is Table 11.3. It should be emphasised that all figures in the table are averages, and that the cost estimates in particular depend on some rather rough calculations. However, the orders of magnitude should be reasonably correct; they represent the fact that both public transport fares and motor car running costs depend on distances covered in such a way that the cash cost per kilometre declines as distance covered increases by all transport modes except walking.

In Table 11.3 separate estimates are given for motor car and for non-motor transport. The reason is that the time/cost tradeoffs are very different for the two, public transport/walking generally being more time-consuming but cheaper. Again, though motorists have the option of using public transport, people who cannot drive or who for some other reason do not own a car have no option but to walk or go by bus or train, and the public transport times and costs reflect the cost to them of life in different parts of Sydney.

---

1. As for example, the following: 'I have found that travelling longer distances is not usually boring or uninteresting. In the morning, reading the paper ... makes the time pass quickly. In the evening, particularly in the warmer weather, sleeping is quite easy... In some cars, card games are other people's pastime. Others read novels, study or in one case a school teacher was marking exam papers.' Coker, 1977, p 230.

TABLE 11.3 *Average Costs for the Journey to Work by Residential Area in Sydney.*

Residential Area	Average Journey Time (Mins)		Estimated cost $/week		% of estimated annual income per worker	
	Car	Other	Car	Other	Car	Other
Column	1	2	3	4	5	6
Penrith	24	67	9.40	6.20	7	5
Blacktown	31	64	9.40	5.60	7	4
Outer South West	27	54	8.00	4.10	6	3
Parramatta/Auburn	24	48	7.00	2.90	5	2
Baulkham Hills/Hornsby	34	57	8.40	4.30	4	2
Ryde/Hunters Hill	27	47	7.00	3.00	4	2
Middle West	25	38	6.50	2.30	4	2
Bankstown	25	50	7.50	3.50	6	3
Sutherland	30	60	8.40	4.40	5	3
St.George/Canterbury	26	45	7.50	3.30	5	2
Marrickville/Leichhardt	24	33	6.00	1.70	5	1
South Sydney/Botany	20	29	6.00	1.50	4	1
Eastern Suburbs	23	39	6.50	2.40	4	1
City of Sydney	21	26	5.50	0.90	3	1
Ku-ring-gai	33	49	8.90	3.70	3	1
Inner North	25	33	6.50	1.90	4	1
Manly/Warringah	27	52	8.00	3.20	4	2
TOTAL	27	45	7.60	3.00	5	2

Note: Cost means cash cost only, with no attempt to convert time costs to cash. This table is therefore not comparable with that in CBR (1975) p.107.

Sources: Col.1: Table 10.8 - typical weekday, 1971. Col.2: Tables 10.8 and 10.2 - typical weekday, 1971.
Col.3: Average costs of $7.60 a wk.(see text) adjusted for average distance (Table 10.4) on the basis of $3.52 a wk. fixed costs + 47¢ a wk. per km. The distance measures are from 1971, but costs 1974/75.
Column 4: Average train/ferry costs of $4 a week (see text) adjusted for average distance (Table 10.4) by relativities from the rail fare table in use in 1974. Average bus costs of $2.95 a week (see text) adjusted for average distance (Table 10.4) by relativities from the bus fare scale in use in 1974. Walking assumed to be free. The figure given is a weighted average of the costs of rail, bus and foot travel by residents of the region, using distance estimates from 1971 but costs from 1974/75.
Columns 5 & 6: Columns 3 & 4, as a proportion of income/worker for each region, from SATS 1974, Vol.1, Table 2.20 adjusted for the increase of income/worker from $4,294 p.a. at the SATS survey to $7,515 p.a. at the time of the household expenditure survey 1974/75. A 47 week working year is assumed.

According to Table 11.3, a typical journey to work by car takes an inner suburban resident about 20 minutes and costs about $6 a week in 1974/5 dollars. Its outer suburban counterpart takes about 30 minutes and costs $9 — in each case about 50 per cent more. (The cash differential may, however, be overestimated, since inner suburban residents waste more petrol in traffic jams.) The difference in cash expenses is of the order of 3 per cent of average household expenditure.

On average, public transport/walking trips in the inner suburbs take half an hour and cost around $2 a week, while from the outer areas they take an hour and cost more like $5; twice the time and more than twice the money. The relative disadvantage of living in the outer suburbs seems therefore to be much worse for public transport users than for motorists; their time handicap is worse, and cash advantage less. No wonder so many outer suburban residents travel by car.

In part the apparent disadvantage of public transport in the outer areas is due to its being the preferred means of travel to the city centre. People who choose to work in the city centre travel by train, and their long journey times and high fare payments discredit public transport. However, much of the disadvantage is a consequence of the lack of local jobs in outer areas. This means that very few people walk to work in such suburbs, while the inaccessibility of middle distance jobs by train or bus causes many non-motorists to work in the city centre. As with the low labour force participation of married women in the outer suburbs, it is impossible to say to what extent the long journeys and high fare payments of outer suburban train travellers are the acceptable cost of working in the city and living on the fringe, and to what extent they are the resented result of a lack of local employment.

High costs of travel affect outer suburban residents irrespective of their income or social status. Though there is some slight tendency for workers in low-income occupations to have shorter journeys to work than others (ch. 6), their cash costs are not very much less, and so absorb a higher proportion of their expenditure. As a result work travel is a doubly severe burden in the typical low income outer suburb. The last two columns of Table 11.3 show average cash costs of the journey to work as a proportion of income per worker in the different residential areas. The estimates are very approximate (they depend on a cursory income question asked in the SATS home interview survey) but once again provide an order of magnitude. In the inner areas, whether poor or middle-class, the fares of those who use public transport or walk typically come to about 1 per cent of income, while the costs of driving to work are 3 to 4 per cent of income. The proportions in the high status outer areas of Baulkham Hills/Hornsby, Ku-ring-gai and Manly/Warringah are not very different from this, but in the low-status outer west they reach 5 per cent of income for public transport users and 7 per cent for motorists. The train ride to a city centre job, or the speedy drive to work, are both bought dearly by the people of Blacktown, Penrith and the suburbs beyond Liverpool. This looks serious, but perhaps the people concerned do not think so, for their response rates to the provision of local employment are low (Table 4.1) and there is at least a prima facie case that more of them could work locally and so reduce their travel expenses.

The Public Costs of the Journey to Work

Following accounting practice, the costs of the journey to work borne by the community at large rather than by individual travellers may be divided into capital and current costs. The latter may be divided once again, the first comprising the noise, pollution, danger and inconvenience which the travelling workers inflict on others, the second being government spending occasioned by the journey to work.

Various attempts have been made to quantify the pollution and other external costs of the journey to work, but no agreed figures have resulted. However, it is clear that congestion, noise, pollution and accident costs per passenger kilometre are higher for motoring than for public transport or walking (BTE 1977 p.149, CBR 1975 p.54, NAPT 1976 p.47).

The quantification of the public budgetary costs of the journey to work by road in Sydney is not much less contentious than the pollution cost. Over all Australia, the Commonwealth Bureau of Roads argues that road users pay for the cost of the roads by way of motoring taxes (CBR 1975 Appendix 2). However, this calculation depends on several arguable assumptions. First, the greater part of the cost of roads lies in capital charges, and is therefore sensitive to the interest rate selected (CBR 1975 appendixes p.38). Second, no charge is made for the rental value of the land used for roads (Manning 1973 p.37). Third, and most important, it is assumed that all motoring taxes are user charges; none is an excise or sales tax (Downing et al, 1964, p.95). If these assumptions are disallowed, it is likely that motoring is being subsidised. In any case, the all-Australia position says very little about the subsidy that may or may not be enjoyed by Sydney motorists driving to work.

The total cost to the state and local governments of the maintenance and construction or urban roads in New South Wales in 1974/5 was about $156 million (BTE 1977 p.9). This was a sharp decline from the previous year, and reflected the scaling down of Commonwealth grants for freeway construction. It is very difficult to separate this total into capital works and repairs, since maintenance work often brings minor increases in capacity. The Commonwealth Bureau of Roads assumes that overall 75 per cent of road expenditure is on capital works (CBR 1975 Appendixes p.38), but the proportion obviously varies, and has recently declined in Sydney. In the early 1970s very large sums — of the order or tens of millions of dollars a year — were spent on particular large projects, such as the Warringah expressway, but such major projects serving particular traffic flows seem to be a thing of the past.

Only a portion of total road maintenance and capital costs are due to the journey to work. Much of the total cost is occasioned by freight transport, and some of the rest by non-work travel. In any apportionment of the total cost of roads freight traffic should be weighted more heavily than its contribution to total traffic (8 per cent of vehicle kilometres on arterial roads in Sydney in 1973/4 — CBR 1975 p.114) since trucks cause more wear on the roads than cars, per kilometre travelled, and require higher standards of road construction. By contrast, work travel accounts for under a third of total vehicle kilometres (above) and a lower proportion of expenses. Perhaps, therefore, the road maintenance costs of the journey to work in Sydney in 1974/5 would have been of the order of $5 to $10 million, while the capital charges and any offsetting revenue would be anybody's guess.

The cost to the government of motor car journeys to work is thus highly uncertain. However, the subsidies to public transport are easier to trace, consisting as they do of the loss on urban passenger services of the Public Transport Commission of New South Wales. This loss in 1974/5 was $69 million and rising (PTC 1975). It represented about 40 per cent of the total operating loss of the Public Transport Commission. The fares of urban passengers covered about two-thirds of the direct costs of carrying them. Once again no true figure is known for the capital subsidy involved, though the Public Transport Commission makes notional interest payments based on historic costs.

The subsidy to public transport operating costs benefits some users rather than others. It is more or less equally divided between the rail services and inner suburban bus services of the Public Transport Commission, and so particularly benefits people travelling to the city centre, and bound on inner suburban local journeys. No subsidy is paid to bus services in the outer suburbs, for these are privately owned and operate at a modest profit (DMT Annual Reports).

The apportionment of bus and train operating deficits between work and other travel is difficult: work travel gives rise to peaks, which are expensive to service, but so too is maintaining services at nights and weekends, when few workers are travelling. As an approximation, the loss may be divided in proportion to weekday passenger kilometres (Table 9.5): 60 per cent to work travel, 40 per cent other. The operating subsidies were thus of the order of $20 million each for buses and trains.

Given these calculations, it is possible to compare the running costs of each transport mode, including maintenance but excluding capital charges, and on the assumption that motorist taxation is a contribution to the general revenue. Such a comparison is made in the last (and exceedingly approximate) column of Table 11.2. Apart from walking (costed at a nominal cent a kilometre, to allow for the maintenance of footpaths) the railway remains the cheapest form of transport, even after allowance for its deficit. Buses, on the other hand, are as expensive as private cars.

The costs given in Table 11.2 reflect the efficiency of the services as they were running in 1974/5. Various means have been suggested to improve efficiency. Average motoring costs could be greatly reduced if car occupancy were increased by car pooling (CBR 1975 p.129). However, actual car occupancy continues to decline (CBR 1975 p.104). This suggests that not only is car pooling inconvenient (Schaeffer and Sclar 1975 p.106) but that few motorists

TABLE 11.4 *The Cost of Selected Capital Works in Australian Cities.*

	km	Original Cost $m	$ (1974/75)	
			$m	$m/km
Warringah Expressway	2.4			
property (1) (2)		8.7	65	27
construction (1) (3)		16.9	37	15
			102	42
Bulli Pass Tollway (4)	22.9	30	42	1.8
Eastern Suburbs Railway (5)	9.8			
property		7.1	11	
works		151	151	
			162	16.5
East Hills - Glenfield Railway (6)				
(estimate)	8.5	21.4	21	2.4
Christie Downs Railway (S.A.) (7)	6(7)	6	8	1.3

Notes: (1) Cost from DMR 1976(a).

(2) Aquisition period approx. 1959/62. During the 1960's land values in North Sydney were increasing by nearly 12 per cent p.a. (Statistical Register, N.S.W., 1962 and 1972).

(3) Construction period 1962/68, updated by the road price index - CBR, 1975, Appendixes, p.90.

(4) Cost from DMR 1976b, p.6. Construction period approximately 1971/75, updated by road price index.

(5) Cost estimates from the Eastern Suburbs Railway Board of Review, 1976. Property assumed to have been acquired ca 1967/73, at price inflation of 10 per cent p.a. Construction period 1967/80: no attempt at price adjustments. In 1975/76 the E.S.R. accounted for 58 per cent of capital spending on urban public transport in N.S.W. - PTC Annual Report, 1975/76.

(6) Cost estimate from BTE 1977: pp.121 and 182.

(7) Cost estimate from BTE 1973: The cost includes 4 km of new double track and 10 km of duplication, plus associated works. Updating 1973/74 to 1974/75 by road price index.

find their work journey expenses sufficiently onerous to put up with the inconvenience of sharing them. Similar cost reductions would accrue if load factors on public transport could be increased, but this usually involves cutting services. Other methods of reducing public transport costs include automated fare collection, newer vehicles to cut maintenance costs, improved signalling on the railways and transit lanes to speed bus services (SATS 1974 Vol 3). It is also significant that private buses in Sydney run at much lower costs per bus kilometre than the government services (compare PTC and DMT annual reports), so there may be scope to reduce costs of the government services. However, as long as around two-thirds of the total costs of running buses and trains are paid out in wages (BTE 1977 appendix B) the relative costs of public transport and motoring will depend mainly on trends in wages as against other costs. Increases in fuel prices are likely to improve the position of public transport a little, since fuel comprises about 10 per cent of public transport costs as against 20 per cent of motoring costs.

Not only do the cost estimates in Table 11.2 reflect current rather than potential efficiency; they give average rather than marginal costs, which means that they give a comparison which is valid over Sydney as a whole, but which cannot be used to predict the changes in cost that would be occasioned were traffic diverted from one means of transport to another. Such diversions often require capital expenditure, and can be exceedingly expensive. Table 11.4 gives examples of recent major investments in urban transport routes. The comparisons are approximate, if only because the projects took years to complete and adjustments have had to be made for inflation while they were under construction. The chief lesson of recent experience as reflected in the table is that the insertion of new routes into the existing built-up area is very costly indeed. In the case of roads this arises largely because of property acquisition costs, though construction costs are also considerable if a new inner urban freeway is to be sufficiently grand to have some hope of carrying the traffic offering. For railways, tunnelling is an alternative to property acquisition, but as the Eastern Suburbs Railway shows it can be just as expensive (much of the extra cost lies in stations built underground, rather than in the tunnels themselves). Projects such as the Eastern Suburbs Railway and Warringah Expressway have absorbed an inordinately high proportion of the funds available for investment in urban transport. They are useful mainly to a small group of city centre travellers. Meanwhile little has been spent on facilitating travel elsewhere in the metropolitan area, even though both roads and railways built on the urban fringe are comparatively cheap. Further, where spare capacity is available on an existing route, or where it can be relatively cheaply bought (as when a road is declared a clearway or a railway is resignalled) small investments can have considerable rewards in increased ability to handle traffic.

In summary, cost conditions for the different means of transport would seem to be as follows:

Walking is cheap, and any localisation of employment would save significant amounts of money for people thereby enabled to walk to work.

Motoring is relatively fast and expensive, but well within the ability of most Sydney households to pay. The obvious constraint on motoring is that many of the roads are taxed to capacity during the peaks, and additions to capacity are very expensive except on the urban fringe.

Trains are relatively fast and cheap, but are confined to specific routes with high traffic densities. They are also running at near capacity for the peak period journey to the city centre, though there may be means to provide additional capacity relatively cheaply on existing lines. New lines are expensive in built-up areas.

Buses are slow and expensive, but additions to capacity are cheap particularly when governments are prepared to shoulder other road users aside by declaring transit lanes. New routes can be started at low cost, and are reasonably economic with low traffic. Even so, buses are hard put to compete with the private car, and their future role, as at present, would seem to be confined to acting as railway feeders, and providing local transport for those who cannot afford a car (or a second car in the family).

Transport considerations, particularly the avoidance of new construction works in areas already built up, therefore favour the localisation of employment rather than the building up of suburban concentrations of employment, or of the city centre once the potential for increased capacity on existing public transport is exhausted. On the other hand, there is ample scope for city centre activities which would draw patronage to public transport during the off-peak, thus utilising spare capacity.

CHAPTER 12

Conclusions and Policies

The conclusions of this study are of two kinds: those which summarise the distribution of employment opportunities and people's response to them, and those which have implications for public policy, particularly policy affecting the location of jobs and investments in transport facilities. This chapter covers the two kinds of conclusions in turn, and also includes a brief comparison of the journey to work in Sydney with work journeys in other parts of Australia.

Facts about Workplaces and Work Travel

In describing work travel in this study, four distinctions were frequently made. Journeys to work can be classified according to destination (workplace), origin (residence), and the sex and occupation of the traveller. These distinctions provide the basis for a summary of the results, which broadly confirm the theoretical predictions in Chapter 1.

Jobs in Sydney are more centralised than dwellings. A quarter of the jobs are in the City of Sydney, a quarter in three other major employment concentrations (two of which are adjacent to the city centre), and the other half are dispersed. People who work in the city centre have, on average, long journeys to work; those who work in the suburban concentrations have journeys of middle length, and those who work elsewhere have, on average, journeys only half as long as those of city centre workers. Workers come to the city centre from all over the metropolitan area, though particularly from the inner areas; they come to the major suburban concentrations mainly from nearby and from areas radially outwards, while those who work at jobs dispersed in other suburbs by and large live locally. City centre workers travel by public transport (particularly train) more than others, while some local workers walk, but in nearly all employment areas except the city centre the main means of getting to work is the motor car.

The population living in any residential area tends to divide into those who work in the city centre, who except in the inner suburbs have long journeys to work, and those who work locally and have short journeys. In most places except the outer western fringe these two together comprise at least 40 per cent of the resident workforce, even when 'local' is defined as working within three kilometres of home. The proportion of resident workers who work locally depends mainly on the local availability of jobs, though such factors as the ease of transport to and from other areas, and the extent of competition from job-deficient areas nearby, also affect the proportion.

The distribution of men's and women's jobs is fairly similar, the main difference being that the major manufacturing areas are relatively short of women's jobs. The sexes have roughly the same opportunity to work locally, roughly the same opportunity to work in the city centre. Despite this equality of opportunity, women's journeys are shorter on average than men's. This is mainly due to the job choices of married women, who tend to have work journeys short in distance and brief in time. Single women's journeys are almost as long as men's, and include a relatively high proportion to the city centre. They take more time than men's journeys, because single women tend to travel by public transport rather than by car.

These sex differences are reflected in journey lengths by occupation (women in any occupation tend to have shorter journeys than men) and are reinforced by a tendency for people on lower incomes to have shorter journeys, and to use public transport more often (women's incomes are lower than men's). However, the average distance travelled by workers in any occupation also depends on whether that occupation has a tradition of living locally (like doctors), and most importantly on the extent to which jobs in that occupation are dispersed around the suburbs. Where jobs are widespread, journeys are short.

These findings confirm the fundamental hypothesis given in Chapter 1, that people (particularly married women) prefer short journeys to work rather than long. However, journeys to work in Sydney are not as short as they might be, for two reasons. First, by historic standards the present metropolitan area is developed at a low density, which provides spaciousness but demands long journeys. Second, people travel further than apparently they need, even with the present spread of jobs and houses, the benefit being that they can choose from among a wider range of each. It is very difficult to weigh these two benefits against the known and calculable costs of the journey to work: the hour a day of an average worker's time; the 5 per cent or so of the household budget. However, the evidence of certain groups (married women, or the citizens of Manly/Warringah) is that where so minded, people can give greater emphasis to short journeys without obvious hardship.

A Comparison with the Rest of Australia

Though this study has concentrated on Sydney, many of its findings should apply in other parts of Australia. Unfortunately the 1971 census material has not been processed for any other city, but some comparison is possible using the Survey of the Journey to Work of August 1974 (ABS Journey to Work

1974). This survey did not give any indication of geographic distances, and the sample was too small to divide cities into areas of journey origin or destination, but certain broad comparisons are possible as to journey times and means of transport.

Sydney is the largest city in Australia, and one might therefore expect journey distances within it to be longer than in other cities. This is true, at least insofar as distances are reflected in times (Table 12.1). Median journey times in the cities and towns of Australia are ranked quite strictly according to their population. In country towns and small cities like Albury/Wodonga half the journeys typically take less than 11 minutes, while in Sydney half take more than half an hour. This gives a difference of three times in the duration of the typical journey, which is quite out of proportion to the population difference of nearly 70 times.

These time differences broadly reflect differences in actual journey lengths, at least for those cities where journey lengths are known. In Albury/Wodonga the

TABLE 12.1 *Duration of the Journey to Work. Australia 1974.*

City	Population '000	Hypothetical Radius of the urban area km	Half the journeys were less than mins	Three-quarters of the journeys were less than mins
Sydney	2874	21	30	44
Melbourne	2583	21	24	43
Brisbane	911	15	22	34
Adelaide	868	13.5	21	33
Perth	739	13	21	34
Canberra	185	6.5	18	26
Hobart	158	6	17	24
S.A. (excl. Adelaide)	various		11	17
W.A. (excl. Perth	"		11	16
Albury/ Wodonga	43	3	11	17

Note Hobart data from before the Tasman bridge fell down.

Sources: ABS Journey to Work and Journey to School 1974.
Cities' Commission: Australians' Use of Time.

median journey to work was four actual kilometres, in Melbourne about 12 actual kilometres (Cities Commission 1975 p.67) and in Sydney about 9.4 straight-line kilometres (Table 3.3). The difference in geographic distance is once again about three times.

This lack of proportion between city size and journey lengths is partly explained by the facts of geometry. In a circular city, with all the jobs in the centre and the population spread uniformly over the circular area, the length of the average journey to work is proportional to the radius, for all journeys are from points within the circle to the centre. To take examples, neither Sydney nor Albury/Wodonga is exactly circular, but supposing that their existing populations were living in circular cities at the same density as now, the radii would be roughly 21 and three kilometres respectively — a difference of seven times (Table 12.1). If journeys to work in both cities were arranged in the same orderly pattern from the edge towards the centre, the difference of average length would thus be roughly seven times — much less than the difference in population, though more than the observed difference in journey length. Average journey lengths greater than the radius of the urban area, such as the four kilometre average in Albury/Wodonga, come about if people are not concerned about how close their job is to their house. The Albury/Wodonga urban area is sufficiently small for most people to work locally (or at any rate within five kilometres of home) without any special effort to select a nearby job. On the other hand, average distances fall substantially below the radius of the urban area when at least some people are trying to get jobs near home, or homes near their job. In a small city people can reconcile their preferred home and job without incurring excessive journey distances or times (provided they travel by car), whereas in Sydney, for some at least, there comes a compromise: a job other than the best available in the urban area, a dwelling other than the most pleasant the family could afford, or perhaps a journey to work that takes more time and money than they would wish.

Given that Sydney and Melbourne are of very nearly equal hypothetical radius, it is of interest that the median duration of the journey to work in Melbourne is less than in Sydney (Table 12.1). This may mean that distances in Melbourne are a little shorter, perhaps because its city centre is relatively less important in its total metropolitan job market. It may also be due to faster average speeds, for a higher proportion of Melbourne workers travel to work by car (Table 12.2).

The importance of rail transport for the journey to work varies with the size of the city (Table 12.2). The importance of cars varies inversely with the importance of trains, which suggests that these are an alternative means of transport — trains being used for city centre traffic which would go by car if there were less congestion. Buses and trams, on the other hand, carry between 9 and 13 per cent of all work travellers in all the capital cities except Hobart, where they are more important. This relatively constant share of total travellers is consistent with the finding that buses are used mainly by short-distance

TABLE 12.2 *Main Mode of Travel for the Journey to Work. Australia 1974. (per cent)*

Area	Train/ Ferry	Bus/ Tram	Car	Walk	Other
Sydney	17	13	62	6	2
Melbourne	13	12	66	8	2
Brisbane	9	11	69	6	3
Adelaide	4	13	73	6	4
Perth	3	13	75	5	4
Hobart	-	19	71	8	2
Canberra	-	9	83	6	2
Rest of Australia	1	5	77	12	6
All Australia	8	10	70	8	4

Source: ABS, Journey to Work and Journey to School, 1974.

travellers who cannot afford a car. Such people are probably a fairly constant proportion of the workforce in all cities. Finally, the proportion walking to work varies between 5 per cent and 8 per cent, again a relatively constant figure which may indicate that the proportion of the workforce working locally is similar in all Australian cities.

Table 12.3 confirms the association between trip duration and the means of transport. Average journey times in Sydney by any particular means of

TABLE 12.3 *Median Duration of the Journey to Work by Main Travel Mode.*

Main Mode of Travel	Sydney 1971 (Table 9.11) mins	Australia 1974 (ABS survey) mins
Car travellers	20	18
Train travellers	57	57
Bus travellers	37	34
Pedestrians	12	11
TOTAL	30	20

Sources: SATS tapes, and ABS Journey to Work and Journey to School, 1974.

transport are but little longer than in Australia as a whole, and the difference in overall average journey times arises almost wholly because more people in Sydney travel by train. Journey times by rail are typically long, not so much because trains are slow but because they carry people long distances (Table 9.4).

Sydney thus differs from other Australian cities as average journey distances are greater, durations are longer, and more people travel by train. All these differences come about simply because it is larger, and has a relatively important city centre. A further difference is that average spending on fares in 1974 by those who used public transport was greater (Table 12.4). This, however, was as much due to the particular fares in force as to differences in distances travelled.

Despite these effects of city size, the behaviour of Sydney people is typical of other Australian workers: married women have the briefest journeys, men next,

TABLE 12.4 *Average Weekly Fares Paid for Work Travel. August 1974.*

Main Mode of Travel	N.S.W. $/worker/week	Australia $/worker/week
Train	4.00	3.55
Bus	2.95	2.88
Total Public Transport	3.50	3.24

Note: Though these figures include travel in provincial areas they are dominated by the respective capital cities.

Source: ABS Journey to Work and Journey to School, 1974.

TABLE 12.5 *Median Duration of the Journey to Work by Sex.*

Population group	Sydney 1971 (Table 9.11) mins	Australia 1974 (ABS Survey) mins
Men	30	21
Single women	34	22
Married women	28	17
Total	30	20

Sources: SATS tapes, and ABS Journey to Work and Journey to School, 1974.

and single women the most time consuming (Table 12.5). Insofar as inferences can be made by comparing journey durations from the 1974 survey with journey lengths from the census, Sydney people are also typical: clerks have the longest journeys to work, and sales, service and process workers the shortest. In these and presumably other behavioural respects, therefore, the results of this study of Sydney should be directly applicable to other places in Australia.

Implications for Public Policy

The policy instruments by which governments can influence work travel stop far short of enabling them to dictate where people shall live, where they will work and how they will get from the one to the other. Even so, town planning regulations can be used to influence the location of jobs and housing areas, as can direct state involvement in land development and redevelopment. And even if governments eschew town planning and land development (as some would do, through devotion to laissez faire or cynicism as to the effectiveness of planning) the state and its municipalities are still responsible for all transport infrastructure in Australian cities, and for the operation of most public transport. Many of the demands for transport investments, and a proportion of the bus and train deficits, are due to work travel. Whether or not governments believe that they can influence urban layout for the better, concern for the use of public funds demands that they try to have a coherent policy for the journey to work.

Yet work travel is only a small part of life in cities. Concern that work journeys are too long, or too slow, or too expensive, should not be allowed to dominate policy to the exclusion of all else. Urban policy should be taken as a whole, and is so discussed by Neutze (1978). A study of workplaces and work travel cannot come up with definite policy recommendations, but only with comments on the effects of particular policies. Such comments were scattered throughout the preceding chapters, and some of them are drawn together here.

One of the most consistent aspirations of Australian politicians, and indeed of the people also, is that as many families as possible shall have their own house and garden, set in a residential area from which most kinds of employment-generating activities have been banned (Stretton 1975 ch. 2). This suburban ideal has been pursued consistently and with some success. On the other hand, there is less of a consensus as to the ideal work environment, which is seen as varying with the kind of job. Some kinds of work are found 'naturally' in small enterprises, like a mum-and-dad shop; others are found in large factories. Some are scattered 'naturally' around the suburbs — teaching, local retailing jobs — while others 'naturally' concentrate in the city centre. However, other things being equal, there is at least a widespread belief that it is better to work in an employment area which is full of things to do, a place vibrant with life, rather than in a neighborhood shop or a factory in a large industrial estate. For many people the city centre is still the archetype of the preferred place to work.

If housing is to be dispersed, and if as many jobs as possible are to be concentrated in the city centre (or that plus a small number of other major employment centres), the necessary result in a city the size of Sydney is journeys to work which are both time-consuming and expensive. The obvious response to this dilemma is to propose that transport be quicker and cheaper. Government responsibility for the transport infrastructure is already established, and there are government engineers anxious to get on with the task of improving it, so administratively this response comes naturally (Sandercock 1975 p.192). Further, there have been occasions in the past when happy technical innovations have meant that transport could be speeded and journey times cut at the same time as costs were reduced. An example would be the substitution of electric for steam traction on tramways and railways earlier this century. However, at present extra speed is available only at extra cost, for it is attained by switching from public to private transport, and by building freeways. Car travel is more expensive than train in private costs, while the public costs of building freeways to carry city centre traffic have proved prohibitive. For this reason increased speed cannot reduce the burden of long city centre work journeys. People therefore turn to policies which would reduce the distance to be covered on the typical journey to work, for such policies would seem to have the benefit of reducing both the time and money costs of the journey.

If it be that dispersed housing and concentrated employment generate excessively long work journeys, it may be that the housing pattern is at fault. People therefore propose that residential densities should be increased, even at the sacrifice of the traditional house and garden. They argue that well-designed medium density housing is at least as pleasant to live in as the single family dwelling on its quarter-acre block, and that redevelopment of the inner suburbs in this form would in the long run be cheaper than adding to the urban sprawl. Those against this policy deny both these arguments, and point to the high costs and lack of public acceptance of inner area high rise flats as substitutes for brick veneer villas on the urban fringe (Halkett 1976 ch. 1, Jones 1972 ch. 5). While some degree of flat building and redevelopment may continue, for the moment the fringe-extenders seem to have won the argument.

If the people do not want to be brought to the jobs, then surely the jobs should be brought to the people. Since this would result from a continuation of present trends it seems the most likely way of reducing the burden of the journey to work. The effectiveness of such a policy of job decentralisation depends on public response in two ways. First, how far will people respond by reducing their travel distances, and second, to what extent will they switch to a more expensive means of transport?

So long as all employment in a city is concentrated in one place the question of providing a choice of jobs does not arise. Anybody who can get to the city centre (and with a developed system of suburban railways anybody can) has the choice of all the city's jobs. But what happens when jobs are dispersed? It cannot be arranged that everybody works at home, so there will still be journeys to work. The crucial question, therefore, is how far people will travel in search of a suitable job. It is conceivable, indeed quite likely, that a policy of job decentralisation would result in longer work journeys (Thomson 1977 ch. 3). This is associated with a third issue. So long as most of the jobs in a city the size of Sydney are at the centre, the main means of transport for the journey to work has to be the railway, with some use of other kinds of public transport. There is little room for motor cars in such high density city centres, and the distances are too long for people to walk. Once employment is dispersed passenger flows become too diffuse to support public transport, particularly the forms with high capacity and low costs. The resulting switch to private motor transport will mean that journey times are shorter, but will costs be less? And what becomes of those who do not have cars? It could be that a policy of job decentralisation would result in people travelling further, and at greater private and social cost, than they would have if most jobs were in the city centre. The bright lights would have been sacrificed to no avail.

To a considerable extent these questions are being posed after the event. Jobs *have* been decentralised, and journeys to jobs in the suburbs *are* shorter than journeys to the city centre. The motor car *has* become the most common way of getting to work. And yet questions still arise: should the trend to the decentralisation of employment be encouraged or resisted? And should its form be changed, with greater emphasis on regional centres, or on dispersed local employment?

The trend towards the decentralisation of employment has reached the stage where only 14 per cent of the jobs in Sydney are in industries classified as highly concentrated (Table 2.1) and but 22 per cent of all jobs are in highly concentrated occupations (Table 2.2). Employment is dispersed in all manufacturing industries, in road transport, in retailing and in most services like health and education. For these, the great majority of industries, the question is not whether the overall degree of decentralisation is too little, but whether the distribution is satisfactory. In manufacturing, for example, the existing pattern of jobs can be criticised in two ways. First, despite the generally high degree of dispersion, a satisfactory local balance between workers and workplaces has yet to be achieved in some suburbs, particularly those on the outer western fringe. Efforts should be made to remedy this, since — as was shown in Chapter 6 — process workers (particularly women) appreciate local employment opportunities, and tend to work locally when they can. Second, modern manufacturing plants are developed at a low density. Most factory jobs are beyond walking distance from any residential area, and indeed are so spread even within industrial zones that it is difficult to provide them with a good bus service. This dispersion of jobs within manufacturing areas comes about for technical reasons, (single storey factory layouts are efficient, and firms like to have spare room for expansion) but there may be scope for improvement of design which would make it easier to provide factory workers with the option of getting to work by public transport.

In retailing and services the problems are often those of excessive scatter:

> 'In North America and Australasia too many hospitals, universities, technical and teachers' colleges and high schools and trade schools, suburban office developments, supermarkets, filling stations, theatres, cinemas, pool halls, squash courts and other high and low entertainments have been scattered like confetti along main roads through characterless expanses of housing, in the name of decentralisation... Not houses and gardens, but that formless uncentred litter of facilities on and off public transport routes...is the true and disastrous meaning of "suburban sprawl". Policies of *re*centralisation should try to gather those activities to support each other...in strong town centres with their own local transport, local government, day-and-night life, and sense of identity.' (Stretton 1976 p.225)

In other words, dispersion 'in the uncoordinated pursuit of cheap sites' can result in a city which is not only visually (and perhaps spiritually?) depressing, but which is expensive to live in, for it depends entirely on motor transport. Is it possible to have decentralisation without these disadvantages?

Much depends on the design strategy adopted. When facilities are most scattered the proportion of workers who can work locally is maximised, journey lengths on average are shortest, and the greatest number can walk to work. However, in most occupations a majority will still choose not to work locally (e.g. the case of schoolteachers, ch. 6) and these people will have to drive, for there is little hope of providing a competitive public transport service in a city where facilities are all over the place. There is, therefore, much to be said for promoting regional commercial centres, situated at intervals along railway lines and at the focus of bus routes for each group of suburbs. Public transport patronage could also be increased by grouping such other facilities as hospitals and tertiary institutions in line nearby, so that they can be served by the bus routes before they diverge. The best new example of such a regional centre in Sydney is that at Mt Druitt.

If there are to be regional centres, would it be possible for some of them to attract the office industries, and so reduce the concentration of clerical employment in the city centre? While it is true that clerks have a low response rate to local employment (ch. 6) and that decentralisation of clerical jobs would invite more long-distance motoring than most kinds of work, it still seems unfair that employment opportunities for clerks should be so heavily concentrated in the city centre.

The most spectacular suggestion is that a 'twin and rival' city centre should be built at Parramatta, able to compete with the City of Sydney itself in the brightness of its lights (Stretton 1975 p.255). This is but a dream, for if employment in the Parramatta business district were increased much beyond its present 11 000, new roads and rapid transit lines would have to be built to bring these people to work. The insertion of such new transport routes into the existing urban fabric would be too costly. On the other hand, where the planning is done in advance and land for the necessary transport routes is reserved, it may be possible to develop major new centres at a reasonable cost. The new centre at Campbelltown provides an example: even if it achieves its planned total employment of 38000 it will be no rival for the city centre (employment 207000) but it will still make a substantial contribution to job opportunities in the outer suburbs (SPA 1973 p.88).

In that none of the proposed suburban centres would be very large, the present city centre would still be very attractive to those establishments which require centrality. This might mean that employment in it would rise, though only slowly. While it is true that journeys to work in the city centre are long (on average), they are mostly by train, the form of transport with the lowest operating costs per passenger kilometre. Any additions to the city centre workforce would likewise have to travel by public transport, but it should be possible to provide for them by works to increase the capacity of the present suburban railways and by increased use of transit lanes for buses, or even trams.

Though continued decentralisation of employment should reduce the average length of journey to work, there will still be people (mostly men) who insist on driving a long way across town to their jobs. Collectively these gentry make considerable demands on the road system. Should expensive arterial roads and orbital freeways be built to meet their requirements? The extra journeying range provided by such roads will be something of a luxury once employment has been dispersed to all suburbs. Again, it may not be a wholly bad thing for a district to have its road access restricted. In Sutherland and Manly/Warringah journeys to work are shorter than elsewhere, without any vociferous complaints that the residents are being denied their due choice of jobs (Chapter 4). The example of these two regions would recommend a policy of traffic restraint rather than roadbuilding (Thomson 1977 ch.7).

A policy to guide the existing trend towards decentralisation of employment would thus try to constrain the amount of motor traffic by limiting construction of new roads in built-up areas and by maintaining public transport services to the city centre and to regional centres. Some local workers might find their journey lengths so reduced that they can switch back from vehicular transport to walking or cycling. However, most workers in local employment will continue to have the same choice as now: bus or the private car. Given reasonably easy car parking (and the proposed regional employment centres will not be large enough to generate severe parking difficulties) present-day bus speeds and costs are not competitive with the private car except where the bus enables the traveller to dispense with car ownership entirely. It must therefore be expected that most workers outside the city centre will continue to drive to work (Smith 1976 p.221). Bus services will have to be maintained for the benefit of those who cannot drive, and by focusing both services and employment on regional centres it should be possible to make bus travel attractive to those who could drive but would rather avoid the expense of car (or second car) ownership.

For the present, therefore, a policy of job decentralisation to suburban centres can be expected to reduce distances travelled to work, without unduly limiting people's choice of jobs, and without depriving them of public transport. In addition to these benefits, job decentralisation would seem a prudent policy in a world in which energy supplies are dwindling. Should a coming energy crisis increase the cost of transport, particularly the energy-intensive (private) forms of it, a policy which enables and encourages short work journeys in the present will have incalculable benefits in the future.

APPENDIX

Definition of Occupations used in Tables 6.1, 6.2 and 6.3

Abbreviation	Full list
Clergy	Clergy and members of religious orders
Teacher	Teacher
Nurse	Nurse, including trainee
Doctor	Medical Practitioner, Dentist
Scientist	Chemist, physicist, other physical scientist, biologist, veterinary surgeon, agronomist, related scientist
Engineer	Architect, engineer, professional surveyor
Lawyer	Law professional
Manager	Employers, managers, workers on own account not elsewhere classified
Clerk	Other clerical workers
Typist	Stenographer or typist
Sales	Proprietors, shopkeepers, workers own account, retail or wholesale trade salesmen, shop assistants, related workers
Technician	Draftsmen and technicians not elsewhere classified
Cleaner etc	Housekeeper, cook, maid, waiter, bartender, caretaker, building cleaner, related workers
Clothing worker	Spinner, weaver, knitter, dyer, tailor, cutter, furrier, leather cutter, laster, sewer, related worker
Storeman/labourer	Storeman, freight handler, labourer not elsewhere classified
Process worker	Workers in printing trades, pottery, glass, clay, milling, baking, food and drink; chemical, sugar, paper, tobacco products, rubber, plastic and concrete products; process workers not elsewhere classified
Metal Trades	Metal tradesmen, mechanics, electricians and related workers

BIBLIOGRAPHY

Abbreviations

ABS	Australian Bureau of Statistics
AGPS	Australian Government Publishing Service
BTE	Bureau of Transport Economics
CBR	Commonwealth Bureau of Roads
DMR	Department of Main Roads, New South Wales

ABS (1968): *Australian Standard Industrial Classification*, (Draft), Vol. 1 Canberra.

ABS (1975): *Income Distribution 1968/9,* Ref 17.17, Canberra.

ABS (1976): *Journey to Work and Journey to School Aug. 1974*, Ref 17.5, Canberra.

ABS (1977): *Household Expenditure Survey 1974/5,* Vol 4 Ref 17.22, Canberra.

ABS (1977): *Year Book No. 61, 1975/6*, Canberra.

ABS: *NSW Statistical Registers*, Sydney.

Black, John (1977): *Public Inconvenience*, Urban Research Unit, Canberra.

BTE (1973): *Review of Public Transport Investment Proposals for Australian Capital Cities 1973/4*, AGPS, Canberra.

BTE (1975): *Transport Outlook Conference 1975, Papers and Proceedings*, AGPS, Canberra.

BTE (1977): *Urban Transport: Capital Requirements 1977/78 to 1979/80*, AGPS, Canberra.

Cities Commission (1975): *Australians' Use of Time*, Canberra.

Coker, Brian (1977): 'Life as a Blue Mountains Commuter', *Australian Railway Historical Society NSW Digest*, Vol 15 p 230.

CBR (1975): *Report on Roads in Australia*, 2 Vols, CBR, Melbourne.

Davis, J.R. and Spearritt, Peter (1974): *Sydney at the Census: 1971, a Social Atlas*, Urban Research Unit, Canberra.

DMR (1976): *The Roadmakers,* DMR, Sydney.

DMR (1976b): *Annual Report 1975/6*, Government Printer, Sydney.

DMT (Department of Motor Transport NSW) (1974): *Annual Report 1973/4*, Government Printer, Sydney.

Downing, R.I., Arndt, H.W., Boxer, A.H. and Mathews, R.L. (1964): *Taxation in Australia: Agenda for Reform*, Melbourne University Press, Melbourne.

Eastern Suburbs Railway Board of Review (1976): *Report*, Government Printer, Sydney.

-vans, A.W. (1973): *The Economics of Residential Location*, St. Martin's, New York.

Halkett, I.P.B. (1976): *The Quarter-Acre Block*, Australian Institute of Urban Studies, Canberra.

Harrison, P.F. (1977): *Major Urban Areas*, Atlas of Australian Resources, Second Series, Division of National Mapping, Canberra.

Hensher, D.A. (1976): 'The Value of Commuter Travel Time Savings', *Journal of Transport Economics and Policy*, 10, pp 167-176.

Jones, M.A. (1972): *Housing and Poverty in Australia*, Melbourne University Press, Melbourne.

Lanigan, P.J. (1976): 'The Spatial Reorganisation of a Federal Government Department' in Linge, G.J.R. (ed): *Restructuring Employment Opportunities in Australia*, Publication HG/11, Department of Human Geography, Australian National University, Canberra.

Liepmann, K.K. (1944): *The Journey to Work*, Kegan Paul, Trench, Turbner & Co., London.

Manning, Ian (1973): *Municipal Finance and Income Distribution in Sydney*, Urban Research Unit, Canberra.

Mumford, Lewis (1961): *The City in History,* Secker and Warburg, London (Penguin edition 1966).

N.A.P.T. (National Action for Public Transport) (1976): *Getting on the Right Track*.

Neutze, Max (1971): *People and Property in Bankstown*, Urban Research Unit, Canberra.

Neutze, Max (1977): *Urban Development in Australia, a Descriptive Analysis*, Geo Allen & Unwin Australia, Sydney.

Neutze, Max (1978): *Australian Urban Policy*, Geo Allen & Unwin Australia, Sydney.

Paterson, John, Urban Systems Pty. Ltd. (1974): *Transport Services Available to and Used by Disadvantaged Sections of the Community*, CBR, Melbourne.

PEC (Planning and Environment Commission, NSW) (1976): *Work Places and Work Trips 1971*, PEC, Sydney.

PTC (Public Transport Commission, NSW) (1975): *Annual Report 1974/5*, Government Printer, Sydney.

Quarmby, D.A. (1967): 'Choice of Travel Mode for the Journey to Work', *Journal of Transport Economics and Policy* Vol 1 pp 273-294.

Ravallion, M. (1974): *Transport Use and Social Costs*, Dept. of Architecture, University of Sydney, Sydney.

Sandercock, Leonie (1975): *Cities for Sale*, Melbourne University Press, Melbourne.

Schaeffer, K.H. and Sclar, Elliot (1975): *Access for All; Transportation and Urban Growth*, Penguin, Harmondsworth.

Smith, A.B. (1976): 'A Review of the Factors Affecting the Outlook for Urban

Passenger Transport' in BTE (1975) pp 201-242.

SPA (State Planning Authority, NSW) (1973): *The New Cities of Campbelltown Camden Appin Structure Plan*, Sydney.

Stretton, Hugh (1975): *Ideas for Australian Cities*, 2nd edn, Georgian House, Melbourne.

Stretton, Hugh (1976): *Capitalism, Socialism and the Environment*, Cambridge University Press, Cambridge.

SATS (Sydney Area Transportation Study) (1974): Vol 1, *Base Year (1971) Data Report* and Vol 3, *Passenger Transport Systems*, Minister for Transport, Sydney.

Szalai, A. (ed) (1972): *The Use of Time. Daily Activities of Urban and Suburban Populations in Twelve Countries*, Mouton, The Hague.

Thomson, J.M. (1977): *Great Cities and their Traffic*, Victor Gollancz, London.

Urban Research Unit, (1973): *Urban Development in Melbourne*, Australian Institute of Urban Studies, Canberra.

Vandermark, E. (1970): *Business Activities in Four Sydney Suburban Areas*, Urban Research Unit, Canberra.

Wheaton, W.C. (1977): 'Income and Urban Residence An Analysis of Consumer Demand for Location', *American Economic Review* 67 pp 620-631.

INDEX